The Moral
Foundations
of
Professional Ethics

PHILOSOPHY AND SOCIETY

General Editor: MARSHALL COHEN

Also in this series:

The Moral Foundations of Professional Ethics

Alan H. Goldman

ROWMAN AND LITTLEFIELD
Totowa, New Jersey

First published in the United States of America, 1980, by Rowman and Littlefield, 81 Adams Drive, Totowa, New Jersey, 07512

Distributed in the U.K. and Commonwealth by
George Prior Associated Publishers, Ltd.,
37-41 Bedford Row,
London, WC1R 4JH, England

Library of Congress Cataloging in Publication Data

Goldman, Alan H   1945-
   The moral foundations of professional ethics.

   (Philosophy and society)
   Includes bibliographical references and index.
   1. Professional ethics.   I. Title.   II. Series.
BJ1725.G64   174   80-11696
ISBN 0-8476-6274-8
ISBN 0-8476-6285-3 (pbk.)

Printed in the United States of America

To Michael and Joan, my favorite people

Contents

Acknowledgments

My interest in the range of topics addressed in this book was born during my attendance at the Institute of Law and Ethics, sponsored by the Council for Philosophical Studies and the National Endowment for the Humanities in the summer of 1977. I am grateful to the participants in that conference for their stimulating discussions and to the Council and the N.E.H. for the opportunity to attend.

Portions of Chapters II and V on judicial and business ethics reproduce papers that appeared in *Social Theory and Practice* and *Philosophy & Public Affairs.* I thank those journals for their permissions. A large part of the section on political ethics was read at a conference at the Center for the Study of Values (University of Delaware) and at the University of Miami Philosophy Colloquium. That section of the book benefitted from both discussions.

As always, I thank my wife Joan for help along the way; also Marshall Cohen and Jim Feather for providing the incentive to complete the project. My debt to all those who have recently written so extensively in the separate areas of professional ethics is, I hope, reflected in the text and in the notes.

1

Introduction

The Question

Laymen typically judge the behavior of professionals by applying ordinary moral categories and principles to assess their conduct. Most often condemned is the dishonest use of professional status for private gain, that is corruption, or simply the excessive prices charged for professional services. These problems, especially the latter, are real, but I shall address a different issue in this book. Certain other charges of misconduct in business and the professions are defended by appeal to special professional goals, norms and roles: the need to pursue profit for business managers, the requirement to place clients' interests first for lawyers, or to prolong life itself for doctors. Such disputes relate often to the well-meaning behavior of professionals in pursuit of the fundamental values of their professions. It is such conduct that will be addressed in the chapters to follow.

The most fundamental question for professional ethics is whether those in professional roles require special norms and principles to guide their well-intentioned conduct. This is the most interesting issue from the point of view of moral theory, since its answer affects the structure of any complete moral system. It is also the most crucial for professionals themselves and for those who attempt to evaluate their conduct, since

1

many decisions and evaluations in this area will differ according to whether special norms are required. For example, should lawyers ignore the interests of adversaries in pursuing their clients' objectives, in apparent violation of ordinary moral demands?

This is not to say that all moral issues regarding the professions await an answer to this question regarding special norms. Many are clearly to be settled directly in terms of principles more generally applicable, or in terms of analogies with cases from elsewhere in the moral arena. One's view on whether people have rights to medical care, for example, will depend on one's more general political orientation. A libertarian would hold that doctors have the right to sell their services on the free market (despite reservations about their stranglehold on the market through control of training and licensing); while an egalitarian would favor public financing of medical care for those in need. The issue can be settled only in relation to a general theory of social distributive justice. The same will be true of other problems relating to professional practice, especially those concerning the availability of services. It will also become clear as we proceed that many of the concrete moral problems faced in everyday practice in the professions emerge in their full complexity only after we have settled the initial question regarding special norms. But that this question must be settled first renders it suitable for an inquiry into the moral foundations of ethics in the professions. While the fundamental values and norms of each profession differ according to the goals and purposes of the institutions of which they are a part, we may inquire of each such norm whether it is to be elevated above its usual moral importance in the institutional context in which it centrally functions. Our question will be the same for each profession, although the values to be evaluated will differ. We should find some interesting parallels and contrasts.

We may define a professional role as *strongly differentiated* if it requires unique principles, or if it requires its norms to be weighted more heavily than they would be against other principles in other contexts. To say that a position is strongly role differentiated is not merely to acknowledge that its occupier must figure in his moral calculations all consequences deriving from the institutional relations with others created by the position. It is not sufficient for the application of this concept that the professional role involve relations with unique morally relevant features, if these features can be evaluated by applying in the usual way moral pinciples applicable elsewhere as well. We may call a role with such institutional relations and obligations *weakly differentiated*. When a person accepts a position, he normally contracts to perform certain tasks.* He thereby acquires contractual obligations more or less unique to the position. But for most jobs, such obligations have the same weight as other contracts or promises, varying with the import to others of what has been promised. When these obligations are opposed by others normally considered more weighty, such as the duty not to harm other persons, the former give way. Normally the excuse, "I was just doing my job," is not acceptable. More sophisticated versions of this excuse are not uncommon, however, in business and the professions, and one of our tasks here will be to evaluate them closely.

For the stronger concept of role differentiation to apply, it must be the case that the occupant of the position be permitted or required to ignore or weigh less heavily what would otherwise be morally overriding considerations in the relations into which he enters as a professional. Professional duty must systematically outweigh these considerations, as it would not if each such relation were evaluated individually from the point of view of general moral theory. The professional must elevate certain values or goals, those central in his profession, such as health, or legal autonomy of clients, or profits, to the status of overriding considerations in situations in which they might not appear overriding from the viewpoint of normal moral perception. In doing so he will elevate certain interests of those to whom he is professionally obligated, e.g. legal clients, political

---

*Use of 'he' etc. is generally to be understood in this text as short for 'he or she' etc.

constituency, patients or stockholders, over other interests or those of other individuals, in apparent violation of rights expressive of these other interests. His authority to protect certain interests will be systematically augmented, and his authority or responsibility for taking account of opposing claims will be correlatively diminished, if his position is strongly role differentiated.

We have at least one model of strong role differentiation outside the professions. In the family we find roles whose differentiation derives not only from the instrumental benefits of recognizing special obligations, but also from the intrinsic value of the relations that define them. Family members are expected to weigh each other's interests more heavily than those of strangers, to provide for each other's needs as they would not for strangers. It is not simply a matter of permitting such favoritism because of the benefits that doing so affords, although everyone benefits from a moral climate in which such relations flourish. It is true that individuals' interests are better served by those close to them, who take a special interest in them, than they could be within a totally impartial and impersonal moral framework, were the latter a possibility. It is also true that individuals value the freedom to choose and develop such relations, the special nature of which is expressed partly in the extreme favoritism they show toward those with whom they become intimate. But more important are the functions of such relations in the inner constitution of the moral framework itself. From the point of view of a theory of value, human intimacy is a primary source of value and self-realization for almost all persons. And from the point of view of a theory of obligation or right, it is doubtful that individuals could develop moral capacities at all, capacities to act morally toward those in whom they take no special interest, if these capacities were not allowed to develop from affective interests in particular other individuals. Such interests naturally create the intial capacity for self-sacrifice. Moral behavior develops outward from intimate relations within families, to those with friends, to behavior toward strangers within acceptable social limits; and we do not know whether it could develop otherwise at all. Indeed there is some evidence that it cannot, since anti-social and criminal behavior is often associated with a prior history of failure to develop normal intimate relations with family or friends.

It is certainly not required then that persons always count the interests of all on the same scale in order to act morally, even when framing fundamental principles to guide conduct. Beyond the crucial instrumental values for the social framework mentioned above, intimate relations involving extreme favoritism are of utmost intrinsic value in the lives of most individuals. These intrinsically valuable relations are properly characterized as role differentiated in the strongest sense. While it is normally not necessary to ignore or violate rights of others in order to satisfy the needs of those with whom one is close, and while this should not be necessary in a well-functioning social system, there may arise situations in which this becomes permissible. In situations of extreme scarcity, for example, a person can ensure survival for his spouse and children (as he can for himself), before attempting to meet more urgent needs of others in the immediate vicinity. Such situations do not involve the breakdown of all moral categories, as is sometimes argued; they simply exaggerate what are always normally permissible preferences.

Thus preference for family may extend even to violation of claims that would normally constitute moral rights of others. Clearly special norms are in operation here. Special authorities and duties obtain as well in family contexts. Parents have authority to make crucial decisions for their children and responsibility to provide for their welfare. Children owe duties of obedience. Such special obligation and authority derive mainly from considerations of the children's welfare. The idea is that the special needs of children would not be met unless by those who have emotional ties to them, who place their interests first, and who are granted moral license to make decisions for them that they are incapable of making in a rational way for themselves. In some of these respects, as we shall see, arguments in favor of strong role differentiation for professionals treat the recipients of professional services as children. It is argued, for example, that the needs of clients within the legal system cannot be met unless their lawyers systematically place their interests above those of third parties, even to the extent of violating otherwise obtaining moral rights. In the medical context it is held that patients lack the competency to make rational decisions regarding their health, and that doctors must therefore be given special authority to do so.

Judging from the most widely consulted codes of professional ethics, those within the professions tend to view their roles as strongly differentiated in the above sense. The Code of Professional Responsibility of the American Bar Association encourages lawyers to pursue their clients' legal rights with utmost vigor within the bounds of law, without interposing their moral evaluations of clients' legal objectives and tactics.[1] The Principles of Medical Ethics of the American Medical Association leaves the question of informing the patient of his own condition (which we might assume to be a patient's right) up to the professional judgment of the physician, presumably in relation to the objective of maintaining or improving the health or well-being of the patient.[2] In the case of professionals, of course, support for such differentiation cannot derive from the instrinsic value of the personal relations between them and their clients or patients. In the present context such relations approximate more closely to contractual agreements among strangers for the exchange of specific services for money than to relations among family members or close friends. The justification for the elevation to near ultimate status of norms relating to the legal autonomy of clients or to the health of patients must be established in more impersonal terms, appealing to the place of legal and medical institutions in our society.

If the responsibility of advocate lawyers for the consequences of their actions upon third parties is to be so systematically diminished, and the authority of doctors to make decisions for their patients so augmented, this must be because doing so is necessary for their fulfilling their proper professional functions. The complete justification for strong role differentiation here requires that the institution in question serve a vital moral function in society. In addition, the elevation of the norm central to that institution, whether legal advocacy, health or profits, with its consequent limitation or augmentation of the authority and responsibility of the professional, must be necessary to the fulfillment of that function. The interposition of the special professional norm between the professional's ordinary moral perception and his action must be justified in terms of the deeper moral teleology of his profession. It must be shown that some central institutional value will fail to be realized without the limitation or augmentation of his authority or responsibility, and that the realization of this value is worth the moral price paid for strong role differentiation. That price is exacted from two sides. First, there are the interests or claims of others that are normally overriding but sacrificed to the demand of the professional norm, for example the interests of parties who oppose the lawyer's client. Second, there is the dulled moral perception of the professional himself, his insensitivity to interests that oppose the norm in question. This insensitivity may generalize into areas of conduct in which it can no longer be justified.

In the chapters to follow we shall evaluate arguments that attempt to provide such justification of role differentiation within specific professions. In Chapter II we will examine the positions of officials in the political system. For judges it is argued that they have a special obligation to the law: they must apply law in their decisions even when it runs contrary to their perceptions of the relative moral rights of the litigants. For legislators the question is whether they should place the long-range national interest above claims of individual right that normally override aggregations of utility across persons. Chapter III will shift to lawyers and to the argument that justice, the central aim of the legal system, cannot be adequately served unless lawyers act as strong advocates for their clients' legal objectives. The last two chapters will concern medical and business ethics: whether doctors can make medical decisions for their patients; and whether corporate managers can place profits above certain ordinary moral responsibilities, as these would be assigned within our common moral framework.

Before proceeding to these specific variations on the theme of our foundational question, it remains to justify this method of inquiry further in relation to certain meta-ethical issues. For some might hold that the question could be answered uniformly in light of these meta-ethical considerations, without examination of norms specific to the separate professions. There are two opposing ways in which a uniform answer to the question of strong role differentiation might be implied. One would be if ethics were radically relativistic. In that case there might be no problem in asserting separate ethics for each profession, or, for that matter, for each professional. Role differentiation would simply express one ultimate way in which normative systems differ, without standing in need of deeper moral justification. On the other hand, a uniform negative answer to our question might be held to follow from a rejection of moral relativism. One author has argued that the universalizability of moral judgments, the fact that every such judgment is meant to apply to all relevantly similar actions, implies that there is only one moral framework. The idea of separate frameworks of different principles of each profession is thereby rejected out of hand.[3] My initial claim is that our general question is open, that it must be evaluated in relation to the central values of each profession in turn. We should not expect a uniform answer across professions. This claim must now be established in light of the possible objections.

The Relevance of Relativism

We may define moral systems as those that provide ultimate justifying reasons for action. As many philosophers since Kant have pointed out, often when we say what a person ought to do, we intend to suggest only what Kant called a "hypothetical imperative." We tell the person what he ought to do *if* he wants to further certain aims, for example if he wants to stay within the law, or maximize profits for his business, or stay healthy. But when we say what he morally ought to do, we mean what he ought to do all things considered. Moral reasons are overriding reasons; at least it is a necessary condition for the justification of any action that it be morally permissible. Of course many actions are morally insignificant. It is mainly in regard to decisions that significantly affect the interests of others that moral justification is necessary. But when it is necessary, it is also ultimate.

This suggests again that the central norms of the various professions must take their place in the common moral framework that provides such overriding reasons: in situations in which these norms determine only hypothetical imperatives, in which they are normally overridden by other more stringent duties, they cannot be elevated to ultimate prominence. It is a truism that professionals, like everyone else, ought to do what is morally required of them in all circumstances. Their institutional obligations must reduce to moral obligations if they are to have binding normative force. We must look through these obligations to the moral rights they are intended to protect, and we must gauge the place of these rights in our more general orderings, in order to decide when professional duties take precedence. But the inference from these points to a dismissal of strong role differentiation in the professions would be too quickly drawn.

THE ARGUMENT TO SKEPTICISM

The purely formal or functional characterization of moral reasons in our definition leaves the content of such reasons open. Normally part of that content implies elevating the interests of others in relation to one's own interests and selfish inclinations. But if we add even this much content to our definition of moral reasons, we seem forced to admit that these need not constitute reasons for the actions of all persons alike. For a consideration to constitute a person's reason for acting, it must be capable of moving him to act. A fact or belief can be a reason for acting only when connected to a value or desire. A person must share our moral values in order for our moral reasons to be personal reasons for him to act or refrain from acting. Moral reasons are in this sense analogous to aesthetic reasons for appreciating works of art, for example features of paintings which we consider grounds for judging them to be good paintings. If an individual is not moved by these features, they will not constitute grounds for his judging these works to be good.

We must add to this premise, that beliefs constitute moral reasons only when connected to values, another premise concerning systems of values themselves in order to derive a relativist conclusion. The second premise is that there may be two or more self-consistent but mutually incompatible sets of values, such that any preference for one set over the others would presuppose values contained in the first but not in the others. In this situation there could be no value-neutral reason for preferring one of these systems over the others. We could not say that one of them as a whole was more rational or morally superior in some objective sense, since the notion of rationality or moral superiority to which we appealed would beg the question in favor of the one system and against the others. And yet what counted as moral reasons in relation to one of these value systems would not in others; actions judged right from the viewpoint of one such system might be judged wrong from others. That such incompatible moral systems, comprising sets of values and judgments based upon them, can exist without objective or value-neutral ways to judge their overall rationality (assuming all are consistent, as actual systems of societies and individuals are often not) constitutes the truth in relativism.

Judgments that fulfill the functional role of expressing ultimate commitments, commitments that at least sometimes override narrow personal inclinations, can be recognized as moral judgments whatever their specific content. That only this functional role is essential to judgments and values comprising a moral system allows for two or more systems with incompatible contents. Others might argue for a more objective notion of moral reasons, according to which a reason for one person to act in a particular way is a reason for anyone similarly situated to act in the same way. It is not necessary to press further the opposing view that reasons are dependent upon subjective values. A more objective notion of moral grounds for action would avoid the problem that relativism appears to pose for our approach to the question of strong role differentiation in the professions. The problem posed is that, if relativism is true in the sense defined, it appears that there is no objective basis from which to argue whether professional norms should take precedence over ordinary moral considerations. Our question would then appear to reduce to the less interesting empirical question whether these norms in fact command such priority within the professions under consideration. My strategy here is to admit the truth of relativism (since I believe it is true in the sense indicated), and yet to counterargue that the conclusion that there is no basis for argument here, or that there is no right moral answer to whether distinct norms should prevail in the professional contexts, does not follow from this premise.

We must admit that differences in orderings of value systems might involve some of those values central in particular professions. We might imagine, for example, one society or group that values health and prolonged life more than personal freedom to make decisions detrimental to health, and another that places the latter value over the former. The first group would then be inclined to grant doctors broad authority to make medical decisions for others and to initiate restrictions upon certain types of dangerous activities, while the second group would reserve such decisions for themselves as individuals. Many moral philosophers would not regard such differences in value or preference orderings as indicative of any ultimate relativity of moral frameworks.

Utilitarians, for example, would claim that their theory can encompass these different value orientations under the common principle of maximizing desire satisfaction or preferences or the realization of values, whatever they may be. Here the principle of utility would mediate between these two groups by simply adding the utilities and disutilities of each method of assigning authority for medical decisions and choosing the method with the greater surplus of aggregate welfare.

I shall argue that the utilitarian principle fails to capture the diversity of our own judgments concerning rightness. The point here, however, is that the possibility of such broader principles that mediate differences in lower level preference or value orderings does not in itself avoid the thrust of relativism. For moral systems may differ on this deeper level as well. An individualist oriented framework might recognize many individual rights that override collective utilities, while a collectivist morality like utilitarianism would not. A perfectionist or ideal-regarding system will posit goals that override the maximization of desire satisfaction, the only goal of a utilitarian want-regarding system. One framework might recognize independent value to allowing moral autonomy and freedom of choice, beyond the extent to which these are desired by agents; another might not. In one moral system duties to family and other intimate groups may come first; while in another, impartiality in striving to satisfy claims and produce welfare for others may be demanded. These last examples are cases of differences among possible moral systems that are fundamental, that are not reconcilable by subsumption under broader normative principles.

It is often assumed that moral relativism is logically connected to skepticism regarding the possibility of truth or rational justification for moral judgments. The issue for us is whether rational criticism of distinct professional or business moral frameworks is possible. One might argue against this possibility from the points made above regarding relativism in the following way. If different professions can endorse incompatible sets of moral judgments and principles, such that any judgment of them by outsiders presupposes value orderings alien to these professions themselves, then such cross-framework judgments appear naive, based upon failure to appreciate the different value orientation, and in any case irrelevant. It seems that the only rational thing to do when confronted by members of a different group with a set of moral beliefs incompatible with one's own is to withhold judgment. Criticism would presuppose the superior rationality of one's own moral system, which, we have said, cannot be demonstrated (assuming internal consistency in both systems). Any comparative judgment across self-consistent moral frameworks would be rationally unsupportable, and therefore ought not to be made. While it will be possible for us to disagree with professionals who obey different moral norms, there will be no rational way to settle such disagreements, at least according to this argument. (Disagreement will be possible as long as 'x is right' does not mean merely 'x is consistent with my other judgments or with those of my group.' Presumably it does not mean that, if the judgment expresses an ultimate commitment, rather than stating a fact about oneself or one's group.)

REFUTATION OF SKEPTICISM

Thus we have arrived at a skeptical conclusion from the relativist premise. Before proceeding to our critical inquiry into the fundamental values of the different professions, we must show this argument to be unsound. As a first step, we should recognize that the call for tolerance or for silence in the face of different moral frameworks does not strictly follow from the truth of relativism. Indeed we should be immediately suspicious of any attempt to draw a normative conclusion, a conclusion about what we ought to do or what attitude we ought to adopt, from meta-ethical claims about the nature of moral systems. Since relativism states a fact about all moral systems, or about the nature of morality in general, the thesis must itself be totally value-neutral. Because it must be value-neutral, it cannot have any implications regarding how we ought to act toward or judge others. We have said that factual theses or beliefs count as moral reasons only when connected to values. This is true as well of reasons for not interfering with the practices of others. Belief in relativism generates an imperative commanding noninterference only when connected to a commitment to tolerance.

Many people do value tolerance in certain circumstances, but it is inconsistent to attempt to elevate this to a supreme value (as it would have to be for disagreement always to imply a moral demand for noninterference). It is inconsistent to elevate tolerance to a supreme value, because if one were ultimately committed to tolerance, one would have to oppose intolerance in all its forms. This would not allow for noninterference or neutrality in the face of intolerance. To have certain values is to reject others; to have moral values is to be committed to certain final guides to behavior; to be so committed is to be prepared to act in accordance with these guides. If one is committed to tolerance, one must be willing to act in its behalf. To do so is to oppose intolerance and to be willing to act to overcome or prevent it. Thus one cannot be ultimately committed to tolerance or noninterference. (One might be ultimately committed to inaction, but this hardly sounds as appealing, except perhaps to certain university administrators and Congressmen.)

It is also inconsistent to believe that moral relativism could support a demand for universal tolerance in the face of disagreement. If this is intended as a universally valid normative demand, it would imply that one value, namely that of tolerance or noninterference, must reign supreme in every moral system. Since other values could not then be pressed in the face of disagreement, and if not so acted upon, could not be properly attributed as values at all, this would render all moral systems more or less uniform, contradicting the relativist thesis itself. Thus again it is clear that we cannot derive from a relativist premise a moral demand for suspension of judgment or noninterference regarding practices within moral systems incompatible with our own.[4] Even if distinct professional ethics rested upon claims that disagreement with common moral principle is simply irrelevant, and even if there were no value-neutral way to criticize them, this would not imply that tolerance or noninterference is required. For one thing, the ethics of professionals strongly affect others in society. Those affected negatively could certainly seek change without charge of moral inconsistency or presumptuousness. Even without personal stake, it is permissible, indeed it may be required, to discourage the practice and change the judgments of those whose moral views are incompatible with our own. This would include the practices of professionals and businessmen, if indeed their practices run contrary to our moral commitments on the deepest level.

But the fact that the relativist thesis in itself does not imply suspension of judgment of others with different moral beliefs may be of little solace, if we cannot define a method for rationally resolving disputes with them. If, regarding the proper place of specific professional norms, one view cannot be better supported than another, if it makes no sense to say that one view is correct and the other not, then we may remain uneasy in opposing our views to those of professionals who give more weight than we would to those norms. The relativist thesis holds that the demands of rationality fail to determine choice among whole self-consistent moral systems (if none rests upon mistaken assumptions about nonmoral facts). This is not to say, however, that there can be no rational way to arbitrate disputes among them regarding specific moral issues or the place of specific norms. There is no way to stand outside all moral systems and judge their objective worth or value; but there is a rational method for bringing incompatible systems closer together, if there is a will to do so.

This method for resolving moral disagreements is basically the same for global differences in frameworks across social groups as it is for more local disputes among individuals. It consists in reasoning from cases (and principles generalized from cases) on which there is agreement to positions on the controversial issues most consistent with this common body of accepted moral data. Such reasoning proceeds by pointing to analogies and disanalogies with agreed cases, or, what amounts to the same thing, by pointing out implications of shared principles. The constraint of consistency requires stipulating nonmoral differences for every difference in moral judgment among cases. Perhaps more important, it requires generalizing these distinctions, counting them as making a moral difference wherever they occur. If I hold, for example, that doctors may prevent patients from making decisions on treatment detrimental to their health, then I must allow that people may always be prevented from making decisions harmful to themselves by others more competent to judge the consequences of their actions. I must judge all such cases alike, unless I can indicate morally relevant differences among them; and these differences must again be generalized to differentiate other situations in which they are found.

We may illustrate this process of moral argument further by citing an example relevant to our discussion later of the property rights of stockholders in relation to philanthropic decisions of corporate managers. I refer to the disagreement between libertarians and egalitarians over the moral status of redistributive taxation. This specific disagreement is of course indicative of broader differences in relative priorities between the value of equality and certain values relating to liberty, especially the liberty to control property. Nevertheless, the dispute is subject to rational argument, if each of the parties is willing to begin from the equally broad area of agreement and attempt to expose inconsistencies in the other's position in relation to this data base. The critic of libertarianism might argue, for example, that the refusal to allow exceptions to property rights in order to alleviate dire needs is inconsistent with other exceptions carved into such rights to prevent harm. Or, if the libertarian bases his position upon a principle of personal autonomy, in which the primary value is the ability to pursue personally formulated long-range plans, to do with one's life what one wants, the critic can point out that poverty blocks such liberty, that economic deprivation is as enslaving as are chains. The libertarian can reply to his egalitarian critic that in simple preindustrial or "desert island" contexts the industrious deserve to keep their products and owe nothing to their nonproductive counterparts. He will then attempt to extend this argument by analogy to more complex industrial contexts in which people are paid according to their productivity. And so on.

The point here is not to resolve this dispute. We shall encounter numerous disputes on specific issues relating more directly to the professions that employ similar forms of argument. The point for now is that even such substantial and fundamental differences in value orientations can be resolved, if there is willingness to reason from the background of shared commitments and judgments. There is of course social value to resolving moral disputes by such rational methods. Then too, a broad enough range of moral agreement among the disputants would indicate that the issue in dispute lies relatively toward the periphery of their moral frameworks (judgments at the center are those that would require the most changes elsewhere in the system if they were to be changed). This should add to their willingness to open the issue to debate (despite the fact that controversial issues often stimulate the most emotionally charged opinions).

It must be admitted nevertheless that there can be no moral imperative to resolve cross-framework differences rationally, at least none that transcends the different moral systems. Those with alien systems of moral beliefs can maintain them intact without violating canons of rationality, as long as they are internally consistent (it is probable that few actually held sets of moral beliefs satisfy this proviso). Once more there can be no reason to meet the challenge of an opposing system by reasoning from the product of the two, from their shared convictions, unless there is a commitment to do so. But, to bring the issue back home, professionals who adhere to distinct moral frameworks, who give weight to certain norms beyond their importance in nonprofessional contexts, are in no position to rest their case in the isolationist refuge of the relativist argument. Professionals are often granted certain privileges within the social framework, especially privileges to control access to their own professions. Presumably the professions themselves exist to serve others in society, not to provide exclusive benefits to their practitioners under the protective shield of an isolated and distinct moral framework. Professionals of course would not defend their moral codes in such stark relativist terms, although they sometimes resist judgment from outsiders. They certainly acknowledge that their particular kinds of expertise are imparted and acquired in order to be applied in the service of others. In fact, we may take it as definitional of professions that they involve the application of a specialized body of knowledge in the service of important interests of a clientele.

When professionals see their roles as strongly differentiated, it is usually because they elevate certain interests or demands of their clients to greater importance than might be granted by others. But this narrowing of moral focus must itself be justified in terms of deeper moral principles acknowledged by those who might question it. It cannot be a matter of mere preference on the part of professionals, if society is not to be justified in resisting it. Nor can it be a matter simply of a moral division of labor, in which certain professions, for example medicine, take care of certain values, i.e. health, while other institutions serve to protect other important values such as justice or personal autonomy. For the crucial issues arise when these values conflict within professional contexts. If, for example, health does not normally take precedence, there is a real question why it should in medical situations. The departure from immediate overriding demands of our common moral framework must somehow be justified in terms of that very framework. This means, incidentally, that outsiders, especially moral philosophers trained to abstract from specific convictions and to apply principles and analogies in approaching moral issues, are fully competent to evaluate professional codes. What is lost in lack of personal experience and technical expertise in the professions should be offset by the more detached and impartial viewpoint that an outsider can bring to these issues. (I hope also that the parallels and contrasts that will emerge from comparisons among different professions can serve to clarify the issues involved.)

Returning from such apologetics to the argument here, the fact that the case for strong role differentiation would have to be made through appeal to shared moral beliefs and principles means that we may feel at ease in assessing its defense by the methods of ordinary moral reasoning. Within this common framework, when parties disagree on specific issues or on the relative weight given to specific norms, we may assume that one of the parties is mistaken on the nonmoral facts, or inconsistent in his specific judgments, or that he takes some principle to have implications that it does not have. I shall level all these charges against various opposing views in the chapters to follow. In the first class, that of misperception of the facts, are certain approaches to business ethics, those whose position relies heavily upon the false assumption that the free market protects against serious harms to consumers. An example of the second type of moral error, inconsistency in specific judgments, would be a doctor's judging that health or prolonged life take precedence over all other values when it comes to patients, but not acting on that value ordering in the conduct of his own affairs. Into the third category fall those who misinterpret the implications of shared principles (or who believe they hold some principle because they fail to recognize its unacceptable consequences), for example lawyers who believe that a principle of individual autonomy (for clients) requires that they pursue all objectives desired by their clients.

Before pursuing such specific issues, it remains to comment upon another attempt to answer our fundamental question uniformly. It might be held that a rejection of the relevance of relativism implies a uniformly negative answer to the question of strong role differentiation. If professionals must share our common framework, how can norms expressing their central values have special weight, import that they would not have in nonprofessional contexts? To see why this remains an open question, we must examine certain features of this common framework.

The Common Moral Framework

THE POSSIBILITY OF ROLE DIFFERENTIATION

It might appear that strong role differentiation involves the rejection of a common moral framework, that it requires ultimately distinct moral systems. How could a particular norm have one weight in normal contexts, and another in circumstances identical except for the fact that a professional and his client are involved? Such a difference would appear to violate a feature of our moral judgments that many philosophers take to characterize them, certainly within our single moral framework, namely their universalizability.[5] When we render a moral judgment, we intend it to apply not only to the single case before us, but to all persons in relevantly similar circumstances. This is simply the other side of the demand for consistency in moral judgment described above: when we judge cases differently, we must specify distinctions between them that generally make a moral difference.

I prefer the latter formulation of the consistency requirement, because the former suggests that we must specify in advance all relevant similarities determining the proper applications of our moral terms. Stating such necessary and sufficient conditions for the application of terms is something we generally cannot do, as Wittgenstein pointed out.[6] But while we cannot do this for moral terms either, we can meet the weaker demand to specify why we refuse to apply a term to a new case that appears to resemble in certain ways former cases to which the term was applied. In the moral context this amounts to specifying some difference when judging a new case differently from an old one. If, for example, we say that abortion is always permissible, but not infanticide, we must show which properties acquired at birth make such a tremendous moral difference in the status of the fetus-infant. (Of course we might have an intuition of a moral difference without being able to specify what it is. But the requirement of rationality imposes an obligation upon us to try to do so. To rely on such ineffable intuitions is to leave rationality behind. In the example just mentioned, we cannot leave it that birth makes a difference, because birth can be analyzed into the acquisition of certain properties, and these must make a difference in other cases as well.)

Given this demand to be consistent when operating from our common moral framework, the question again presses itself upon us of how strong role differentiation in the professions is possible. The problem is that it is not immediately clear how simply being a professional can itself make a moral difference. And yet on the face of it this would appear to be necessary for professional positions to be strongly differentiated. For if norms are given weight in professional contexts that they are not otherwise given, even when all other circumstances are relevantly similar, if, for example, moral rights of outside parties that would otherwise override can be ignored or demoted by lawyers acting in behalf of their clients, then it would seem that being a professional itself is what matters. But why should our single moral system contain principles singling out professionals for special moral status? Why should it count being a professional as making a moral difference?

In answering this question we may first remind ourselves briefly of our earlier discussion of family relations. The family context makes it clear that who you are, e.g. a father, and not simply what you do or what you know, can make a difference. It is not the special expertise of fathers in relation to their children that gives them special authority and responsibility. Certainly others with similar expertise would not be permitted or required to make decisions relating to their children. The parental relation itself is what counts. I commented above on why it counts. We have also seen that role differentiation for professionals cannot be supported solely by analogy with the family context, since special professional authority, responsibility, or limitation upon authority cannot derive from the intrinsic value of the relation between professional and client. It must derive rather from the fact that more important values will be served by the profession when such special norms are introduced to bar actions on the basis of ordinary moral perception—more important in terms of our common moral framework itself.

I am assuming that special institutional obligations exist when their recognition has better moral consequences than would refusing to recognize them. (Included among moral consequences are not only effects on social welfare or utility, but the satisfaction of moral rights.) The special obligations that comprise strong role differentiation are unique in that they obtain (somewhat) independently of the moral content of the actions they require in specific circumstances. There is some analogy here with the obligation to keep promises. Once one has made a promise, one has a duty to keep it that is somewhat independent of the moral consequences of doing so. But it is also true that one ought not to make promises to do things that one knows to be morally objectionable. One should promise to perform only actions that are independently morally permissible. Our question is why we should recognize in advance standing obligations that require their bearers to ignore ordinary moral considerations. Promise makers cannot do so when deciding whether to make the promises. It still seems odd to maintain that institutional obligations must reduce to moral duties under general principles, and that they nevertheless obtain independently of the content of the actions forbidden or required, that indeed they prohibit the professional from appealing to ordinary moral considerations. Yet such obligations define strong role differentiation. If, for example, judges have a special institutional duty to apply the law and render legally correct decisions, then, except in extreme cases, they ought not to ignore this duty by ruling according to their own moral perceptions.

Granted that the actions of professionals affect the institutions of which they are a part, for example that judicial decisions affect the law itself, we still want to know why the professionals cannot estimate these effects directly in their moral calculations. Why can they not estimate the values at stake from the point of view of the profession or institution in question, and weigh these against the interests of other parties that may oppose them? The answer to our puzzlement lies in the recognition of moral fallibility. If all agents were infallible in their moral perception and perfectly consistent in their moral judgment, if all could estimate correctly the interests and values at stake in every relation into which they entered, then there would be no strong role differentiation in the professions. Our question could be answered uniformly. Because agents are not infallible, the question of authority to act on one's moral perceptions is distinct from that of the moral content of one's actions according to more general principles.

Institutional obligations amounting to strong role differentiation systematically augment or limit the authority and responsibility of those in institutional roles to act on direct moral calculation. Imposing them is morally best when error would be likely if all agents involved acted on their own general moral principles. The interposition of special norms is to simplify the moral universe, and to shift decisions toward consequences that are cumulatively best, but unlikely to be achieved by individual well-intentioned agents acting on their own. Moral fallibility gives rise to a distinction between authority to act and the nature of the action, and this distinction to the possibility of moral obligations independent of the moral content of the actions they require. Those who would dismiss the idea of strong role differentiation out of hand must ignore this important distinction.

To be more specific, fallibility in judgment is relevant to professional role differentiation for three reasons. First, those who consult professionals may lack expertise or competence themselves to make decisions in their own interests in the problem areas in which they seek professional advice. This might argue for specially augmented professional authority and responsibility to make decisions for clients. It can be argued that doctors may override normal rights of patients to information and to autonomy in decision-making on these grounds. Second, the cumulative effects of individual actions within institutional contexts can be difficult to predict in direct moral calculation. Actions judged right from an individual's point of view might have cumulatively detrimental effects upon the institution itself and the values it exists to uphold. This might be true, for example, of the administration of justice and the cumulative effects upon the law of separate judicial decisions according to the moral perceptions of individual judges. If such effects would be detrimental to the operation of the legal system, this would argue for a limitation on the authority of judges to decide cases on moral perception alone. Third, professionals typically act in behalf of their clients, and that in itself raises questions about authority for decision-making. Personal autonomy may be at stake in such contexts of seemingly divided authority and responsibility. So it is argued that the moral autonomy of legal clients depends upon lawyers' allowing them to make all decisions regarding objectives within legal bounds.

MORAL RIGHTS

Before pursuing such specific issues more fully, it remains to make more precise our general question in relation to the parameters of our common moral framework. The problem of authority to act in professional roles on direct perception of ordinary moral considerations is not to be settled in terms of aggregate social welfare or utility alone, but primarily in terms of the satisfaction of moral rights. Since talk of rights will figure prominently in the discussions to follow, we require some initial clarification of their origins and orderings. Rights express interests of individuals important enough to be protected against additions of lesser interests across other persons. When they are exercised, the resultant claims to goods or freedoms are to be honored even at the expense of the aggregate collective welfare. The number of people with opposing lesser interests becomes irrelevant when a right is at stake. Rights themselves are ordered nonaggregatively. If I have a right to speak freely, for example, then it is irrelevant how many people might be offended by what I have to say. If I have a right to my property, then it is insufficient reason for forcibly transfering it that several or many others might collectively benefit more from having it.

Some philosophers would consider this characterization of the absolute priority of rights over utilities to be extreme, but I believe that it does capture a feature of our common moral reasoning. It is also not as extreme as it may sound. The spectre of a trivial right having to be honored at the cost of many lives, for example, does not arise. It does not arise first because rights are not trivial, but express interests vital to the integrity of the individual. Sometimes in ordinary language we refer to rights that appear trivial—my right to eat dinner when I like or to wear a pink shirt with a green tie. But such reference is really to a very important right, the right to be free from excessive interference. The point is really that no one else has authority to dictate my dining habits or dress. Honoring this important right does not require refusal to interfere in all cases such as those just mentioned, if there is good reason for interference. It does require that reasons such as the convenience or offense of others not be routinely accepted. Second, while rights are absolute in relation to utilities, they are themselves ordered, so that rights to life would take precedence over lesser ones. Third, positive rights, rights to have certain goods, are relative to the availability of the goods and the costs of providing them. Thus the spectre of honoring some right at the expense of enormous economic gains for all society does not arise either from the claim that rights are not to be overridden by mere utilities. Normally we do not recognize rights to such economic benefits, but this is because they could not be provided, except perhaps at the expense of more important interests of other peoples. But if such economic means to the free adoption of different life styles could be afforded so cheaply, simply by overriding a single less significant right, then we would recognize rights to such economic gains.

The complaint might now become that we have expanded talk of rights beyond manageable bounds. The reply is that utilities talk has been greatly exaggerated in the history of moral philosophy. The former is common in ordinary moral discourse; the latter is not. The difference between saying that rights at a certain point may be overridden by utilities, as some philosophers do, and saying rather that they may be overridden only by other rights, concerns the extent to which aggregative calculation, the addition of satisfactions across different individuals, is proper to moral decision. The framework of rights emphasizes that such additions are rarely of relevance. Numbers do count, but only when the interests on opposing sides are of equal importance, only when rights are opposed by others of the same type, or when it is a matter of mere utilities.

Given this priority of rights over utilities, the latter may be ignored in most of the discussion of the following chapters. In fact we should now rephrase our fundamental question in terms of the framework of rights. The issue becomes whether professionals may ignore or weigh less heavily individual moral rights that normally constitute overriding considerations. Authority to do so (or limitation on authority to take such rights, those of non-clients for example, into account) would have to derive from the protection of rights more central in our common framework. We may then get a final better grip on our question by delving somewhat deeper into the origins and priorities among various rights.

Certain interests appear intrinsically more important than others, the satisfaction of which is counted as mere utility. An example mentioned previously is the interest in free expression versus that in not being offended. Other interests generate rights not because they differ intrinsically from those opposing them in specific contexts, but because they relate to more fundamental concerns of individuals. My interest in my property, for example, is not necessarily of a different nature than interests others might have in possessing it. Personal property rights are justifiable because they allow individuals to maintain stable expectations and formulate plans in accordance with them. Such priorities among interests and concerns show up as discontinuities in the self-regarding valuations of most persons. Rights relating to basic material needs, security in expectations, opportunities, freedom from unwarranted interference, and self-respect represent interests so vital that individuals generally would be unwilling to trade them for additions of utilities, or for money as the means to obtain such utilities beyond basic needs. While unwilling to trade rights protecting these interests for aggregates of lesser utilities, persons would, if necessary, sacrifice less vital rights to preserve others more fundamental. These discontinuous orderings can be extended to the interpersonal context once we accept the equality of persons from a moral point of view. They then help to explain why we refuse to allow aggregations of utilities across individuals to outweigh individual rights.

Recognition of rights, however, does not derive solely from the strength of desires associated with the interests they express. Rather there is a common thread of content uniting these different interests. What unifies the vital interests in the list above is not merely the intensity of desire associated with them, but their relation to the ability of individuals to formulate and pursue their own plans of life. The truth of relativism suggests that values originate in the distinct valuations of persons with goals and desires. If it is in relation to such freely valuing individuals and their central projects that other goods acquire their value or utility, then it makes sense that the preconditions for the exercise of creative individuality and valuation should take absolute precedence. Such preconditions include satisfaction of basic material needs, the ability to form stable expectations and make plans in accordance with them, the provision of equal opportunities, respect, and freedom from harm and excessive interference. There is therefore an ideal-regarding source of the priority of personal rights independent of the strength of desires in particular individuals to retain them. (That a reason is ideal-regarding does not mean that it is independent of our actual valuations, only that we may count it as a reason for treating others in certain ways whatever their wants might be.) Even if certain persons were willing to sell their rights, their doing so would be objectionable as a sacrifice of their own worth as the creative source of values. Certain interests are important as protective of the integrity of the individual person, which is lexically and logically prior to the other particular goods he enjoys.

Thus rights stake out a moral space in which individuals can develop and pursue their own values within a social context. They serve to assert the dignity and inviolability of the individual symbolically as well. A person with rights is freed from dependence upon the benevolence of others: he can demand satisfaction, and these demands must be reckoned with and respected. The moral space of individual rights exists within a framework that at the same time protects the moral equality of all, since rights derive from universal interests of individuals. If this space is to comprise also an area of increased freedom of choice, then persons must have some choice whether or not to exercise their rights. Such freedom extends to the authority to exercise rights even when doing so is wrong because unnecessarily insensitive to the interests of others. Continuing with the example of free speech, I may have a right to speak freely even when doing so would be wrong because unjustifiably offensive. It is important for later discussion, especially of legal ethics, to appreciate the extent of this discretion in the exercise of rights. It does not extend, of course, to discretion to violate more central rights of others, but does entail authority to act in ways not on balance beneficial or even neutral toward them. Thus, within the very structure of moral rights, we find already an implicit distinction between authority to act and the moral content of the acts. The former is limited, but not fully determined, by the latter.

I have been emphasizing that recognition of rights in general expresses the fundamental liberal values of individual autonomy and equality. Both tend to become fundamental once the relativist thesis is accepted, and it is admitted that persons create values in relation to their autonomously determined goals and projects. This admission naturally elevates these two formal values over those with narrower content, since it implies that no individual's internally consistent priorities take objective precedence over those of others. Recognition of this implication inclines one toward acceptance of the moral equality of others, which, together with a preference for diverse values in society, and the discontinuities in personal valuations mentioned above, recommend the liberal framework of rights. I argued above that tolerance is not demanded by acceptance of the meta-ethical thesis. On the other hand, once individuals do accept it, it may well become to their mutual advantage to establish a rights-based social framework. We may then speak of foundational rights to autonomy (to pursue one's own life plan) and equality (to have one's choices and interests considered on the same scale as those of others). These values are presupposed in the recognition of other rights: the first because all rights protect individual choice against collective interests; and the second because rights protect common individual prerogatives, not idiosyncratic privileges. The framework itself is only one possible social outcome and has no objective warrant over more purely aggregative or collectivist moralities. But I am presupposing for the discussion to follow that rights figure prominently in *our* common moral framework, in terms of which professional objectives are to be evaluated.

Given that rights to autonomy and equality are fundamental within this framework, a useful criterion for establishing priorities among other rights is found in the notion of a hypothetical contract among relevantly equal agents. Rights are to be recognized on this account in the order in which they would be granted by such initial contractors. This criterion is relevant because it captures the autonomy of agents bargaining from their own interests and values. It also defines them as morally equal, as it abstracts from the irrelevant advantages and disadvantages of real persons.[7] Its validity as a general criterion depends entirely, however, upon its ability to capture our convictions in specific cases. Moral differences are where we find them, as long as we count them as morally relevant wherever we do find them. For this reason it is impossible to state any interesting general and absolute priorities among types of rights. We cannot say, for example, that rights not to be physically harmed take precedence over other types. Even more specific priorities among particular rights have exceptions at the borders, as the threats to the interests represented become extreme. Thus we cannot say that the right to free expression always overrides a right not to be offended: a proposed lewd billboard on Times Square is a counterinstance.

While our specific convictions are too fine to be captured by such absolute orderings, certain less sharp distinctions are usefully drawn. Some fundamental rights necessary for the protection of individual integrity obtain simply in virtue of being a moral agent; others result from actions of individuals that create specific relations among them, e.g. contracts. The former generally make claims against all persons, while the latter do not. A distinction mentioned earlier and related to this one, that will figure in our discussion of political ethics, is that between negative and positive rights. The former are rights not to be treated in certain ways, while the latter are claims to goods that others are obligated to provide. Again the former generally hold against everyone; the latter do not. The right to have basic materal needs satisfied is an anomaly from the point of view of these distinctions. It is fundamental, since necessary to individual survival, yet positive. It therefore makes direct claims only on those to whom one is related in certain ways, for example parents and children or government representatives, and indirect claims on others. The latter do not generate obligations to provide personally for basic needs, but obligations to support social institutions that will guarantee their provision. The reason why even a fundamental positive right generates only such limited obligations relates to the underlying rationale of all rights, the provision of moral space for individuals to pursue their own projects and plans of life. If individuals had to provide personally for the basic needs of others, they would have little time or resources to pursue their own interests. On the other hand, they can honor negative rights by limiting their own pursuits to the realization of objectives not seriously harmful to others. This is a far less obtrusive limitation and one in the interest of all relevantly equal rational agents.

Fortunately for the limited purposes of this introduction, we need not press further at this point into priorities among specific nonfoundational rights. For much of the discussion to follow will concern only those fundamental rights on our initial list and the rationales for recognizing them. The discussion of judicial ethics, for example, centrally concerns the ability to form stable expectations and make long-range plans free from the fear of interference by legal authorities. The issue for the lawyer regards the extent to which personal autonomy of clients requires demotion of moral rights of others and of his own autonomy from primary considerations in his decisions. Our discussion of medical ethics centers on the question of whether the patient's contractual right to adequate health care and his right to life override from the doctor's point of view certain of his rights relating to personal autonomy. Our other discussions will be somewhat broader in relation to rights: whether aggregate social good for politicians, or pursuit of profit (as a means of maximizing social good or honoring free consumer choice) for business managers, can override normally predominant rights (primarily negative), whichever specific ones they may be.

The burden of proof must lie with those who would have professionals defer to special norms, rather than make decisions according to perceptions of ordinary moral rights. For strong role differentiation to be established, it must be shown not only that more fundamental rights than those downgraded require it, but also that the effect on the character of professionals themselves is not too detrimental. We must realize that a demand to ignore moral rights can affect moral character, even if the justification for that demand is itself rights-based. The immediate appeal will be to institutional goals, rather than to ultimately justifying considerations. Part of this effect might perhaps be mitigated by sound professional ethics courses that critically inquire into such moral foundations, as this book will attempt to do. But in the present context, even a justified insensitivity to ordinary rights might cause serious problems of conscience for morally sensitive professionals, or, conversely, might generalize into a global insensitivity to moral considerations.

Thus the burden of proof must be rather strict. My impression is that professionals themselves assure that it is met, while moral philosophers tend to assume that a single moral framework must prevail directly. We shall proceed with the inquiry profession by profession. As indicated, I include among professions politics and business, but omit discussion here of such clear-cut professions as journalism and teaching. My reason for this choice relates to our fundamental question, which is central to the practice of law and medicine, as well as to politics and business. While there are questions of differentiation in teaching, for example the requirement to ignore consequences to students in assigning grades, and in journalism, when newsmen seek to protect their sources, these issues do not strike as much at the heart of professional practice (and opposing rights are less often at stake) in these areas as in law, medicine, business, and politics.

I therefore have not sought painstakingly to define 'profession' in any way that might exclude the latter two endeavors. My interest is not in such analysis, but in normative ethics; and the parallels and contrasts that will emerge from discussion of these institutions make their inclusion natural. In any case, the definition briefly suggested above in terms of the application of specialized knowledge in the interest of a clientele fits the case of business management and politics without much difficulty. We must only conceive of stockholders and constituencies in the place of clients and patients. Typical additions to this definition in terms of distinct moral codes or control of access to practice would, of course, beg too many questions from our point of view.

The central problem in professional ethics as actually practiced is not that professionals often fail to live up to their unique official codes and professional principles; nor that they lack the will to enforce them. It is rather that they often assume without question that they ought to live up to them. We may now proceed to question that assumption.

2

Political Ethics: Applying the Law and Washing the Dirty Hands

Judicial Ethics (Strong Role Differentiation)

I shall argue in the first part of this chapter that law enforcement officials, including judges, prosecutors and police, have special obligations to law that private citizens lack. It is not simply that the law grants them special powers and imposes special duties to apply its force to others. Beyond this platitude, I want to argue that these officials have a moral duty to accept these institutional obligations even at the expense of seemingly more important moral rights of others. By contrast, ordinary citizens lack this duty to accept as independent moral obligations the legal obligations that the law seeks to impose upon them. The position of these officials is therefore strongly role differentiated. They have a moral duty to obey law (somewhat) independent of the content of its demands in specific applications. Furthermore, since the requirements of law constitute for them independent moral reasons for action, such reasons can override the moral weight of ordinary rights and the obligations they impose. No such relation to law exists for private citizens.

My argument here will run exactly counter to the major traditional analysis of these matters. The classic view of legal obligation developed by Hobbes and the Positivists was that citizens have obligations to obey the law, but that officials, at least higher officials as representatives of sovereign power, can have no such obligations. This view resulted from the identification of being obligated with being obliged, and of being obliged with being under the threat of sanction for disobedience. Its attempted moral justification lay partly in the claim that rational prudence demands support for such sanctions in order that others will be controlled by them as well. On the other hand, to accept the restraint of a legal or moral obligation without a threat of sanction applying equally to others is in Hobbes' view to place oneself at an unfair disadvantage, to expose oneself to the agression of others. Thus threats backed with power were held to be both necessary and sufficient for recognition of obligations to obey law. On this view the sovereign or its representatives, not being threatened with sanctions from others, could not be under such obligations.

With the distinctions of de facto from de jure authority, and of obligation from threat, and with the recognition that social order based upon threat and force alone is precarious at best, came the tradition of arguing that rulers as well as ruled are morally obligated to obey law. From Locke through Rawls the assumption that all have at least prima facie duties to obey law has predominated. In the more recent literature several philosophers have articulated the opposing view that there can be no obligation to obey the law as such,[1] and that a social order based upon the idea of a duty to obey law irrespective of its moral content is as morally bankrupt as one based upon brute force. Some hold this claim to be compatible with support for legal authority, as recognition of a right of some to legislate and enforce the law. We can recognize that coercive rules are necessary for social order without accepting that they create moral obligations to obey them. Both those who presently support a duty to obey law and those who presently oppose it seem to agree in presupposing that either all members of society are so obligated or all are not. The position to be defended here rather agrees with the early Positivists that we must distinguish officials from private citizens in discussing this issue. I will derive the contrary conclusion, however, from that reached in their analyses.

To admit a special obligation to obey law is to elevate the concept of legal obligation from a descriptive to an independent evaluative or normative category. It is to say that the applicability of law to a given case constitutes a reason *in itself* to act in the way that the law specifies. A duty to obey law amounts to an obligation to give separate consideration in moral deliberation to whether some law applies to the issue at hand. To recognize such an obligation is to recognize a demand of law as an independent reason for action, beyond normal consideration of the actual effects of one's action upon expectations developed in relation to law, or upon the stability of the legal system itself. (The latter considerations could be admitted to be sometimes relevant by those who recognize no independent obligation to obey law as such.) My claim in this section is that officials are obligated to give special consideration to the demands of law in their behavior; while citizens need give only usual weight to effects associated with law, for example the possibility of punishment or liability, the frustration of expectations for actions within the bounds of law, etc. Citizens need calculate only moral consequences of their actions for the welfare and satisfaction of rights of others. They need not defer to the demands of law when these oppose their moral calculations regarding such consequences. It is the latter duty to which I refer as the obligation to obey law.[2]

When I say that enforcement officials are obligated to obey law, I of course refer to that part of law that governs their official powers and activities and stipulates their duties.[3] The specific duty in question is to enforce and apply the law itself, as opposed to acting on what is thought to be the moral weights in each case irrespective of law. In arguing the case, I shall use the example of judges throughout, although the arguments could be applied with slight alteration to other enforcement officials. A full theory of judicial decision procedure is not at issue here. I assume only that the legal system requires judges not to decide each case on what they consider to be the moral merits alone, but to apply the law when possible in their decisions. Whether applying the law is possible in some cases or in all, whether it amounts to applying explicit rules alone or also broad principles implicit in those rules, or whether it includes application of some concept of the overall teleology of the legal system, are also not at issue here. I simply want to point out contrasts between the moral positions of officials like judges and private citizens, such that, while the primary moral purpose in all cases may be to maximize justice by satisfying moral rights, judges ought not to do so directly in each case, whereas citizens ought to do so. For a judge the question of the moral merits of a case is distinct from the question of his authority to rule on those merits directly, even when a normally obtaining moral right of a litigant is at stake. Supposed recognition of ultimate criteria for a morally correct decision does not entail a right to apply those criteria. Rather the judge ought normally to defer to the legally correct decision. Not so for a citizen in his private actions. For the obligation of the judge to amount to strong role differentiation, both these claims must be established.

We want to see then why citizens ought to decide each course of action on what they consider to be the moral merits alone, why for citizens demands of law are relevant only in so far as they alter consequential calculations, while judges ought to stick to law wherever applicable, except in extraordinary circumstances. It is of course tautological and redundant to say that there is a legal obligation to obey law. But this obligation is hypothetical: when specific legal requirements are filled in, we know only how we must act *if* we want to stay within the bounds of law. Hence such obligations are not necessarily independent moral duties. They may simply express a set of rules, like rules of a game, that could be observed, but need not, and perhaps should not be. The major difference with rules of law is the threat of punishment for disobedience. In the case of laws with sanctions attached, there is always prudential, but not necessarily moral, reason to obey. Because we do not trust moral conscience alone to prevent antisocial activity, we require such prudential incentive. But it is one thing to justify coercion, another to claim that demands of law must be accepted as moral reasons independent of their content. The latter is what we mean by a moral duty to obey law as such. To say that an obligation is moral is to say that it has weight (beyond other consequences of disobedience) in any calculation of what should be done all things considered. Our question is whether the demands of law must be so weighed when applicable to a proposed course of action.

It makes sense to talk of obligations to obey laws independent of the moral content of the laws in particular cases, which nevertheless reduce to moral obligations, because of the distinction between perception of moral content and authority to act on that perception. It can be best to limit such authority because of moral fallibility. I stated in the introduction criteria for an institutional obligation to be elevated to the status of a moral duty. The institution in question must serve moral ends, and the obligation held to exist within it must accord with the broader teleology of the institution.[4] In the case of law, the ends are justice and social tranquility. I shall try to show why the former is maximized, and the latter not seriously damaged, by recognition of officials, but not citizens, of an obligation to obey laws as such, that is to give the law extra weight in calculations of the best decisions. Our argument will appeal to the goals of making judicial decision consistent, manageable and predictable, of eliminating bias and error from such decisions, and of dividing and checking official authority.

THE OBLIGATION TO LAW OF JUDGES

Having clarified the nature of the obligation in question, we may turn directly to the distinction between officials and citizens regarding the desirability of its recognition. How is the moral position of enforcement officials differentiated such that they sould accept institutional obligations of a moral kind that citizens do not have? To begin with the judge, the first important factor is his effect upon the consistency and predictability of the law itself. It is important for citizens to be able to know what the law demands in various areas of their conduct. If they want to stay within the bounds of law, they must be able to predict how it will be applied. In order to find this out, it should not be necessary to learn the personalities and prior behavior patterns of each official. It is especially important for lawyers to be able to predict judicial decisions in potential litigation, in order to be able to decide whether to litigate or advise out of court settlement of disputes. Only when such prediction is reliable can the amount of litigation be kept manageable. It is generally easier to predict a decision according to law than it is to predict a ruling on the moral merits alone, since the latter would require detailed personal information about the litigants which could not be found in law books, and only part of which would probably come to the attention of the judge. The judge's own moral opinions also would play a greater and more unpredictable role in reaching decisions on the moral merits alone. Thus in order to preserve consistency and predictability in the legal system, we want judges generally ruling on cases according to applicable law.

It is true that there is a difference in this respect between decisions of lower courts and those of courts of final review. It might be claimed that, while inconsistencies in decisions of lower courts render law in the areas in question unsettled and hence unpredictable, once a decision is rendered by a court of final review, that settles the law regarding the issue in question. In fact, however, inconsistency in high court decisions over time, that is frequent reversals, would leave the state of the legal system in greater disarray than would inconsistency among lower courts at a given point in time. High courts rule on more fundamental issues, and their decisions affect more individuals in and out of the legal system. Even if a decision of a court of final review were taken to settle the law on the issue for the time being, a history of inconsistency would always leave it uncertain how long the time being would be. One could never be sure when a new case might be considered a new test case to be decided on its moral merits. And at this level too decisions on the perceived moral merits could be expected to be less consistent over time than decisions (including decisions to review lower court judgments) according to accepted legal sources.

One might object also that prediction of judicial decision according to law is reliable only in relatively easy cases. When cases go to court, it is often because lawyers disagree in their predictions. For hard cases prediction on the basis of law may be no easier than prediction on the basis of moral merits. Furthermore, decisions which are consistently perverse from a moral point of view are no better for their consistency. Indeed inconsistency might be preferable in that context. In any case consistency is only one factor to be weighed in rendering judicial decisions that are best overall. It certainly can be overridden as a consideration by the moral perversity of extending earlier decisions and existent rules in particular cases.

These objections would call for decisions according to the moral perceptions of judges, but they do not show this to be proper in the average case. The first point about predictability in hard cases does not touch the original argument in relation to relatively easy legal cases, which constitute the bulk of those initially brought to lawyers for potential litigation. Agreement is more easily reached in this majority of cases regarding the demands of law than regarding the demands of morality (as the latter might be perceived by the judge). This objection nevertheless will require a complication regarding those rare cases that are legally hard but morally every easy, a complication to which I shall return later. As for the second objection, we shall see that the law itself provides means for avoiding consistently perverse decisions, and so should not force judges to exceed its bounds for obvious moral reasons. Thus both these points are relevant only in extreme situations, when moral departure from law may be required. They do not show that judges have no special obligation to give the law extra weight in their decisions. Such obligation exists even when moral rights appear to oppose the application of law. A bank's foreclosing on the house of an impoverished debtor might result in the denial of a basic need, but its legal right to do so must be upheld by the courts.

A judge's moral perception might be colored by his political views or by any personal identifications he might feel toward one of the litigants or lawyers. Perhaps a principled judge would overcome such biases or disqualify himself when they came into play; but the increased opportunity for them to influence decisions, were judges given total discretion, would itself be damaging to citizens' respect for the legal system and to their willingness to settle disputes within it. The demand upon officials to act according to law is meant partly to avoid such inconsistency or bias, or even the suspicion of such bias. Since suspicion alone is damaging here, it is not only the consistency of official decisions, but their acceptability to those who agree to submit their disputes, that demands deference to law in rendering those decisions. The fact that legal tradition, the seemingly impersonal aura of the law, commands more respect in the eyes of litigants and criminal defendants than would moral opinions of judges itself constitutes a reason why we should want individual judges to defer to that tradition. The myth of the rule of law rather than of men and women serves a useful function for the stability and tranquility of the legal and social systems, and this useful fiction is supported by the deference of judges to their predecessors and to legislators.

Given that the decisions of judges have effects upon the law and upon expectations built in relation to law different from the effects of private actions, given that consistency among judges is more important than consistency among citizens, cannot judges simply include these effects in their consequential calculations in rendering morally best decisions? They then would normally have to take account of consequences safely ignored by citizens, but this would not generate an obligation different in kind from the moral obligations of others. The duty to consider all morally relevant consequences of one's actions is standard and does not amount to an obligation to obey law as such, that is a special obligation to obey law, independent of normal consequential calculations. That the existence of law can alter those consequences again does not imply the special obligation to obey law as such. Why could not judges simply figure the effects on the legal system of their decisions as one consideration among others, a consideration of which citizens must sometimes, though rarely, take account as well? The positions of enforcement officials would then be weakly, but not strongly, role differentiated. According to this line, a judge might justifiably resolve to stick to law when long-range consequential considerations demand this, but resolve to rule on other moral merits when the effect on law and legal expectations seems minimal, or at least not overriding. In the example of the bank foreclosure, a lower court judge who accepts this reasoning might find ways of at least delaying the morally regrettable outcome, predicting that his action would have little actual effect upon the legal system and upon credit practices. To maintain an independent legal obligation, I must show why this is not the correct moral to draw from the distinctions between official and private decisions enumerated above and below.

Before proceeding to further distinctions, I can indicate initially why a judge's obligation to render decisions consistent with those of other judges and with legislative enactment does not reduce to an obligation to consider expectations derived from such sources or possible effects upon future analogous cases. It is the maintenance of the ability to form such stable expectations that is crucial, and the effect of each decision upon this capability cannot be judged in isolation. The potential effect of each departure from law to render a supposed more equitable decision may appear slight, especially if the judge assumes that the precedent will be limited by future cases rather than extended; but the cumulative effect of a general policy to aim at morally optimal decision in each case would be seriously damaging. In the case of the bank foreclosure, for example, the cumulative effect of judicial efforts in seemingly isolated cases to ameliorate the moral consequences might be to alter credit practice to the detriment of the public. Rights to adequate housing might be satisfied less rather than more often.

The situation here is an instance of a widely recognized general problem in social decision-making. The problem is that decisions that are rational and even moral from an individual point of view may be collectively irrational and morally inoptimal. A standard example of this in the literature is the "prisoner's dilemma." In this story each of two prisoners can maximize his own welfare by confessing and turning state's evidence, if the other does not confess as well. If the other does confess, each is also better off confessing, since the worst situation is to plead innocent and have the evidence presented. Thus it seems to each better to confess no matter what the other does. But both would be far better off not confessing than both would be confessing, since there is no independent evidence that could convict. Thus acting individually from rational calculation they will produce an outcome that is collectively irrational.

This type of situation was brought to the attention of social philosophy in Hobbes' description of the pre-political state of nature. There Hobbes held it to be in no one's individual interest to accept moral restraints, since this would expose one to deadly risks if others were not accepting them, and would prevent one from securing advantages if they were. Yet again it is in everyone's collective interest that restraints be imposed upon all alike. The answer to this problem in the state of nature, and in many real life analogous situations, lies in the introduction of sanctions to tip calculations involved in individual decisions toward behavior that otherwise would not be chosen in particular cases, perhaps not even on moral grounds, but which is required when cumulative effects are recognized. One real life example is the case of industrial pollution. Here the effects of particular decisions to dump wastes may appear minimal in themselves, even from a moral point of view. In the case of air pollution, for example, if others have already fouled the air, then there may appear to be little reason for a single additional plant not to utilize this cheap means of waste disposal; and if others have not polluted, then one plant's doing so might not create any problem. To avoid the unwanted cumulative result of such reasoning, either individuals must become convinced of the wrongness of contributing to the collective problem (which may not be sufficient if their own interests are at stake), on grounds of fair play for instance, or else sanctions must be applied to those who so contribute, making it uneconomical for them to do so.

Judicial decisions share this common structure. We have seen that from the bank foreclosure example. But in the case of official actions for which consistency is desirable, the recognition of an obligation to act according to legal requirements must replace the threat of sanctions. Recognition of this obligation tips judicial decisions toward a cumulative consistency, the demand for which could not be calculated on a case by case basis otherwise. As in other situations in which individually rational decisions result in cumulatively detrimental outcomes, we require either nonconsequentialist rules or alteration of consequences through sanctions or incentives. In the case of officials, in which the latter is not practicable, an obligation beyond normal consequential calculations must be accepted, in this instance an obligation to obey or apply the law. Fortunately, while sanctions are out of place, the recognition of this obligation can be effective, since judges do not have a strong personal interest in rendering decisions according to one criterion rather than the other. Thus judges and other enforcement officials normally ought to apply law, even when they believe that the best moral decision for the particular case lies the other way, and even when this belief has been formed after figuring probable effects of the decision upon future law and existing expectations.

A second distinction between the position of officials like judges and private citizens relates to the capability and desirability of knowing or finding out all the morally relevant facts concerning the parties affected by their decisions. If a judge is to decide each case on the moral merits rather than through application of law, he must investigate the personal situations of the litigants, look into aspects of their situations that would be legally but not morally irrelevant.[5] For example, to decide whether it is morally right for a bank to evict someone from his house by foreclosing on the unpaid mortgage, it would be relevant and necessary to consider the person's financial position, his ability to find somewhere else to live, the bank's need for capital, etc. But the legal right of the bank to foreclose is much more easily ascertained. Similarly, when one person sues another for damages, whether it is morally best that he collect might depend upon the moral gravity of the injury, the motives of the other party, the relative financial positions of the individuals involved, what they proposed to do with the money, the motive for the suit, etc. But the applicability of the law may be far more clearcut. Many similar examples could be provided.

It is doubtful that we would be willing to provide judges with the means to carry out the investigations necessary for intelligent moral judgments on such cases, or that we would be willing to entrust them to evaluate our overall moral needs and deserts in rendering decisions. Furthermore, the economic costs of providing those means while accomodating the required number of cases would be great. Thus, once again, in order to keep the law and the process of adjudication manageable and acceptable to the parties who submit their disputes, we require that judges fulfill their legal obligations to adjudicate by applying law, even when they feel that the moral merits balance the other way. They lack the means to make intelligent moral decisions in every case. A primary function of the law is to simplify the moral universe in which social disputes can be peaceably settled. The more complex moral universe that would result from direct application of ordinary moral principles in judicial decisions would be socially inefficient. In addition, the resultant uncertainty in the legal system would prevent individuals from forming stable expectations free from interference from legal authorities. Preservation of stability in expectations is a primary motive for recognizing rights.

Thus there are good reasons why citizens would not want to delegate the authority to judges to decide cases on perceived moral merits, but would desire them to apply law in normal cases. There may be still some question, however, why from the judge's own point of view he ought not to do what he considers morally best. I do not deny that he should do what is morally best, and what he considers morally best if he calculates correctly. I claim only that in his calculations he must give the demands of the law extra weight. He is not simply to consider such factors as expectations based upon law or consistency as equal considerations among others. From the citizens' points of view, this limitation on judicial authority derives as well from an appreciation of the moral fallibility of judges and from a desire to check their authority with that of legislators and of the judicial tradition itself. In a democracy it is ultimately up to the citizenry to decide how official power is to be delegated, divided and limited, and we have seen why it is rational from its point of view to limit judicial authority in this way by imposing the obligation to rule by law. While a judge may fail to render a just decision occasionally because of a mistaken belief that some prior case is binding on the present case, with adequate training in the law there is less chance of such a mistake in law than there is regarding the decision with morally optimal consequences. If hard cases had to be decided always on moral merits alone, and if each such decision created a fixed rule forevermore, then application of law in other cases might simply compound errors of prior decisions. But since precedents derive from whole lines of cases, and since wrong decisions will normally contradict other principles implicit in prior law, there is less chance of extension of error in this way.

The obligation to obey law by applying law is therefore to be viewed as an important check upon the power of individual officials to make decisions having great effects on the lives of others by their moral sense alone and without firm guidelines. From the point of view of the officials themselves, the obligation in question can be plausibly viewed as contractual in nature. They derive whatever power and authority they have from the political system and ultimately from the citizenry who agree to submit their disputes to them, but acquiescence in their power of decision is not a blank check or one way agreement. It is not implausible therefore to construe acceptance of official roles as agreements or voluntary commitments to act officially within the confines of the limited institutional powers of those roles. Such agreements amount to voluntary assumption of obligations to obey laws governing their official duties, and for many officials obligations to apply law where called for. Their duty to defer to law thus can be viewed as arising both from the advantages to the community of their doing so, and from their having promised in effect to do so. Like other promises, these carry independent moral weight. It is a reasonable answer to an official who asks why he should not act according to his conception of how his role *ought* to be construed that he assumed the position as institutionally defined, that he was entrusted by the public to perform the role as institutionally defined, and that, if he thinks change in the role's functions desirable, he ought to work within the political system to change it. (As we shall argue later, no such answer is available to the citizen who asks why he should accept an obligation to obey law irrespective of content.)

Another crucial difference between the positions of officials like judges and that of private citizens was hinted at above, namely the applicability of sanctions for failing to do what the law requires. In the case of actions by citizens or private corporations, the threat of sanctions (together with other recognized moral obligations) can be relied upon to slant decisions toward cumulatively desirable courses of action; while the recognition of an obligation to obey law is necessary to render official actions and decisions consistent with what the law requires. We cannot demand punishment of judges for every legally incorrect decision, first because in many cases the correct decision is a matter of controversy and honest disagreement, and second because few would seek careers on the bench under such threats. Only criticism within the profession and the possibility of being overruled by higher courts approximate to sanctions for failing to apply law correctly (assuming no gross moral abuse of the position for which impeachment or recall might be demanded). But criticism itself proceeds from an assumption that law ought to be applied in decisions. It can be ignored as misguided by a judge who feels no such obligation, but remains convinced that he ought to decide each case directly on its moral merits. As to the chances of being overruled, they diminish as we ascend the judicial hierarchy. But the desirability of applying existent law according to our previous justifications remains constant; hence so does the obligation to do so with or without this threat of being overruled or limited by future decisions.

Thus, because of legal sanctions, it is easier to incline actions of private citizens toward socially desirable outcomes without an assumption of an obligation to obey law as such than it is in the case of officials acting in their legal capacities. Greater consistency in the behavior of officials is both more desirable and more difficult to achieve without recognition of this obligation. The fact that legal sanctions and liabilities are required to alter some types of morally objectionable and cumulatively detrimental private actions affords yet another reason why officials must feel obligated to apply the law consistently, despite what otherwise might be morally relevant differences among the individuals to whom it is applied. For the threat of sanctions against citizens also diminishes if the sanctions are not applied more or less automatically according to law when violations occur.[6] If those in need could regularly expect sympathy rather than adverse judgment for default of debt payments, for example, they would feel far less inclined to pay their debts, and the entire credit structure from which they and others often benefit would be in jeopardy. The effectiveness of legal sanctions in the area of citizens' behavior depends upon the obligations of officials to fulfill their legal roles by applying the law. This dependence therefore again reinforces the duties of officials to obey the law defining their institutional roles. Because of the need for consistency, the impossibility of making well-informed moral decisions, the democratic ideal of legislative supremacy, the function of the idea of rule of law, and the moral fallibility of individual judges, they ought to subordinate their moral judgment to the legal requirements that specify their institutional duties. They ought, that is, to accept a special institutional obligation to obey laws that define their positions by applying other law in their decisions.

LACK OF AN OBLIGATION TO LAW FOR CITIZENS

Few writers on jurisprudence would deny that officials have this obligation to law, that at least sometimes they ought to defer to legal requirements even when their moral perception of the situation disagrees with these requirements. Most, however, would refuse to characterize this obligation as entailing strong role differentiation in the sense in which we have defined that concept. While the obligation of officials to law creates special specific duties in application, i.e. the duty to apply law in regulating the actions of others, most would deny that this general obligation is itself unique to law enforcement officials. Most would argue that citizens too have a prima facie duty to obey law, a duty which, while not absolute, can sometimes override other perceived moral considerations. If they were right, then the positions of these officials would be weakly, but not strongly, differentiated. We must therefore deny the second half of their contention in this section, as we affirmed the first half in the last.

We may begin by contrasting the positions of citizens from those of officials as characterized above. The argument of the previous section appealed first to the need for predictability and hence consistency in the actions and decisions of enforcement officials. We may contrast the demand for consistency and predictability in the actions of citizens. First, it is obvious that inconsistency in actions among different citizens will not affect the law as inconsistency in actions among different officials does. If different citizens act relevantly differently in relevantly similar morally significant situations, then at least one is probably acting wrongly (or at least morally inoptimally from our point of view). But the inconsistency is not in itself a wrong, in that normally no bad effects will result from the fact in itself that the agents disagree in their behavior. The ability to form stable expectations might require predictability and thus consistency in the actions of particular individuals, but not necessarily congruence of their actions with those of others. The degree to which we are entitled to form expectations about a person's conduct in a morally controversial sphere normally does depend upon our knowledge of his beliefs and prior behavior patterns. Individuals are expected to be more or less consistent in their own behavior, but not with the behavior of others in morally controversial matters. Furthermore, an individual need not act in the same way toward all other persons. A private citizen who acts one way toward a stranger and another way toward a friend normally does nothing wrong. But for an official acting in his official capacity, such favoritism would constitute a serious wrong. (At the opposite end of the scale are roles that demand different treatment according to personal relation, for example the role of parent.)

Thus a primary rationale for the requirement that officials defer to law in their decisions is not present in the case of private citizens. It was also argued that officials are not in a position to learn all the morally relevant facts about the many persons in whose affairs they must intervene. Again there is a contrast here. Private citizens, who need not adjudicate disputes between parties who are total strangers to them, are normally in a better position to know the relevant overall situations of those toward whom they act. There is not the same reason to limit their responsibility to learn all the relevant moral facts before acting in morally significant situations, or the same need to have them defer to authority or to general rules which render only certain facts relevant to their decisions.

Certain other points made above in support of an official's obligation to law have been used in parallel fashion by those who recognize this duty as universal throughout society. From my point of view these claims constitute further contrasts between citizens and officials. We said, for example, that an official can view his obligation to defer to legal requirements as partly contractual in nature. I take it that no such appeal to contract or promise is available for the private citizen who asks why he should accept an obligation to obey law irrespective of content, although such appeals are common in the historical literature. The notorious stumbling block of contract arguments for such duties is that no voluntary acts of private citizens can be plausibly construed as assumptions of duties to accept laws as moral reasons for action. Certainly living in a particular place does not constitute such a consensual act, even if one is legally free to leave or work to change the law. Except in extreme circumstances one does not choose one's residence on criteria of preference for the laws there. One's place of birth is not a matter of free choice. Hence even if residing constitutes promising (how could it?), it would not be binding, since only promises freely given are binding.

It has been argued, somewhat more plausibly, that taking part in a political process, by voting for example, constitutes an implicit agreement to abide by its outcome. Abiding by the outcome is then construed as accepting the laws that issue from the political process as creating genuine obligations. One cannot agree to a decision procedure and then refuse to accept the result.[7] This would be like agreeing to assign the first move in a game by a flip of a coin and then refusing to accept an unfavorable outcome. Again, however, this argument is not sound when applied in the political context. One minor problem with it is that it would apply only to democratic political systems. Another somewhat more serious objection is that it would appear to obligate only those who actually take part in the legislative or electoral process. The really insuperable problem lies in the second premise. Agreeing to the outcome of the political process need be construed only as agreeing to the rights of legislators to issue laws with coercive sanctions attached, not as accepting these laws as independent moral reasons for actions. We saw earlier that one can consistently recognize a legitimate function of law in providing coercive prudential reasons to act in ways deemed collectively desirable, without accepting laws as creating moral reasons beyond consideration of the consequences of disobedience. Refusal to accept the obligation in question does not entail anarchy.

In general, one does not consent freely to assume obligations when one is not conscious of doing so or when one denies having so consented. There is something inherently suspect in the idea of unconscious promises. It is true that freely assuming a job or institutional role entails accepting the responsibilities and duties that go with it. But citizens do not normally choose freely to be so. In any case, it begs the question to presuppose that a duty to obey law goes with the position of citizen. This brings us to a second point, made above in a different context, namely that one is justified in promising only that which is independently permissible to do. If it is not permissible to relinquish part of one's moral autonomy to the judgments of legislators, then it is not permissible to promise to do so. I shall argue for the antecedent below; accepting it makes it far more implausible to claim that such promises are unwittingly made by us all.

The fact that a claim of obligations unconsciously assumed is morally suspect tells against another standard argument for an obligation to obey law as such. This is the argument from "fair play." It holds that since each citizen benefits from the respect shown by all others to law, each owes it to the others to restrain himself equally in the face of law. To disobey those laws with which one disagrees is to assume an unfair advantage over other citizens according to this line. It is to be a free rider, to accept the benefits of a stable social order while refusing to do one's share to maintain that stability. This argument assumes first, however, that all do benefit from the acceptance of obligations to obey laws irrespective of opinions regarding their moral content, and this will be disputed below. Second, as has been argued elsewhere,[8] disobedience of laws places others at a disadvantage only when the laws are such that obedience benefits those others. This is not always the case, especially when the laws are judged to be immoral or discriminatory. In the latter context obedience may itself continue to impose unfair burdens upon those who are disadvantaged by the law. Third, to deny the obligation in question is not to claim an advantage over one's fellow citizens as long as one is willing to grant to all the same discretion to disobey when ordinary moral calculations call for disobedience. One would assume an unfair advantage only if one denied the same moral authority to others, but the denial of an obligation here applies equally to all. Finally, free riders are those who seek out advantages without being willing to pay a fair price for them. Even if citizens did benefit from uniform obedience of others (something I wish to deny), if they did not actively seek such benefit, if in fact they could not avoid it, then they could not be said to owe anything in return.

Thus, whereas it has been argued that considerations of fairness demand that enforcement officials give legal considerations extra weight (in order to treat similar cases similarly), arguments from "fair play" will not work to generate obligations to obey law on the part of citizens. As for their owing the state itself a debt of gratitude, as some philosophers (including Socrates) have claimed, citizens collectively pay for public goods through taxes. These goods are not freely bestowed and do not therefore generate debts (except the national debt). Furthermore, one cannot owe the state anything, as opposed to owing legislators or other citizens. The claim in relation to citizens reduces to that considered in the previous paragraph. Regarding legislators, one surely owes them nothing (beyond their salaries) even for passing good laws, except perhaps a vote in the next election. Finally, even if debts were owed to legislators, it is doubtful that any debt could amount to a duty to accept anything and everything the creditor says as a moral reason for action. An obligation to obey law on the part of citizens amounts to such a duty to accept judgments of legislators as moral reasons in themselves, irrespective of moral content. We have not yet seen a sound reason for doing so.

Despite the soundness of these counterarguments to the standard reasons offered in the literature, the crux of the matter, as with any question regarding the recognition of an obligation, is whether its recognition has overall favorable moral consequences. Within our framework this reduces first to the question of whether more central moral rights will be better protected if it is recognized. Regarding the obligation to obey law, on the negative side is the fundamental right to autonomy, to make one's own decisions on the basis of one's own moral perceptions. On the other side it must be admitted that a central function of law is the protection of other moral rights: to life, to property, to fulfillment of contracts, etc., all of which relate to fundamental rights to autonomy, opportunity, and stable expectation. If such rights were better protected through respect for law as such, then it would indeed be better to view the law as having independent moral force.

In weighing the negative against the positive arguments here, we can first point to one final difference indicated above between the positions of officials and those of citizens, namely the applicability of coercive sanctions. The law always gives prudential reasons for private citizens to obey, always slants decisions toward courses of action deemed cumulatively desirable by legislators. But to say that the threat of sanctions operates in relation to private behavior as a recognized obligation operates for office holders is perhaps to suggest that social order among citizens relies too heavily upon these threats. It is certainly true that social order cannot be maintained by threat alone—to attempt to do so would be oppressive and extremely costly even if it were possible. Perhaps the strongest argument for recognition of a prima facie duty of all to obey law is that society must be based upon freely accepted obligations which respect the rights of others, rather than upon threats of force alone. This premise is indeed correct, but to complete the argument one must ignore the fact that the obligations in question can be our usual moral obligations, rather than a special duty in relation to law. Society can better rely upon the good moral sense of its citizens than upon their deferential attitudes towards its laws. Laws which for the most part embody moral content will require actions which there are independent moral reasons to perform. To say that there is no independent obligation on the part of citizens to obey laws as such is not to condone disobedience to laws that require refraining from immoral conduct. It is to question only whether there is any moral reason whatsoever to obey a law when the act itself is considered immoral or morally neutral, all things considered apart from legality (but including expectations based upon the existence of law). Disobedience in such cases should not threaten social chaos or place others at an undeserved disadvantage. (In the extremely rare case in which social chaos would be threatened, this would be figured in the normal moral calculation of consequences.)

Sanctions add to the force of laws which are moral in content in several desirable ways. First, of course, they provide prudential reasons for committing or refraining from certain acts for those who fail to act on moral reasons. For such individuals, the attempt to convince them of an obligation to obey law is unlikely to be any more successful than attempts to convince them to accept their other more basic moral obligations. Trying to influence them to obey law in this way would be like trying to convince someone who cannot appreciate the logical law of universal instantiation that he should always apply that law in his reasoning. Thus the notion of an obligation to obey law can have no use for those for whom it might be needed, while for others, who normally do what is moral, it is not needed. Of course sanctions work only if lawbreaking is infrequent. But the recognition of an obligation to obey law either cannot or should not remedy this fact. If a law commands what there is independent moral reason to do and yet is frequently disobeyed from selfish motives, then once again the attempt to convince those who neglect their first order moral obligations that they have a second order institutional obligation is likely to be of little avail. If a law is frequently disobeyed because widely believed to be immoral or unnecessarily restrictive of individual rights, then it is better that such conduct check the power of officials to force compliance than that it be further suppressed. But while individuals in the majority are likely to accept most laws as independently moral, what of their acceptance of judicial decisions that go against them and are therefore unlikely to appear morally optimal to them? Routine acquiescence in these decisions is also necessary for a stable society. Here sanctions can again play a role, for these are cases in which disobedience is immediately detectable and hence easily punishable.

The third major use for sanctions occurs in those situations described above, in which the cumulative effects of behavior differ from the predicted effects of instances taken singly, and in which abstention from the behavior in question represents sacrifice or undeserved disadvantage when others are not abstaining as well. In such cases we may add to the force of sanctions a moral obligation of fair play on the part of citizens not to contribute to the cumulative detrimental effect when others are refraining from doing so. In the pollution example, it would be unfair to contribute to pollution when others are restraining themselves, even if the actual effect of one's contribution is minimal. Here we do have a case in which each benefits from the restraint of all, in which the benefits (e.g. breathable air) would be sought by all rational persons, and in which the duty to fair play is therefore genuine. Thus individuals are morally, and not merely prudentially, motivated toward the desirable practice once others are cooperating. Whether the third motive of deference to law is desirable in such contexts must be decided in light of further negative considerations.

Given that actions would conform more closely to the requirements of law if an obligation to obey were recognized in addition to the threat of sanctions and the duty of fair play, why not recognize it? One reason stated earlier is the moral autonomy of individual citizens, which requires authority to act on direct moral perception. Restriction of this authority for officials acting in official capacities allows them to retain it as private persons. But deference to law on the part of private persons would restrict more severely the range of independent moral judgment. A further reason why it would be wrong to recognize this obligation as an additional inducement to act within the law lies in the notion of checks and balances to the exercise of official powers. It is healthy for society to have the moral sense of citizens act as a check to the legislative power to command conformity with laws that may not always serve moral ends. If the moral sense of judges ruling on cases were to have free reign as a check to legislative power, this would have the effect of nullifying legislative authority entirely. But in the case of citizens, recognition and acceptance of legislative authority can consist in the acceptance of the power of legislators to attach sanctions to their laws and have them enforced by other officials. Since the threat of sanctions inclines actions of citizens toward obedience to law on prudential grounds, citizens will not disobey generally on moral grounds unless these are felt very strongly. Recognition of additional moral force to law irrespective of content would establish too great a power of legislators to determine conduct. It would be not only to entrust them with the power of the state, but to set them up as moral experts, which they cannot be.

Given that citizens have strong prudential reasons to act in accordance with laws considered immoral, do we want to give them even more reason to do so? If anything, I believe recent history (during the Viet Nam war, for example) has shown not only that it is better that they feel no obligation to obey law irrespective of content, but also that an attitude of "respect for law" or deference to law is impermissible. Not only is one not obligated to give the fact of law extra independent weight in one's moral calculations, but it is not morally permitted to do so. Only by assuming full responsibility for the moral consequences of his actions can the citizen assume a position as a check or balance to the great power of legislators and enforcement officials to determine conduct.

This claim does not imply an anarchist political stance, as long as it is acknowledged that a coercive legal framework is necessary for social order. It does imply, together with the claim that officials have a special obligation to the law, that the positions of those officials are strongly differentiated.

EXTENT OF STRONG ROLE DIFFERENTIATION FOR ENFORCEMENT OFFICIALS

Having now stated my position in as stark and contrasting terms as possible, I will proceed to soften and fill it out somewhat, retaining its basic claim. First, in relation to the permissibility of deference to law on the part of citizens, we may distinguish different types of cases. For there are laws which command behavior thought immoral (e.g. draft laws during unjust wars); laws which are morally neutral or beneficial, the obedience of which at certain times may contribute to unjust causes (e.g. tax laws during unjust wars); and laws morally neutral or beneficial, the obedience of which in certain circumstances is not necessary to fulfill the moral purpose of the law (e.g. traffic regulations). Deference to law may be impermissible only in relation to the first of these types. For none of them it is obligatory, although in regard to the last type, the principle consideration may be the lack of good arguments for such obligations, rather than the force of the arguments against them. We may also admit that in a just society, the existence of a law may create an epistemic or inductively justified presumption that what it commands is moral. If most laws serve moral purposes, a citizen may even be obligated to think more seriously of the reasons for and against actions to which laws are applicable. But this does not amount to an obligation always to give the existence of law extra weight in the final calculations.[10] The existence of law in a just state may be reason to believe that what it commands is just; it will not be a reason to act in a certain way in itself, although the belief that what it commands is just may be a reason to act. In morally controversial matters there is always reason to look beyond law for support for one's moral beliefs, and the existence of law need be given no independent moral weight when deciding how to act once the beliefs have been formed. (As mentioned before, one also ought to count the expectations of others that may have been built in relation to law where relevant.)

Just as we need to distinguish different types of law in relation to citizens' obligations and permissions, so it is necessary at this point to distinguish different types of cases in relation to official, obligations to apply law. I have argued that judges normally are obligated to apply the law rather than ruling by their own moral senses, since they have accepted positions institutionally defined and limited in this way, and since there are reasons having to do mainly with consistency, predictability and fallibility why this institutional limitation is rational from society's point of view. But in those relatively rare cases which are legally hard but morally very easy, judges may make exceptions and decide on moral grounds. The law must evolve and cannot always await legislative action. It is a legal commonplace that rules of precedent may be limited, ignored or overruled. When this happens in accordance with other more fundamental principles implicit in prior law, there is no reason to view it as a departure from normal procedure in accord with judicial obligation. But there may also arise cases in which legal principle or the teleology of the law, all (legal) things considered, implies a morally perverse decision. Here it has been argued plausibly[11] that the legal institution itself condones moral departure from legal obligations to apply law (presumably only when the decisions would not, if generalized or extended, constitute rules of precedent with bad cumulative effects). In terms of our previous argument, we may say that it does so because those considerations which led to the recognition of the obligation to apply law figure less prominently in these cases. Stability of expectations may be better served, for example, by rendering the morally obvious decisions than by rendering the legally difficult but perhaps correct ones. Nor should expectations for morally perverse decisions carry as much weight as other expectations for legally correct decisions. Nor in a morally very easy care is the moral fallibility of judges as crucial a consideration.

An alternative, but I think less preferable, way of describing the situation in which decisions on moral grounds alone are permitted is to say that the obligation to apply law dissolves in that situation. This is the way we speak of certain obligations in ethics, for example, when fulfilling them would entail morally outrageous results. A promise to murder carries no moral weight whatsoever as a promise. But in the case of official action, it is never inappropriate, in fact always required, to give extra weight to the demands of law. It is therefore better, even in these cases, to say that the legal obligation to apply law remains, that there is a moral obligation to meet this institutional demand, but that this obligation can be overridden in exceptional cases, and that the law itself recognizes and accepts this possibility.[12]

I shall conclude this section by attempting to make clearer the relations between the normative force of the legal obligations of officials (and lack of such force in the case of citizens) and broader moral considerations including moral rights. In the case of citizens, the existence of other moral duties and rights obviates the need to recognize independent moral force to legal duties. The honoring of moral rights and their protection through the sanctions of law are sufficient to serve those moral purposes for which we recognize obligations to obey law on the part of officials. I do believe that consistency and the ability to form stable expectations is desirable in the sphere of private actions beyond that which would be possible if everyone acted on utilitarian calculations all the time. But I believe that the recognition of moral rights allows for the formation of stable expectations without recognition of an obligation to obey law. If one has not only a legal but a moral right to his property, for example, then considerations of utility will not justify taking it from him. He can then be secure in his possession of it in relation to the moral, and not merely legal, motives of most other persons. For the others, whose actions are not guided by what we consider to be moral motives, the threat of sanctions against theft hopefully will suffice. A major rationale for the recognition of many moral rights lies in the need for security and stable expectations. These in turn are required for the ability to formulate and pursue one's own plan of life, which I have called the most fundamental right. Morality must honor these requirements apart from obedience to law.

One moral right of citizens that we recognize at least partly for this reason is the right to actions and decisions of officials in accord with law. This right is correlative to the obligation of officials to obey law: an obligation *to* citizens to honor this right. Viewed in this way, we can see more clearly why the obligation amounts to a moral demand to accord the law extra weight in moral calculations. If we say that the litigants in a judicial case have a right that the case be decided according to law, this means that their claim to such a decision will not be overridden by considerations having to do only with the maximization of utility or interest satisfaction (by what the judge believes would lead to these goals). The right can be overridden only by other stronger moral rights. This makes more precise the claim made earlier that a case must be morally very easy for a judge to be justified in departing from law. What this means is that there must be clearly overriding moral rights involved. The moral right of citizens to official actions and decisions according to law is only one among others, which is why the obligation of officials to obey the law cannot be absolute. A necessary condition for justifying this right is showing how its recognition benefits its holders. I have tried to show how citizens benefit from the obligation of officials to obey law, and also why officials cannot have competing claims that would annul this obligation. Finally, I hope to have shown why citizens would derive no overall benefit from imposing a like obligation upon themselves. They have no general right that other citizens obey all laws, because in many cases they could not benefit from this obedience. They benefit more from the defiance that sometimes results from opposing the moral sense of their fellow citizens, with no moral fetters, to that of even well-intentioned legislators.

Morality and Politics

The previous section provided us with an illustration of strong role differentiation within an institutional context. We have seen that the actions of certain agents occupying roles within the political system must be guided by special norms, in this case legal norms. The discussion there, however, did not focus upon political ethics in the usual sense, since judges and other enforcement officials are not those normally thought of as politicians. They do sometimes engage in political activity, especially if their positions are elective, but the real business of politics is carried on mainly by those in the legislative and executive branches. There is no question of strong role differentiation in the same sense for them, since they are engaged in making the law rather than applying it. If they fail to pass legislation in accord with the rules stipulating their authority, then their statutes will not constitute law in the eyes of the courts. Thus there is no real question of their failing to defer to that part of the law that defines their institutional role. It is commonly argued nevertheless that political ethics is strongly differentiated in another sense. The moral framework for politics is claimed to be more lenient in some of its demands (and less lenient in its demands on the private lives of legislators) than our common moral framework. I shall assess this claim in this section.

THE PARADOX OF DIRTY HANDS

At least since Machiavelli it has been common for political and moral philosophers to accept that politicians or statesmen ought sometimes to set ordinary moral scruples aside. Sometimes, it is held, they must do what is wrong from the narrower viewpoint of personal morality in order eventually to promote the greater good or national interest. Politicians are sometimes permitted, even required, to lie, deceive, mislead, threaten, coerce, break promises, etc., actions condemned by ordinary moral principle. Saints are not cut out for the rough and tumble of political life. Ruthlessness is sometimes required in the pursuit of the public good, and scruples as to means, even prohibitions relating to individual rights, must sometimes be ignored or overridden. If such prohibitions are absolute or even simply more stringent in private life, then moral judgment of politics must indeed proceed from a different perspective. The role of politician would then be strongly differentiated. It has seemed to many philosophers that this moral framework for politics is more purely consequentialist, more oriented, as are the actions of politicians themselves, toward the longer range end of aggregate public welfare, less concerned with personal rights and their relation to political means.

This dichotomy has its contemporary adherents too. In fact, in a recent collection of papers on the subject of private and public morality, there was unanimity among the three distinguished philosophers who addressed this issue that the difference is real.[13] There prevails in these recent articles, as in the writing of Machiavelli himself, a tone of bemused condescension toward the naive moralist who would deny it, like his counterpart greenhorn politician who learns more quickly in the real world of politics that he must dirty his hands almost as soon as he wets his feet. In the more contemporary nationalist political context, as opposed to the Machiavellian politics of the city state, the modern politician may conceivably be required not only to deceive, coerce, and deal with the unscrupulous on their own level, but in more desperate contexts of war or internal strife, to order the bombing of civilian populations, the killing of innocent adults and children, or even perhaps to order the torture of a terrorist to prevent deaths within the politician's constituency or social disaster.[14] The differences between ordinary and extraordinary political contexts, and between this and earlier times in politics, are matters of degree; the reasons for the difference in moral assessment of politicians, as opposed to private citizens, remain the same: that the public figure is more concerned with the broader and more remote public good. Pursuit of this aggregate social welfare sometimes requires overriding individual claims or rights that would obtain absolutely in more personal contexts. Political morality is thus claimed to be less individualist and personal, more purely consequentialist or utilitarian, than is ordinary private morality, in which rules respecting rights are to be more strictly observed. The politician is to be judged not so much in terms of the deontological status of his acts, whether they involve lying or even killing if necessary, but more in terms of their longer range historical effect on the achievement of worthwhile national or social goals.

There is, however, one new twist in the analyses of the contemporary philosophers befitting the development of heightened moral sensitivity since the time of the Florence of the Medicis. The contemporary philosophers who recognize a dichotomy between political and private morality are not thoroughgoing utilitarians or consequentialists. They take rights seriously; hence the claim that the violation of individual rights or of the deontological rules corresponding to them is wrong not simply in a weak or prima facie sense, but genuinely wrong. The politician who violates them is genuinely guilty of a breach of duty, of treating another person in a way that he ought never to be treated. There is a real injustice, and the person may rightly complain or seek redress. The Machiavellian precept that the politician must learn to do wrong is taken in its most literal sense, and a full-fledged moral paradox results. The broader aggregate consequences of which the public figure must take account can overwhelm rules or rights that are nevertheless to be taken as absolute prohibitions. Such rights retain their force even when overridden in political contexts. It therefore may become morally necessary for the politician to do wrong, impossible for him to do what he ought to do, and he becomes guilty for doing what is morally required. Or so claim those who recognize this paradox of dirty hands. Their position results first from their belief that certain absolute moral prohibitions, certain rules regarding things one simply must not do, nevertheless give way in political contexts. Their second premise is that a good man will accept guilt from having treated people wrongly, while a good politician will recognize the necessity of sometimes doing so.[15] Politicians remain persons even while acting politically. Treating people wrongly does not become right when morally required. Lying to someone who deserves not to be deceived, ignoring just claims, torturing or killing innocent people are always wrong, but sometimes politically necessary. Such actions may be directly required in the formulation of policy for the general good, or indirectly necessary in order to attain or retain political power so that one can serve the general good. Certainly the requirement of public support fosters aggregative moral reasoning and acts in behalf of one's constituents that might not be proper in the context of personal morality.

THE PARADOX RESOLVED

In this subsection I shall defend the allegedly naive view that the framework of ordinary moral principles suffices to determine what ought to be done in political contexts as well. Thus I shall reject the view that the position of politician is strongly differentiated. Rejection of the split between political and ordinary morality will also dissolve the paradox of dirty hands. In order to accomplish this, it will be necessary first to remind ourselves of certain features of our common moral framework, as described in the Introduction. The seeming paradox, as well as the claim that political ethics must diverge from that applicable in personal contexts, derive, I believe, from confusions regarding the nature of rights and the rules that recognize and express them. Clarity on the ordering of rights in relation to each other, and on their relation to utilities, takes us a long way toward appreciating both why political life must be guided by our common moral framework, and why political ethics has nevertheless seemed to many philosophers to differ from private.

THE ORDERING OF RIGHTS   The first relevant point made earlier regarding moral rights is that they are never to be overridden by aggregations of utility across different individuals. Rights express interests that are not to be sacrificed to lesser ones, the satisfaction of which results in mere utility, no matter how many of the lesser satisfactions are at stake. If there is a right to dine in public facilities, for example, then a person cannot be justifiably refused service according to how many others might be offended at his presence. Aggregations of these disutilities, each in itself inimical to the self-respect and integrity of individuals, are simply irrelevant. This lexical priority of rights over aggregations of utility or disutility is one source of the mistaken claim in the position characterized above that rights are absolute, that it is always wrong to ignore or override them, and that all consequentialist reasoning is out of place in relation to them. In fact the denial that rights can ever be overriden by aggregations of mere utility does not imply such moral fanaticism, since they are clearly to be ordered internally and non-aggregatively in relation to each other. The right to free expression must sometimes be overridden if another person's life or most valued property is at stake. There is a right to free speech *except* when this would conflict with certain other even more important rights expressing more fundamental interests. If rights were absolute, then indeed we should have to conclude that sometimes it is right to do wrong and sometimes impossible to do what we ought to do. But even without appeal to such implied contradictions, it becomes obvious that this is not the case when we think of certain specific rights, the right to be told the truth for example, which can be overridden for a variety of reasons.

If we had available a complete ordering of rights, these relations of priority would be expressed in exceptive clauses that narrow the domain of each in relation to more important interests. Each right would then remain absolute within its properly narrowed domain, and we could if we wished avoid talk of conflicts among rights or of their being overridden in such contexts of conflict. But the latter expressions remain useful in bringing out that certain rights may continue to have force even when overridden by others. Some such cases require only an apology or excuse; in others the rights can and should be honored at a later time. In yet other cases, when persons' lives are severely disrupted and their vital interests sacrificed, profound regret and reparations in so far as possible are due. (All compensation may be insufficient to the person sacrificed.) This last class of cases constitutes a second source of the false intuition that rights are absolute, never to be overridden. A third source perhaps is the fact that most of us thankfully rarely or never encounter situations in which conflicting rights obtain against us, and in which we must override some in order to honor others.

The rarity of such disturbing situations for private persons, *as opposed to politicians,* derives from the varying claims that different types of rights make upon us. Such claims often vary according to our relations to the right holders in question. Negative rights, rights not to be harmed, mistreated or denied respect, generally hold against everyone. But these are relatively easy to honor simply by staying out of the way of most people. Rarely need we encounter situations in which we must harm one person in order not to harm another; normally we can refrain from harming anyone. Positive rights, on the other hand, rights to have certain needs or interests satisfied by the actions of others, would be far more obtrusive if they held equally against all. But partially for that very reason, they make strong and specific claims only against those to whom their bearers are related in certain specific ways. As a private person I have no obligation to meet even the basic needs of all those who lack necessities, although I do have an obligation to support institutions and political processes that will tend to guarantee their provision.

That positive rights generate only such weaker claims against the general public was explained by appeal to a fundamental source of the existence of rights: their preserving moral space for the free development and integrity of individuals who can formulate and pursue their own life plans, in relation to which other goods derive value. The asymmetry in the private sphere between obligations not to harm and those to provide positively for needs and wants of others derives from what would otherwise be the obtrusiveness of positive rights on both ends. If individuals felt obligated to take steps constantly to satisfy the interests of others, they would have little time to pursue their own interests, and they would be often obstructed in that pursuit by others mistakenly attempting to aid them. For persons in private life, therefore, morality consists for the most part in refraining from harming others, and also in providing benefits to those with whom they stand in naturally close or contractual relations. It is mainly in the latter cases, and then relatively rarely, that they must take seriously orderings among different rights in having to sacrifice some in order to honor others. The promotion of general aggregate utilities is not a major duty and certainly of no concern when rights are at stake.

RIGHTS AND POLITICAL OBLIGATIONS   These further comments on rights allow us to judge better the question posed regarding political morality. The claim in dispute was that politicians must sometimes ignore personal rights when our framework for personal morality would require honoring them, i.e. that the politician's role is strongly differentiated. We cannot, of course, reject this thesis out of hand, since we have seen that others in the political system must indeed march to a different drummer. The case of the judge is, however, instructive in its contrast to that of the politician. The reason for role differentiation for the former related to some of the underlying purposes of recognizing moral rights in the first place. Especially the ability to acquire stable expectations, to formulate long-range plans with the knowledge that one will be free from interference by legal authorities, requires a stable legal and social framework. This in turn requires consistency in judicial decisions according to law, rather than decisions on perceived moral merits alone.

The argument regarding the formulators of public policy is

the converse. The purposes for which moral rights are recognized would be defeated were politicians permitted or required to place aggregate welfare or utility above the observance of individual rights. If the purpose of recognizing rights is precisely to protect certain interests vital to the integrity of the individual against aggregations of lesser wants or desires, then why should we permit this to happen when instigated by politicians? The political context is important in providing a framework in which individuals can exercise choices in developing life plans as centers of diverse values. Certainly some individuals can rise above repressive social contexts to assert their individuality creatively, but there is no doubt that the degree of respect shown personal rights in the political system influences patterns of free expression on the one hand, and blind conformity on the other, in society. Even without this more subtle but pervasive influence, so many moral issues in which rights are at stake are decided in practice in the political arena, that rights would be fragile indeed if not protected there.

In fact, governments pose so much more visible threat to personal rights than do other individuals that historically rights were often conceived first as holding against the state, and only derivatively against the aggregate of other individuals represented by the government. Our Bill of Rights was framed precisely to protect the interests named there against appeals to broader national welfare when seemingly opposed in specific contexts. There is of course a class of moral rights that relates specifically to the political and legal process: rights to due process and equal protection of law, to participation in political decision and to public disclosure by representatives. These arise from the same source as other moral rights, but, because they relate specifically to and are typically threatened only by political action, they are more often explicitly asserted against governments than are other moral rights. Presumably those philosophers who argue for a more purely consequentialist or aggregative political ethic would not endorse violation of such political rights in its name. But all moral rights share this formal feature of priority over aggregative considerations, and some are difficult to classify as political or nonpolitical, e.g. the civil rights of minority group members. There is no more reason to violate those unconnected with political participation. Finally, all moral rights, including those related most closely to the political process, become endangered by claims implying special less personal political ethics, whether the appeal is to the conservative's reasons of state or national security or to the radical's people's demands.

Moral rights are then to be conceived as constraints upon political action taken to satisfy majority wants. Equally important is the positive duty of government to protect moral rights by law. This is a major rationale for the existence of a coercive legal and political framework. From Locke through Nozick there is another tradition of political philosophy that recognizes as the *only* function of government the protection of moral rights. This tradition, however, notoriously fails to acknowledge or honor positive rights to the satisfaction of basic needs. Beyond the protection of negative and positive rights, we may recognize also legitimate political decisions that have to do only with the maximization of utility—decisions relating to the economy, highway or dam construction, and so on, where basic needs are not obviously at stake. But if we believe in moral rights at all, if the priorities of our common moral framework are as described above, then it is simply inconsistent to acknowledge rights as trumps on aggregations of lesser interests, and yet deny that this priority holds in relation to politicians.

We have seen one sign of this inconsistency in the paradox of dirty hands, the contradictory claim that politicians ought to do wrong and are guilty for doing what is right for them to do. The source of this paradox can now be better understood. It arose from a mixture of truths and confusions: first, taking rights to be absolute because never overridden by aggregate utility and rarely overridden in private contexts; second, recognizing that rights must be overridden far more often in political contexts; then concluding that political morality must be different, must be more purely consequentialist or cost-benefit oriented, and that the politician who adopts this stance is nevertheless guilty as a person of violating absolute moral prohibitions. When we recognize that the same moral framework applies to both the private and public domains, that within it rights are prior to utilities but ordered in relation to each other, and that the politician more often than the rest of us must make decisions within a context of conflicting rights, the paradox dissolves. The moral framework for political decision does not differ from the usual, but the occasions for its application in the political context do. People indeed must occasionally be lied to, deceived or coerced by political acts, but only when more fundamental rights are at stake. The reason for the politican's more often facing situations in which he must honor or protect some rights at the expense of others is the fact that he is entrusted with the protection of rights that impose no such perfect obligations upon the rest of us. This is a primary rationale for the existence of his position. But it is not a matter of a different moral framework, certainly not one more lenient in regard to rights, only of a special additional contractual obligation attaching to the office. Like many other roles, the politician's is weakly, but not strongly, differentiated.

The examples provided by those who accept the paradox in which personal rights are ignored by politicians may then be genuine, but they are never cases in which mere utility or aggregate interest constitutes the overriding moral requirement. The test is always opposition by stronger rights, as we can see by noting some of the examples. A candidate may have to make a deal with an unscrupulous boss to fix a contract in order to get elected, if he is convinced that his opponent, if elected, will fail to honor rights more precious than economic rights to fair bidding.[16] Otherwise he has no excuse. And if the contract will result in shabby construction which may endanger health or lives, for example, then he has no excuse in any normal election for agreeing to the deal. At the other extreme in circumstance, it is true that a terrorist without an urgent cause may have to be tortured to find out where bombs that will kill innocent people are hidden, but this is certainly not a case of mere utilities overriding rights. Appeal to national interest or security may be legitimate if the appeal is to rights of citizens that are genuinely threatened from without or within, otherwise not. Such cases in which rights must be overridden to protect others more precious do not involve guilt or wrongdoing by the public official entrusted with their protection, but they may be occasions for profound regret and reparation. The regret is not for having violated a rule that is sacred, but for having harmed someone or having failed to provide for his needs. Speaking in terms of guilt is an exaggeration, but it does express a well-taken reluctance to allow politicians to make a habit of ignoring rights. Even in politics conflicts not already settled by well-defined exceptive clauses should be relatively rare, and the more central a right is to personal integrity, the more certain and immediate must be the opposition of an even stronger right to justify overriding it.

Proponents of a special political morality have one further argument not yet addressed here. Appeal is sometimes made to a supposed division of moral labor within legal and political institutions. The idea is that the courts are to protect rights, while legislatures are left free to pursue aggregate community welfare within this context of judicial protection for minorities and individuals.[17] This claim derives what plausibility it has from the fact that purely consequentialist reasoning is out of place in judicial decision, but often not in legislative enactment, from the fact that representative democracy encourages aggregate or majoritarian calculations by legislators, and from the historical circumstance that courts in recent years increasingly have come to defend minority rights against objectionable majority sentiment through appeal to the Constitution. The first fallacy, however, emerges from the realization that courts, as argued above, must confine themselves to protection of legal rights, those recognized explicitly or implicitly in the body of law. The class of rights recognized in law is not coextensive with those that figure in ordinary moral reasoning. It may be that one explanation for the courts' recently stretching beyond appeal to legal rights is the acceptance by those in control of political processes of exclusively aggregate consequentialist reasoning. Second, even if the protection of moral but not legal rights were a legitimate concern of the courts, they could attempt to correct for the violation of these rights by politicians only after the fact, which would leave the rights still inadequately protected. Thus we are left with a position nearly opposite to that advocated in this final argument for a special political morality. I have argued that judges may sometimes ignore otherwise existing moral rights in order to apply the law, but that legislators may not do so in its formulation.

The only difference we have found in the moral framework for political decision is a contractual obligation to defend and honor moral rights and promote utility through legislation and political action. The order of specific duties imposed by this general obligation is the same as that imposed by our ordinary moral framework: first, to protect negative rights of citizens through the police force and defense system, the criminal code and civil system of remedies for injury; second, to provide for positive rights, i.e. to enforce relations of positive right among citizens mainly through contract law, and to ensure the provision of basic necessities for all; and third, to promote aggregate welfare or utility by regulating the economy and providing public goods and services. This order of goals for public policy argues for the politician's adopting the same constraints in all his political decisions. The additional contractual obligation not only to refrain from violating rights, but actively to defend them and provide for their realization, explains why public officials may rely upon coercion to effect what would be illegitimate for citizens to do for themselves. Redistributive taxation, for example, would be theft if attempted by private citizens; but it is legitimate for legislators to enact it as a way of meeting basic needs and honoring the positive right to a fair share of society's resources. The draft would be enslavement if attempted for a private army, but may be legitimate as public policy when the freedom or quality of life of all citizens is threatened from without. Again these added powers do not represent a more lenient moral framework in relation to rights, but in fact more prefect obligations in regard to their protection and realization than those incumbent upon private citizens.

Redistributive taxation is not in violation of property rights, since we recognize an exceptive clause in these rights in order to contribute to the satisfaction of basic needs of others. It is the politician who has the duty to determine the specific scope of this obligation so as to distribute burdens and benefits fairly throughout the community. Private citizens acquire specific obligations to contribute to the satisfaction of other citizens' positive rights (in noncontractual situations) when these burdens are distributed fairly by the political system. This cannot be the whole story behind the justification of taxation, however, since tax money is not used only for the protection of rights. It is not used only for defense and police, to protect rights against harm, and for minimal welfare, that is to provide for basic needs. Tax revenue also purchases public goods and contributes to higher education and the arts. Regarding the latter uses it might be said that rights to property are being violated or overridden to provide mere utilitarian benefits to the public. If we do not wish to deny the propriety of government support for science, humanities and the arts, and I do not, must we then admit either that utilities may indeed sometimes override rights in our common framework of moral reasoning, or else that politics really does require a more utility oriented framework?[18] Either admission would be damaging to the position defended in this section, but neither is necessary.

Part of justification for spending on public goods appeals to the notion of consent. Citizens do have some control over the rate of taxation through election of officials and direct referenda. They normally do vote to provide certain public goods and services from government resources. The problem of free riders, those who would benefit from such goods even if they did not contribute to payment for them, makes public funding from coercive taxation not only fair, but required if the goods are to be provided at all. Appeal to consent by vote cannot supply the full justification we seek for this restriction or exception to property rights, however, since there remain those of libertarian orientation who would vote against taxes for these purposes, even after understanding the free rider problem.

The deeper answer derives partly from the point that positive rights to goods are relative to the (moral) price of satisfying them. The interest in having these goods must be weighed against the interests that must be sacrificed to provide them in deciding whether to recognize such rights. But this is not a simple utilitarian calculation. Rather, these interests are weighed relative to the fundamental liberal value of freedom, including positive means for the individual to develop his own values, to pursue what he considers worthwhile and express his own personality. In this light it may well be that persons in an affluent society have rights to such goods as recreation and opportunities for cultural enjoyment and expression.

On the other side, there is no reason from this point of view to recognize rights to every penny that can be acquired in a free market. Rights to a certain *amount* of property exist to satisfy basic needs. Rights to a certain *proportion* of what one earns derive first from the link between concepts of personal desert and a person's effort and productivity. Second, recognition of these rights allows individuals greater freedom to pursue what they consider worthwhile, including styles of life that are materially expensive. But recognition of a right to keep all that one can earn in a free market, upheld by right-wing libertarians on the grounds that anything less is unjustifiably coercive (in forcing some to contribute to the welfare of others), would actually result in far less freedom and opportunity for many to formulate life plans, develop values in relation to them, and pursue these autonomously chosen goals. Poverty, the inevitable result of such "free" market distribution, is enslaving in a literal sense. Without such rights to full earnings, payment from taxation for public goods amounting only to utilities, such as improved roads, can be justified as well. It becomes a matter of weighing interests of the rich to additional marginal wealth against the interest of the public to the goods in question (this *is* a straightforward utilitarian calculation).

As mentioned earlier, the politician also has a stricter duty to promote public welfare or aggregate utility than does the private citizen. In freely conferring benefits the private individual can prefer his family or friends, but this is impermissible for the politician when he distributes public benefits and burdens. On the other hand, as representative of a certain constituency, his preference for his interests and those of his own country is not merely permissible but obligatory, although it does not extend to violating negative rights of others (unless through their government's aggressive acts they have forfeited them). Once more these differences do not signal a different moral framework for politics, but simply special contractual obligations that attach to various positions that exist for particular social purposes. We said in the previous section that the judge's strongly differentiated obligation to law could also be viewed as contractual. The difference is that the judge's duty extends to ignoring moral rights of litigants that might otherwise override, while in the case of the politician this is not true. In fact in his case the obligations obtain precisely to enact and enforce certain demands of our common moral framework.

UTILITARIAN ACCOUNTS OF RIGHTS

A major thesis of this section has consisted in a denial that aggregate utilitarian analyses suffice as moral frameworks for political decision. I have been presupposing from the Introduction until now that rights cannot themselves be captured by analyses of these types. In this subsection I shall take a brief look at some of the recent more or less sophisticated attempts to account for rights in these terms. This will carry us back eventually to a somewhat altered thesis of distinct private and political moralities, which I shall again reject.

THE ECONOMIC ANALYSIS   One major recent movement in legal philosophy views rights as utilitarian devices to promote economic efficiency.[19] On this view we think of rights initially as claims to goods that can be bought and sold on a free market. They gravitate therefore toward the highest bidders, toward those who would be willing to pay most for them. Willingness to pay is supposed to reflect value to the party in question. If the right is to resources to be put to a productive use, the value to the producer in turn reflects greater potential value to others who will benefit from the product. The reason we do not simply allow these claims to be bought and sold relates to the transaction costs involved in having to enter into contracts to secure them. Prior assignment of the rights avoids such costs and hence promotes efficiency. We are to recognize rights as if they were the results of free market distribution in the absence of transaction costs involved in transferring them to the highest bidder. In so doing we eliminate costs that might prevent the rights or goods in question from being assigned where they are of most worth. Assigning rights in this way therefore minimizes the costs and maximizes the value of joint and potentially conflicting activities, for example ranching and farming, or polluting and breathing. The deeper rationale for the recognition of rights on the economic analysis appears to be the maximization of aggregate social utility. If this analysis were able to capture our beliefs about specific rights, then assignment of legal rights by courts and legislatures could properly proceed according to utilitarian criteria, and much of what I have claimed in regard to both judicial and political ethics would be nullified on a deeper level.

The first problem with this analysis relates not to its utilitarian underpinnings, but to the free market as a mechanism for maximizing utility (more on this in the chapter on business ethics). Willingness to pay is a function of initial wealth; hence the first obvious criticism of the economic analysis is that assigning rights to those willing to pay most for them favors the rich. Others have dwelt upon this point,[20] so I shall not, except to note that the bias favoring the rich is one way in which rights conceived in this manner fail to express the equal dignity of individuals central to their real function. If this problem could be discounted, then assignment of rights on economic criteria in two party cases, in which potential activities or use of goods conflict, generally accords with our intuitive judgments of which parties possess the rights. This is simply because rights represent important interests, and individuals in general would be willing to pay more to protect their more important interests. In two party cases problems of aggregation, often crucial in political contexts, do not arise. The economic analysis achieves its partial intuitive fit partly from this fact, and partly from the fact that the rights it analyses often represent adjustments of property rights not antecedently assigned. Genuine moral demands do not always determine such precise adjustments, and efficiency therefore may be a proper guide. Natural property rights exist as an expression of the objectification of personal labor or creativity. Beyond that some conventional assignment is demanded to allow stability in expectations. But the boundaries of this assignment are flexible and therefore able to be captured by economic analysis.

Even where the economic assignment of rights is intuitive, however, it appears to be so for the wrong reasons. Property is not viewed as an extension of the individual's work, or as security enabling him to form realistic plans or projects, but as an incentive to encourage investment of resources and labor in their most valuable or efficient uses. (The idea is that if the products of those investments could then be freely appropriated by others rather than owned as property, the investments would never be made.[21]) Property rights are transferrable on economic criteria not to allow freedom for individuals to do so, but so that goods can gravitate toward their most productive uses. Clearly benefits to others, and not simply the interest of the right holder, are counted here. Such calculation is contrary to the idea that personal rights assert the independent worth of the individual against additions of lesser interests in the collectivity. The criminal law is viewed not in terms of prohibitions against acts inherently wrong because in violation of moral rights central to personal integrity, but as a way of imposing penalties for bypassing the economic market and hence acting inefficiently.[22] The thief or rapist who simply takes what he wants fails to ensure that the good in question resides where it has the most value. The wrongness of his action seems to be equated with the sin of bypassing the market on this analysis. This appears to us ludicrous precisely because we are unwilling to weigh the satisfaction of such individuals against their violations of personal integrity and security. The anti-utilitarian thrust of rights on the deepest level comes to light here.

Once we encounter cases in which numbers of people with opposing interests figure, we find potentially counterintuitive assignment of rights on the economic criterion, and not simply assignment for the wrong reasons. We may cite some examples from Richard Posner, the leading proponent of the economic analysis. If the cost to the manufacturer of inspecting cans of food for wholesomeness is less than the cost of illness to those who might be poisoned, then Posner approves of demanding inspection in the factory; otherwise presumably not.[23] In a case in which only one or two persons would be poisoned and inspection is costly, an economic analysis would find no violation of these persons' rights, indeed no rights not to be so harmed. A slightly cheaper price for thousands would be permitted to outweigh the harm to a few. To cite another example, Posner addresses the pornography issue not in terms of antecedent rights to read or view what one likes (as part of the more fundamental right to free expression or choice of life style), nor in terms of the dehumanization claimed by conservatives to be implicit in pornographic works, but rather in terms of the size of the market and the total amount of offense caused, both questions of utility.[24] It is true that aggregation here is not equivalent to taking a majority vote, since intensity of utility or disutility may figure as well in willingness to pay. But there is still room here for the tyranny of numbers, for a mere disutility like offense to override a right central to individuality, like the expression or development of personal tastes.

Assigning rights on the basis of efficiency fails to capture their force as trumps against utility.[25] If rights have this feature, then they belong to individuals whether or not they would or could purchase them in a free market from all concerned, even in the absence of transaction costs. And even if individuals were willing to sell their rights, they might be wrong to do so for ideal-regarding reasons. Rights exist percisely to correct for inequalities in wealth, power or numbers, to assert the vital interests of individuals against aggregates. The tyranny of the majority, which rights counter-balance, is ignored here, or at least prevented only until the numbers become great enough to outweigh the intensity of desires on the part of the minority in a straightforward quantitative calculation. This turns out to be the insuperable problem for any attempt to absorb rights into utilitarian accounts. I mention the economic analysis only because it is an obvious illustration of this difficulty.

UTILITY AND FALLIBILITY   Thus, to return to our main topic, if political morality is to be constrained by moral rights, then a utilitarian framework (of which cost-benefit analysis is another recently popular instance) is insufficient on a deeper level as well. There is one more sophisticated, if also more old-fashioned (in its conception of utilities themselves), recent attempt to incorporate rights into a thoroughly utilitarian framework. Here we encounter a more subtle argument that attempts to show how honoring rights is utility maximizing in the long run. This version admits that there will be both apparent and real exceptions to the claim that overall utility lies on the side of honoring any particular right, yet holds that it is better on utilitarian grounds to honor the right even when utility seems to call for ignoring it.

It may be better to treat the rule creating the right as absolute, as barring direct appeal to utility as a reason for overriding it, for either of two reasons. First, an almost exceptionless practice may be necessary for the utility attached to a certain type of right or obligation to be realized in particular cases. An example is the practice of promise-making, where no one would rely on others' promises if utility were allowed as a ground for breaking them in all cases. Second, for other rights it is claimed that attempts to identify exceptions to the rule that utility lies on the side of honoring them (since they represent important interests) will be mistaken more often than not. Such attempts are likely to be in error because those judging utilities are likely to be partial to their own interests and to underestimate certain disutilities systematically attached to violations of the rights. This might be the case, for example, with temptations to violate property rights on grounds of greater need or benefit. Potential Robin Hoods will tend to overestimate their own needs or those of persons close to them and will tend to underestimate the frustration of expectations involved in losing one's property. Since there is no criterion for reliably identifying exceptions, it is better not to try to do so, but to treat the rule as an absolute prohibition in relation to direct utility calculations. Thus in order to maximize aggregate welfare in the long run, it is better to allow rights to stand as trumps against utility in particular cases. Here the utilitarian also recognizes the problem of authority to act on one's moral (utilitarian) perceptions, the problem with which this book is centrally concerned. Indeed he views moral rights as a kind of restriction on that authority, justified by the recognition of moral fallibility. On one level rights are absolute in relation to aggregate welfare; on a deeper level their justification is utilitarian according to this position.[26] If it were correct, then utilitarian reasoning would reenter as the fundamental framework for political morality.

The first problem with this argument has been noted by others, and so again I shall not dwell on it. It is that the principle of utility here seems to require its own suppression. If publicity is a demand on moral principles, then this one would seem to violate it.[27] But perhaps it is not after all a genuine demand, or so the utilitarian might maintain. A potentially more serious question is whether the utilitarian himself, even when aware of this argument, can accept the force of rights against direct utilitarian calculations. Can he estimate utilities to the best of his ability in particular cases and yet not act on these estimates in the belief that they are probably mistaken? It might seem then that he must both believe and disbelieve his calculations at the same time. An analogy shows, however, that the utilitarian analysis of rights might escape this objection as well. If I am not good at solving a particular kind of mathematics problem and am given a set to solve, I might work out the answers, yet rationally disbelieve their correctness and be unwilling to bet or act on them. A person's higher level beliefs about his general competencies might outweigh his immediate beliefs in the area in question. It is still problematic whether utilitarians really would believe themselves, as opposed to others, mistaken in their direct calculations. Then too there is at least some paradox in the idea that a utilitarian might be forbidden to do what is really utility maximizing, which would be the case on this account when real exceptions to the rules of thumb regarding rights exist. Perhaps the paradox diminishes when we recognize this as the price for overall utility maximization.[28]

The really insuperable objection to this argument is that even when we do have a genuine exception, even when utilities genuinely fall on the side of violating a right, and *even if this could be known with relative certainty,* we ought not to violate it. Those who take rights seriously enough see them as fundamental and not merely superficial constraints on aggregative calculations. To return to the example of free speech, even if the disutility of the offense taken by large numbers of persons outweighs the satisfaction of some activist in speaking his mind, as well as any long range good that might come of what he says, even if the case would not be generalized to others, and even if this could be known as well as any utilitarian prediction, it would be wrong to silence him. A final move open to utilitarians is to call for sanctions to attach to rules creating rights, in order to tip utility calculations in the direction of obeying those rules. They might endorse sanctions for the two reasons that they recognize rights in the first place, and this added factor would allow utilitarians to make direct calculations while still inclining them toward protection of the rights in question. But the example of free speech shows this move to be insufficient as well in failing to protect the right adequately. Application of sanctions has costs in disutility that make it impracticable in many cases to apply them, for example against a crowd that shouts down a speaker. That silencing a speaker may be utility maximizing, and that sanctions are inapplicable in such cases, do not show that he is not wronged, his right violated, when he is prevented from expressing himself.

All utilitarian arguments, no matter how sophisticated, must fail to incorporate the discontinuities in reckoning of interests and the ideal-regarding reasons that I have claimed to underlie rights. Such rights arise not from an epistemological problem in identifying exceptions to rules of thumb, but within the very foundations of morality, as expressions of respect for individuals who are independent sources of value. This last and most sophisticated of utilitarian arguments is defective in yet another way. Its appeal was to the lack of a criterion for identifying exceptions to the rule that utilities favor honoring rights. But our description of political contexts suggests one such criterion: when the desires of enough people oppose some single individual's right, a straightforward utility calculation would most often favor the majority. It is hard to believe that if enough people are offended by some speaker's clearly objectionable thesis, overall utility might not lie on the side of silencing him. It is not really all that difficult to identify clearly worthless viewpoints on particular issues, and the negative feelings of a proponent who is silenced may not match in combined intensity those of all who may be offended. But to silence him is to wrong him, to show him a lack of respect and violate his right as an individual to free expression. This wrong is independent of the intensity of feelings in the particular case. Thus, even if there is a criterion for identifying situations in which utilities really oppose rights, and even when this criterion is satisfied, the right nevertheless obtains, and the utilitarian has no way to account for it. The problem of moral fallibility is indeed important, as I have been maintaining all along, but it is not the source of moral rights.

As a final thrust, the utilitarian might at this point attempt to resurrect the theory of two moralities with which this section began, the thesis of a distinct political ethic. Since the criterion for identifying when utilities call for violation of rights is most often met in the political arena, where the interests and wants of great numbers are at stake, the utilitarian might allow a more thorough and immediate utilitarianism as a framework for politics, treating rules and rights as constraints upon aggregative calculations only in the private sphere. Thus we are taken back to the question of political role differentiation in a different light. The phenomenon of dirty hands would here receive a different but perhaps equally satisfying account along thoroughly utilitarian lines. Of course the difference in moralities would now obtain only on the first or more superficial level. The same underlying moral framework would generate both the political and personal ethics.

I have made the same claim in relation to the framework of rights and the contrast between *judicial* and personal ethics. The very reasons for recognizing moral rights in the first place call for restriction of the judge's authority to rule on direct application of rules that express these rights. The utilitarian might say the same of the principle of utility and restrictions on its direct application in the private, but not the political sphere. The thrust of his claim would be opposite to mine: that the official can apply the common principle of utility directly because of the numbers of persons affected, while the private agent would be better off respecting rights (on his view a restriction on the common principle). But the form of his reasoning and of his moral system would be similar. In making this final move, however, the utilitarian does not escape the charge, elaborated above, that he simply cannot take rights seriously enough. As argued in the second subsection, it is no more permissible to violate rights for mere utilities in political contexts that it is elsewhere. This attempt to justify strong role differentiation must then be rejected as well.

As pointed out in the Introduction, there is always a moral price to be paid for the insertion of special institutional norms or ethics between an agent and our common moral framework of rights. The insensitivity to moral rights that is thereby encouraged, even if justified in the institutional context, is apt to generalize to areas of conduct where it is not justified. For judges this tendency may be less marked, since justice and the underlying purposes of rights themselves animate the primary allegiance of those in the judicial branch to the law. But the subordination of rights to aggregate utility would be more dangerous and easily generalized; and when being elected or remaining in office are viewed by the politician as clearly for the public good, allowing such reasoning to bypass personal rights threatens our moral framework itself. We may interpret Richard Nixon's reminder that he was not a crook as a sincere if crude allusion to the fact that his violations of rights were for the perceived national good, not merely for personal gain. Certainly not only in our country does the government remain the greatest single threat to individual rights. In this respect the need to win votes and the aggregate majoritarian thinking that this need provokes verify the observation that democracy is the worst form of government except for the others. But democracy itself entails a right to informed participation, and the professionalization of politics under a separate moral framework would be alien to that ideal as well.[29] The politician, like the businessman, rather needs to be reminded that the moral constraints imposed by rights sometimes require sacrifice, not only of private gain, but of aggregate social good.

POLITICIANS AS REPRESENTATIVES

There is one further argument in favor of strong role differentiation for legislators that I shall consider briefly. The premises here refer to the legislator's role as representative for his constituency. Under one theory of representation he has a duty in this role to vote as his constituency prefers, at least when their collective preference can be clearly ascertained. The justification for this claim appeals to the ideal of pure democracy. According to this view representation is a necessary expedient that should approximate as closely as possible in practice to that ideal. The democratic ideal itself can be supported either on want-regarding grounds, given the assumption that people tend to know their own interests best, or on both want- and ideal-regarding grounds, since autonomy is both desired and instrinsically valuable as a necessary condition for other creative values.

This argument seeks, then, to place a direct limit upon the legislator's authority to vote according to his own moral perception. The reason for the limitation here relates not to the content of the principles that he might invoke in his own decisions, but to values inherent in or affected by the decision-making process itself. Fortunately we do not require a full political theory to answer it. We may rely first upon our earlier claim that rights are not to be overridden by collective welfare in the context of political decision-making, together with the observation that majority preference, even when easily ascertainable on particular issues, is unlikely itself to be fully restrained by perceptions of moral rights. When expressing political preferences, people often press for self-interest, on the reasonable assumption that others are as well. Rights exist precisely to protect individuals against such collective preference. Furthermore, even if constituents attempted to be adequately deferential to the interests of others, majority opinion would be still no criterion for minority or individual rights.

Of course a legitimate question arises as to whether the legislator is likely to be more enlightened in this regard than his constituents. Several additional considerations can be brought forth to answer it. First, whether or not he is more enlightened, he is likely to be more impartial on matters in which interests of his constituents conflict. Second, and more important, to allow a legislator to override majority preference among his constituents, when he perceives that rights of individuals are at stake, is not to free him totally from their control, not even from the influence of their opinions regarding such rights. This partial control and influence is exercised at election time. The politician does have a duty when running for office to state honestly his views of the orderings of rights and values, as these pertain to the issues likely to arise. He also has some duty once elected not to change his stance radically on these matters.

Accepting these duties, and given the political pressure to conform to majority will, a legislator will have to perceive rights clearly, to feel the demands of conscience strongly, in order to oppose that will. As in the question of citizen obligation to obey law, we want to know here whether we should add to a powerful prudential reason to conform a moral duty to do so. Since the legislator's opposing the majority will tend to oppose his own political self-interest, and since the majority preference will tend to express self-interest even at the expense of rights, the legislator's judgments as to when rights require protection against lesser majority interests are to be the better trusted. Of course his decisions extend only to the making of law. Citizens have an additional protection because, as argued earlier, they have no moral (as opposed to prudential) reason for obeying the law when they perceive moral (as opposed to prudential) reasons to disobey it.

A final consideration here is the moral autonomy of politicians themselves. Other things being equal, it is better to grant each individual autonomy to make his own moral decisions, whether in professional or private life. If the legislator were bound to vote majority preference, he would provide no moral input to the decision-making process. If he votes his own conscience when he believes rights to be at issue, then both he and his constituency contribute such input, the latter during elections. For all these reasons we should not grant the majority a right to determine directly legislative votes on all issues. It has long been recognized that pure democracy must be restricted if minority rights are to be adequately protected. The role of the morally autonomous legislator is a reasonable restriction built into the decision-making process itself. To fulfill this role the legislator must have the authority to apply principles respecting rights directly. Such authority might not be necessary if it were possible to define a set of morally sufficient political and legal rights once and for all, and then trust the courts to protect them. But moral rights must progressively become institutionalized in new ways; and the scope of such rights, especially positive claims to goods, shifts with changes in productive capacities.

That legislators are not to ignore moral rights in order to vote majority preference itself negates the idea of strong role differentiation on grounds of representation. The authority of the legislator is indeed delegated from his constituents, but it is delegated authority to apply principles protective of moral rights directly in his role as lawmaker. I have argued, on the other hand, that this role is weakly differentiated in the preference owed by the legislator to his constituency first, and to his countrymen second. When utilities alone are at stake, majority preference among the citizens enters more directly into his calculations. In fact majority preference among constituents should be determinative, with two exceptions. One is where the intensity of wants among the minority outweighs the majority preference in a quantitative calculation. (Such intensity does not always indicate that rights are at stake, just as lack of it does not always indicate that they are not.) This situation is unlikely to reveal itself to the legislator, however. If the majority expresses its opinion, it normally will be difficult to estimate the intensity of opposing preferences; and, if the majority does not bother to reveal itself, then the minority will appear to outnumber their opposition. In either case the legislator should go with the apparent majority.

When rights are not at stake, the lawmaker should have no reason to oppose his values to those of his constituency. His purpose is to act in their interest. Accepting the relativist thesis, that interest is almost always determined (in the absence of ideal-regarding values connected to rights) by wants or preferences. Thus the legislator's belief as to the right vote should coincide with his belief regarding citizen preference. The deeper exception to this rule occurs when the preferences in question appear to be inconsistent. They may be so when satisfaction of the short-range expressed preference would block the realization of some longer-range stronger want, or when the expressed preference is based upon ignorance of fact and hence not the true preference. I shall argue in detail in the chapter on medical ethics that this is the one situation in which purely paternalistic interference is justified, despite the relativity of values. In parallel fashion, when rights are not at stake, the legislator is justified in opposing his judgment to the expressed preference of his constituency only when the latter appears clearly inconsistent with other wants higher on the scale, or when it appears based on clearly mistaken fact. The legislator is sometimes in a position to recognize such mistakes on the basis of superior information or greater personal distance from the issue in question. He must only guard against substituting his values for those of his constituents, if he is to serve their interests rather than his own.

The preference to be shown by a lawmaker for his own constituency is justified by a premise that applies to the family context as well—that interests of individuals are better served by those with special interests in them, or special responsibilities for them. But it is important to reemphasize at the end of this chapter, as it is relevant also to the next, that such preference cannot extend to the violation of rights of others. Regarding negative rights, there should be no conflicts in the political sphere, as there should be none in the private. (When negative rights are threatened, the aggressors forfeit their rights not to be subdued.) Regarding positive rights, the legislator's perfect duties are first to his constituents, although those of his other countrymen come before considerations of utility. When any of these rights are at stake, the autonomy of the individual that they protect is itself better protected by the autonomous judgment of the legislator than it would be by any institutional restraints upon that judgment. The restraint must come from our common moral framework, in which respect for moral rights, and the demand that they be respected and protected in law, take priority over aggregate interest and, as goes without saying, over political ambition.

3

Legal Ethics:
The Problem of Immoral
but Legal Means and Ends

It is accepted dogma within the legal profession, as reflected in the Code of Professional Responsibility of the American Bar Association, that a lawyer should pursue his client's interests as vigorously as possible within the limits of law. This means that he should not interpose his own moral opinion of those objectives of his client that are legal. He should not block on moral grounds any attempt by his client to exercise legal rights; nor should he refrain from using the most effective legal means to realize these rights and objectives. The purpose of this chapter is to question this cornerstone of legal ethics, and to propose an alternative fundamental principle that subjects legal behavior more directly to moral rules that apply elsewhere as well.

Our question here is the by now familiar one applied to lawyers: we want to know whether their role is strongly differentiated. It is a logical truth that no one, lawyers and other professionals included, ought to do that which is overall immoral to do. The question for lawyers is whether the fact that certain legal courses of action are in their clients' interests, or demanded by their clients, is sufficient to make it morally obligatory or permissible for the lawyers to pursue those courses. If considerations relating to clients' interests within the legal system justify courses of action by lawyers that would otherwise be immoral, then their position is strongly differentiated.

We saw in the previous chapter that the legal system does demand such moral differentiation for judges. In deciding a case, the judge ought normally to defer to the legally correct decision, even when he recognizes that the moral consequences of doing so in the particular case before him are not optimal. The arguments there related to the effects of decisions upon the law itself, to the requirement that the law be manageable and predictable, to the greater predictability of decisions according to law than according to moral judgment, to the inability to estimate cumulative effects of decisions considered singly, and to the principles of majority rule and legislative supremacy. These considerations generate an institutional obligation of judges to weigh the demands of law more heavily in their decisions than if they were private citizens, and to ignore (or weigh less heavily) certain moral consequences of their particular decisions. In the Introduction we saw also positions whose role differentiation derives not only from the instrumental benefits of recognizing special institutional obligations, but also from the intrinsic value of the relations that define them. Such are the roles of close relatives and friends. In these cases it is either obligatory (in the case of close relatives) or permissible (in the case of friends) to weigh the interests of those to whom one stands in the relation in question more heavily than one weighs the interests of others.

Our question is whether the position of a lawyer allows or requires him to favor his client in a similar way, to give the interests or demands of his client ultimate weight within the limits of law. Is the role of a lawyer analogous in relevant respects to either of the two types described above as strongly role differentiated? The answer, I believe, is no, but the arguments in favor of the accepted view are not initially implausible. They appeal, as we might predict, to the broader legal institution within which lawyers operate. The lawyer's role as advocate and adversary is seen to contribute most effectively to the morality and justice of that institution. By providing a legal expert and spokesman for each individual or corporation that requires one, the overall system is seen to place no one at an unfair legal disadvantage. And by requiring lawyers to pursue all legal objectives of their clients vigorously, the legal framework is seen to operate as intended by legislators and judges, who first define legal rights according to democratic and historically rooted social principles.

The Principle of Full Advocacy

THE A.B.A. CODE

As mentioned previously, the official view of the A.B.A. is that the answer to our question is affirmative. We may examine relevant sections of its Code of Professional Responsibility, as arguments are suggested there which may then be analyzed in more detail.[1] The A.B.A. code is the most developed of any such professional document, and portions of it have the force of law in relation to lawyers' conduct. It is therefore appropriate to begin our discussion of legal ethics from consideration of its relevant sections, especially as the view of lawyering projected from them presents the lawyer's role as differentiated to an extreme degree.

The Code is divided into a set of Canons, or basic principles, Ethical Considerations, and Disciplinary Rules. Although there is variance from state to state, generally only the latter have the force of law. The Ethical Considerations reflect the Bar's ideal of legal practice, however, and we may consider them equally in appraising the ideal. The provisions of both the Code and older set of Canons of the Bar have been interpreted and amplified by both informal and formal opinions of its Committee on Ethics and Professional Responsibility, and some of these are relevant as well in appreciating the degree of role differentiation suggested by the Bar.

Section 7 of the Code calls for zealous advocacy within the limits of law. Here we find that it is not the lawyer's place to forego on moral grounds any legal objectives that his client seeks or thwart any attempted assertion by the client of his legal rights. The lawyer may offer moral advice to his client, but, as long as he continues to represent him, he must allow the client to pursue whatever objectives within the law he desires and act to realize those objectives as vigorously as he can.

In assisting his client to reach a proper decision, it is often desirable for a lawyer to point out those factors which may lead to a decision that is morally just as well as legally permissible. He may emphasize the possibility of harsh consequences that might result from assertion of legally permissible positions. In the final analysis, however, the lawyer should always remember that the decision whether to forego legally available objectives or methods because of non-legal factors is ultimately for the client and not for himself . . . the authority to make decisions is exclusively that of the client and, if made within the framework of the law, such decisions are binding on his lawyer. . . The professional responsibility of a lawyer derives from his membership in a profession which has the duty of assisting members of the public to secure and protect available legal rights and benefits.[2]

If a lawyer feels strong moral disapproval of a client's course of action, he may withdraw from his employment, *but only in a non-adjudicatory context.*

In the event that the client *in a non-adjudicatory matter* insists upon a course of conduct that is contrary to the judgment and advice of the lawyer but not prohibited by Disciplinary Rules, the lawyer may withdraw from the employment.[3] (emphasis added)

While in these restricted circumstances the lawyer may withdraw, he need never do so for moral reasons alone, and indeed he need not personally approve of any of the client's objectives in order to pursue them vigorously:

The obligation of loyalty to his client applies only to a lawyer in the discharge of his professional duties and implies no obligation to adopt a personal viewpoint favorable to the interests or desires of his client.[4]

It is part of the law cited by the Code that a defense attorney in a criminal case is guilty of invading his client's constitutional rights if he foregoes any potentially successful and customary legal tactic on grounds of conscience or in the belief that his client is guilty:

when defense counsel, in a truly adverse proceeding, admits that his conscience would not permit him to adopt certain customary trial procedures, this extends beyond the realm of judgment and strongly suggests an invasion of constitutional rights.[5]

There are, it is true, certain limitations to zealous advocacy built into the Code. The lawyer is not to take legal action that "serves merely to harass" or delay, advance a claim not supportable by any good faith argument, make a false statement of law or fact, fail to reveal an adverse precedent when the opposing attorney fails to do so, fabricate evidence, aid in illegal or fraudulent conduct, threaten criminal action to obtain advantage in a civil matter, degrade a witness by irrelevant questions, or inflict "needless harm."[6] Such prohibitions may appear at first glance weighty, but the omissions and hedging phrases (*"merely* to harass," *"needless* harm," etc.), surely nonaccidental in a legal document, remove most of the bite. Tactics appear to be permissible as long as they are not otherwise illegal and are in the client's interest. Needless harm, for example is naturally interpreted here as harm irrelevant to the client's cause. Since the lawyer is to give his client every benefit of doubt as to construction of law and pursue all legal means to his goal, harassing or delaying actions that can be claimed by any stretch of the legal imagination to have any other legal purpose seem permissible according to the Code. The lawyer is to reveal adverse law to the court, but *not* adverse facts known to him. He is not to degrade witnesses by *irrelevant* questions, but can (and perhaps must) degrade them if it is helpful to his client's cause. He is not to threaten criminal action in a civil context, but certainly may threaten to bring civil suit that may be costly to defend. Finally, the demand to reveal adverse law does not apply to negotiations with an opposing attorney that might lead to settlement. There is therefore great latitude as to tactics in behalf of a client's cause. The Code prohibits mainly what is otherwise illegal. Within legal limits the client's interest reigns supreme.[7]

Clearly these demands and permissions, even together with the prohibitions, effectively absolve the lawyer of moral responsibility for his client's actions within the bounds of law, actions that he aids as vigorously as possible. Whatever the effect on the moral rights of others of his client's decisions, the lawyer must act to realize them as long as he continues to represent the client. And he may justifiably withdraw on grounds of conscience only when withdrawal does not seriously damage the client's cause in an adversary proceeding. It appears from the point of view of the Code that, as long as legal restrictions do not apply, a lawyer has no obligations whatsoever to persons whose interests may clash with those of his client, no obligations to respect the moral rights of such persons unless these are explicitly protected by law. In the absence of law, such rights have force only when the interests of the client are not at stake. Section 5, which primarily concerns conflicts of interest, contains the following Ethical Consideration:

The professional judgment of a lawyer should be exercised, within the bounds of the law, solely for the benefit of his client and free of compromising influences and loyalties. Neither his personal interests, the interests of other clients, nor the desires of third persons should be permitted to dilute his loyalty to his client.[8]

This degree of role differentiation, excusing the lawyer from all moral consequences of legal actions in behalf of his client, is extreme. He may do for his client what he could not morally do for himself, his friend, or even his wife or child (if the action involves violating rights of others for trivial interests of his family). He may do what is immoral for the client to even suggest for himself. Normally when we act for ourselves or for our friends whose interests we share, we must balance those interests against those of others with which they might conflict. We may prefer our own interests or those of our friends, in disposing of our possessions for example, but only when moral rights of others are not at stake, when no one else has a right to those possessions in that example. We certainly may not pursue our own interests or those of our friends to the limits of the law, when this would involve degrading others, denying them what they morally deserve, or imposing harm upon them. Sometimes it is morally permissible, or at least excusable, to do for another what one would not be permitted to do for oneself. A person might lie for his spouse or child when it would be wrong for them to do so. The love or concern expressed through such an act might excuse it. But in the case of lawyer and client, there is no such intrinsically valuable intimate emotion to express. If the lawyer is to be absolved of responsibility for the moral consequences of his pursuit of client objectives, this must be justified in terms of extrinsic considerations relating to essential values within the legal system, values lost without such role differentiation for lawyers.

This extraordinary reduction in moral responsibility for actions in which the lawyer cooperates is indeed to be justified according to the Code in terms of his place within the broader legal system. To render moral judgment on his client's legal rights and objectives, to refuse to aid in their exercise or realization on moral grounds, when this might block their being realized at all, is to usurp the roles of legislators and judges:

In our government of laws and not of men, each member of our society is entitled to have his conduct judged and regulated in accordance with the law; to seek any lawful objective through legally permissible means; and to present for adjudication any lawful claim, issue, or defense.[9]

Thus the argument initially appeals to the right to have legal rights, as determined by the majoritarian legislature, honored, and to be judged by judges and juries, not by lawyers. The autonomy of the client within the legal framework is held to be at stake. As long as he acts within bounds set by legislators and judges, he is held to have a right to his lawyer's aid "unfettered by his attorney's economic and social predilections." Anything less places those without legal expertise at an unfair disadvantage to those who have such expertise. In a criminal proceeding, for the lawyer to interpose his opinion of guilt is for him to rob his client of the right to trial by jury, fundamental in the American system. The lawyer thereby usurps the role of judge and jury.

There is some recognition in the Code of different roles that the lawyer may play, roles other than that of criminal defense attorney. Prosecutors, for example, must disclose not only adverse law, but adverse fact or evidence unknown to the defense,[10] while defense may conceal fact and must only follow local law in requesting his client, if required, to disclose evidence.[11] In his role as counsel or advisor, the lawyer need not construe the law as favorable to his client. He is encouraged to give moral advice and permitted to withdraw on grounds of conscience. But despite these differences, it is clear that the Code extends the model of strong advocacy from the criminal law context to other roles that lawyers might play—advisor, negotiator, drafter, etc. Again the first presumed justification for this extension must appeal to the moral autonomy of the client, his right to make his own decisions within the bounds of law.

While the first argument suggested in the Code points to the lawyer's limited role as legal spokesman for his client within the system, a second deeper argument, only briefly hinted at, appeals to the virtues of the adversary system itself.

An adversary presentation counters the natural human tendency to judge too swiftly in terms of the familiar that which is not yet fully known; the advocate, by his zealous preparation and presentation of facts and law, enables the tribunal to come to the hearing with an open and neutral mind and to render impartial judgments. The duty of a lawyer to his client and his duty to the legal system are the same: to represent his client zealously within the bounds of law.[12]

Presentation of opposing sides in the strongest terms possible before an impartial body is seen as an effective way of arriving at truth and justice. It is to counter a tendency to judge too easily on the basis of initial impressions and insufficient evidence. Initial biases will be successfully countered only when opposing points of view are presented in their best lights, and they will be so presented by those who have an interest in winning the case. Whatever distortions may be introduced by the operation of such interests on each side are to be balanced by the position of the other. Of course truth and justice are not guaranteed outcomes of such a process; but it must be compared on this view to alternatives in which initial inclinations may remain unopposed by other viewpoints.

If the opposing side is presenting its case as effectively as it can, a lawyer would place his client at an unfair disadvantage if he did not do the same.

While serving as advocate, a lawyer should resolve in favor of his client doubts as to the bounds of law . . . The lawyer may urge any permissible construction of the law favorable to his client, without regard to his professional opinion as to the likelihood that the construction will ultimately prevail.[13] Lawyers are accused of taking advantage of 'loopholes' and 'technicalities' to win. Persons who make this charge are unaware, or do not understand, that the lawyer is hired to win, and if he does not exercise every legitimate effort in his client's behalf, then he is betraying a sacred trust.[14]

Once more it is not the lawyer's place to judge his client's cause or case. He is hired by his client to do his best for him, and a third argument suggested here appeals to the breach of trust involved in his not doing so.

Section 4 of the Code requires maintenance of strict confidentiality: nothing learned from a client is to be used to his disadvantage.

A lawyer should not use information acquired in the course of the representation of a client to the disadvantage of the client; and a lawyer should not use, except with the consent of his client after full disclosure, such information for his own purposes. [15]

Reasons cited are both backward- and forward-looking. Clients divulge information with an understanding that it will be kept confidential. Allowing such an understanding to develop and persist amounts to an implicit promise by the lawyer. It is again a breach of trust arising from past actions later to divulge client secrets. In order that clients feel free to contact lawyers and give them sufficient information to conduct effective cases, this trust must also be maintained for the future.

Both the fiduciary relationship existing between lawyer and client and the proper functioning of the legal system require the preservation by the lawyer of confidences and secrets of one who has employed or sought to employ him. A client must feel free to discuss whatever he wishes with his lawyer and a lawyer must be equally free to obtain information beyond that volunteered by his client. A lawyer should be fully informed of all the facts of the matter he is handling in order for his client to obtain the full advantage of our legal system. It is for the lawyer in the exercise of his independent professional judgment to separate the relevant and important from the irrelevant and unimportant. [16]

Such lawyer-client privilege is supported in case law as well, cited in the Code:

While it is the great purpose of the law to ascertain the truth, there is the countervailing necessity of insuring the right of every person to freely and fully confer and confide in one having knowledge of the law, and skilled in its practice, in order that the former may have adequate advice and a proper defense. This assistance can be made safely and readily available only when the client is free from the consequences of apprehension of disclosure by reason of the subsequent statements of the skilled lawyer.[17]

This duty to confidentiality reinforces the lawyer's duty to do his best for his client's cause, rather than to defeat that cause or refuse to aid in it on moral grounds. For knowledge of morally objectionable aspects of a client's behavior would normally be learned only from the client himself on the understanding that it would not be used against him. However, since the lawyer must keep secret not only confidences learned directly from the client, but anything learned from other sources that might be "embarrassing or detrimental to the client,"[18] it seems clear that the principle of full advocacy supports the principle of confidentiality here, as well as the converse. Clients' future inclinations to disclose all information to their lawyers might be more encouraged by a rule that protected only such confidences, and not information learned from other sources.

We have seen that the Code holds it to be an invasion of a client's constitutional rights in a criminal proceeding if his lawyer refrains from adopting all potentially effective legal procedures in defense, irrespective of the lawyer's opinion of guilt. It was decided in a formal opinion of the Committee in 1932 (Op. 90) that a lawyer may not withdraw upon learning of a client's guilt and must continue to raise all available defenses. The duty of confidentiality and the principle of advocacy with which it is closely linked is again extended from this criminal context to others. For all clients the former is limited only in relation to client intentions to commit future crimes. As amplified by the opinions, the A.B.A. position here appears to be that a lawyer must disclose client intention to commit crime when public safety or national security are at stake, may optionally disclose other future intended crimes, and may never disclose past crimes, although he may advise his client to do so and may withdraw if he refuses. (The scandalously self-serving character of the Code is revealed by its permission to disclose all client confidences in order to collect fees or protect the lawyer against charges.)

Here as elsewhere the principal prohibition is against aiding in criminal activity:

A lawyer should never encourage or aid his client to commit criminal acts or counsel his client on how to violate the law and avoid punishment therefor . . . The law and Disciplinary Rules prohibit the use of fraudulent, false, or perjured testimony or evidence.[19]

The limit regarding perjury also undoubtedly derives from its legal, not its moral, status, since lawyers are to do many things for their clients otherwise far more objectionable than lying. This prohibition too is therefore consistent with the fundamental principle. The prohibition regarding illegality derives not only from the respect that the legal profession must show the law, but appears to be logically required as well. If the justification for the lawyer's extreme partisanship is to appeal to his proper place in the legal system, then he cannot violate demands internal to that system itself. But even with this limitation the principle of full advocacy remains a prime example of proposed strong role differentiation.

TEST CASES

I want here to propose an alternative framework for legal ethics. To see how the implications of my fundamental principle differ from those of the principle of total advocacy within legal limits, we may keep in mind several sample test cases for the lawyer. I claim no originality for these. Some are standard and have been long debated; others derive from texts containing materials for legal ethics courses.[20] My purpose here is not to invent new legal situations, having no experience in legal practice. I choose these examples because I believe they show the serious shortcomings of the Code's principles from a moral point of view. They will be used as well to test our alternative principle after evaluation of the arguments.

(1) Lawyer *A* represents a wine producer who is about to send a shipment east from California. To preserve the wine in shipment, a chemical preservative is added, but this is about to be banned as carcinogenic by the Food and Drug Administration. Loss of the shipment would have serious financial consequences for the producer, who therefore asks his attorney if delay is possible. In six months the shipment will be complete, and the case will be moot as far as the client is concerned. There is strong evidence that the use of the chemical imposes real risk of cancer, but the lawyer knows that expert witnesses can be found who would be willing at least to question that evidence. The lawyer is convinced from preliminary study of the evidence that the substance should and ultimately will be banned. Filing for a hearing, however, should delay the order at least six months, and, with the help of appropriate witnesses, a "good faith" case could be made for further study prior to implementation. Should the lawyer file for a hearing as his client demands?[21]

(2) Lawyer *B* has accepted as a client a woman whose child has been taken from her by the Department of Family Services. Originally convinced by his client that this was the unjust result of certain Puritanical moral views of the client's sexual preferences held by the department worker, the lawyer later learns that there is evidence of serious physical abuse of the child by the mother. He also knows that the department is overworked and understaffed, and that he probably could succeed in returning the child to the mother, as she demands. The child himself has no legal representation. Should the lawyer take the legal action demanded by his client?[22]

(3) Lawyer *C* is defending an accused rapist. His client privately admits to him midway through the trial that he did force himself upon the victim, but claims that "she was asking for it." He insists on continuing a plea of not guilty on grounds

that the woman was a willing sexual partner. She has taken the witness stand and can be cross-examined. The lawyer knows that she has been suffering from an acute nervous condition since the incident, and she appears to be still in a mentally fragile and vulnerable state. Should he aggressively cross examine to destroy the credibility of her testimony, when he knows her to be telling the truth?

(4) Lawyer D is defending a client against a criminal charge of which she believes the client to be innocent. The client confesses to her that he committed a prior murder for which another man is now spending life in prison. Should she reveal this confidence to the authorities?

(5) Lawyer E is attorney for a childless married couple who desire an amicable divorce. The law of their state forbids divorce by mutual consent. Should the lawyer counsel them as to legal requirements most easily met in knowledge that this information will be used by them to fabricate evidence for false claims? Should he cooperate with them beyond advice on the law in fabricating a case?

(6) Lawyer F is counsel to an appliance corporation. One of its products has a defective part, about which there have been numerous complaints. Replacing the part or reimbursing consumers would cost $100 per appliance. The lawyer knows that even though the company would be held liable in court, costs would prevent consumers from ever filing suits, and the company can therefore avoid payments in most cases. Should he reveal this knowledge to the client?

(7) Lawyer G represents a service station and its mechanic, who serviced the brakes on a woman's car shortly before they failed and she was seriously injured. The mechanic denies that he was at fault to the woman's husband, but later confesses to Lawyer G that he was and would admit so in court. The law of negligence in the state has recently changed from disallowing payment of damages when the victim contributes to the negligence to allowing proportionate payment. In this case the woman was not wearing a seatbelt, which contributed to her injury. The opposing attorney for the couple seems unaware of

the recent change in the law and unsure whether the case can be made against the mechanic. He therefore is probably willing to settle for far less than could be collected in court or is deserved by the woman, who is presently bearing exorbitant medical costs. Should Lawyer G press for settlement on these terms?[23]

(8) Lawyer H, a public interest lawyer, represents a welfare recipient with five children, who makes $60 a week babysitting, and whose family barely survives. She has not reported this income to the welfare agency, and it would disqualify her as a recipient. Her action constitutes criminal fraud. Lawyer H must file reports of all income in a court in which she is suing for divorce, and these reports may well be forwarded to the welfare agency. What should he do?[24]

(9) Finally, Lawyer I has been attorney to a wealthy family for many years. The father is recently deceased, having left all his money to his wife. She strongly disapproves of her son's liberal political leanings. When he decides to marry out of his religion, she considers this the last straw and wishes to disinherit him. Should the lawyer accomplish this act that he believes to be morally wrong by drawing up the new will?

We might first consider the implications of the Code regarding proper behavior in these cases. In case 1 *(wine)*, the Code prohibits actions for the sole purpose of delay, but allows, and even requires under the principle of zealousness, actions in the client's behalf that he demands, and that can be supported by some legal argument under a construction of the law favorable to the client. In case 2 *(abused child)*, the lawyer may withdraw if he has moral qualms, but he is not required to. He may suggest that the child should be represented, but otherwise must pursue the mother's objective vigorously as long as he represents her. In case 3 *(rape)*, the Code would have the lawyer cross-examine vigorously if necessary to his client's defense, whatever the harm to the victim. In case 4 *(confessed murder)*, the lawyer apparently may not reveal her client's confidence according to the Code and the Opinions. In case 5 *(divorce)*, the lawyer must not cooperate in fabricating evidence, whatever his opinion of the oppressive law. Likewise in case 8 *(welfare recipient)*, in which he also may reveal his impoverished client's continuing illegal activity. The Code does not prohibit the lawyer in case 6 *(appliance corporation)* from aiding his client in avoiding payments, as long as a court has not ordered them. And Lawyer G in case 7 *(mechanic)* should indeed achieve a settlement most advantageous to his client, no matter how unfair to his opponent, and no matter whether based only upon the ignorance and incompetence of the opposing attorney. In case 9 *(will)* the lawyer must, of course, draw up the will if he continues to accept the woman as his client. (Only in this last case I shall not disagree. It is included for a different purpose.)

If these implications seem to lack all moral sensitivity to the situations of the clients and victims, the more elaborate Opinions of the Bar's Committee on Professional Responsibility seem even more narrowly legalistic, almost amoral in their emphasis on legal detail, important to the lawyer's liability, but seemingly irrelevant in light of moral considerations ignored in the Opinions. To cite one example, Formal Opinion 287 concerned a criminal case in which the court was about to sentence a lawyer's client to probation under the misapprehension that the client had no prior criminal record. The question is whether the lawyer, who knows of the prior record, should correct the court's mistake. The Committee's answer is complex, but not with real moral distinctions. Its main considerations are whether the lawyer learned of the record directly from his client, and whether the court directly asks him about it or obviously relies upon his corroboration. The Opinion holds that if the lawyer is asked, he cannot answer falsely. If he is not asked or relied upon, then he should remain silent. In the former context, if the information was learned in confidence from his client, then he should say that he must remain silent, rather than reveal a confidence or lie to the court.(!) This is clearly legal hair-splitting. When the lawyer is not asked, there is no moral difference between remaining silent and deceiving the court. And, when he is asked, there is no difference between his telling the truth and remaining silent, since the judge will have no problem inferring from his silence to his client's record. On the other hand, despite these overly fine distinctions without a difference, there is no regard in this Opinion for the seemingly obvious real moral questions: how dangerous the criminal is if released, and whether he deserves the sentence otherwise imposed. Surely these questions seem of more moral moment than the precise phrasing of the lawyer's response or whether the judge thinks to ask him.

THE ARGUMENTS FOR THE PRINCIPLE REVIEWED

I have suggested thus far that the implications of the Code and interpretations of the Opinions fail to accord with principles of ordinary morality. Perhaps no sophisticated practitioner of legal ethics would deny this; it is exactly what is to be expected from strong role differentiation. And no one could deny that the principle of full advocacy meets the criteria for placing the lawyer's role in that category. It remains to be shown that the principle is unacceptable and some other preferable. Before presenting counterarguments, suggesting an alternative principle, and testing its implications for our sample cases, we may review and summarize the arguments for the principle of full advocacy.

The first argument for this principle appeals to the virtues of the adversary system and to the role of the lawyer as zealous advocate of his client's interests, taken to be necessary for the proper functioning of that system. Adversary proceedings are held to be the best means by which judges and juries can ascertain the facts and applicable law of cases before them, the best means to counter initial impressions based upon insufficient evidence. Without strong presentation of the opposing case, initial set, probably most often against the accused suspect, is likely to determine in itself the verdict. In a criminal trial the defense attorney is alone in protecting the accused against the vast power of the state. Only zealous advocacy can put the state's evidence to a full test, affording maximum protection for those who are accused of crimes but innocent.

In a civil proceeding the opposing party will be making every effort to achieve legal objectives contrary to the interests of one's client. At least the opposing client and his attorney will have strong economic motives for doing so. A lawyer's client will therefore be at an unfair disadvantage if the lawyer fails to represent his interests equally zealously. Even in routine nonlitigious transactions, only lack of expert legal knowledge might prevent each individual or organization from pursuing desired legal objectives. Lawyers must be certified by the Bar for entrance to the profession, and through the Bar they may therefore constitute and control a monopoly in legal expertise. For those with a monopoly of such knowledge to refuse to provide assistance in realizing objectives to which there are legal rights is again to place individuals without legal expertise at a disadvantage vis-à-vis the legal system. It is to block that degree of autonomy in pursuit of private interests that the legal system officially allows to every private individual or corporation.[25] In order to prevent inequalities in ability to pursue legally permitted objectives by legally permitted means, lawyers must pursue such objectives on behalf of their clients.

If moral rights are recognized in the first place to grant individuals autonomy within the social setting, to allow them to assert certain personal interests against the aggregate weight of the collectivity, then it might seem reasonable that limits to such assertion should be established in an orderly fashion and otherwise left to the individuals' own moral consciences. The legal framework itself constitutes such institutionally sanctioned and collectively approved limits. Not that law exhausts morality; this argument would hold only that it exhausts the authority of those in legal roles to impose their judgments on others. No one should be limited in his autonomy because of lack of legal expertise.

Several other features of the lawyer-client relation as well call for client supremacy in the choice of overall objectives.

There is first the easily overlooked because all too obvious fact that clients pay their lawyers to perform certain legal functions in their interest. The lawyer who placed the interests of others on a par with those of his clients would be ignoring the fact that his clients are paying him to do otherwise, if indeed anyone would pay a lawyer who had acquired such a reputation. The type of contractual agreement involved in the lawyer-client relation is that of payment for services, and the person paying seems to have more right to dictate terms within legal limits, at least to have his legal interest placed first. For a lawyer to count interests of others equally would be like an airline awarding seats on a need or merit basis after the seats had been bought and reserved, or like a restaurant giving dinners to the hungriest after the meals had been paid for by others. Given the functioning of the adversary system, clients will legitimately expect their attorneys to advocate their interests fully within the limits of the law, and it will be a betrayal of trust for a lawyer to accept a client and then refuse to further those interests because of personal disapproval.[26]

Second, if lawyers interpose their own moral judgments for those of their clients, they penalize those who differ in social, political, or moral outlook from the dominant (rather conservative) views of those in the legal profession. If lawyers, even those in criminal practice, accepted only clients with whom they agreed in moral outlook, this would constitute large scale denial of constitutional rights to legal representation. For this reason it is important that lawyers not be identified personally with the causes they represent. The Code therefore holds it improper for a lawyer to state publicly his personal opinion regarding the merits of his client's cause. Even in noncriminal contexts, for the lawyer to impose his views is for him to usurp not only the roles of others in the political and legal system, but whatever roles of responsibility his clients may play in the social and economic system. If a business client, for example, cannot implement a decision within legal bounds because of his lawyer's refusal, then the lawyer becomes a business manager in regard to that decision, and that is not his proper role.

Many rules of the legal system serve to protect the autonomy and dignity of the individual at the expense of other values, even when this results in occasional injustice, deceit, and harm to the innocent public. I refer, for example, to rules against certain forms of police interrogation and evidence collection. Such methods might result in many more deserved convictions, but they would violate rights to privacy, dignity and self-defense, all connected to the ideal of autonomy for the individual. The principle of strong advocacy for individual clients can be seen in its best light as a further expression of and support for that same value. If the interpretation of the principle calls for advocating the client's decisions and demands, rather than the lawyer's opinion of his interests, we can emphasize the anti-paternalist argument here.[27] There is value to each individual's making moral decisions for himself. While the lawyer may offer advice, he should not usurp this capacity of his client.

As pointed out earlier, and as will be emphasized in the chapter on medical ethics, there are three sources to the value of autonomy. The first is directly want-regarding: individuals themselves desire to make their own decisions and derive satisfaction from doing so. The second is indirectly want-regarding: those who might seek to control us might have different value priorities and lack knowledge of our interests; hence they might not satisfy our priorities regarding other desires. The third is ideal-regarding: creative individuals worthy of respect tend to develop more naturally where social decision allows space for autonomous individual choice. The problem of authority to make moral decisions for others, or to prevent them from making or implementing their own decisions, that underlies the issue of strong role differentiation for professionals must always be addressed in terms of this triple value of individual autonomy. Indeed, from the point of view of a rights based moral theory, this value is foundational. The fact that the principle of full advocacy is intended as an expression of this value is a powerful (although, I shall claim, misguided) argument in its favor.

The next argument for this principle relates to the duty of confidentiality. When a lawyer has the opportunity to thwart his client's interests on moral grounds, it is often only because of information he has received from the client himself under an assumption of strict confidentiality. If the information is then used against the client, for example by refusing to impeach the testimony of an opposing witness known on the basis of the client's information to be truthful, or by refusing to press for acquittal of a client learned to be guilty, this is a breach of trust. Breaking a client's confidence is both intrinsically wrong and instrumentally destructive to the proper functioning of the legal system.

Let us consider the instrinsic wrong in breach of confidence first in the context of the lawyer-client relation. Such betrayal exceeds the wrong involved in violations of trust per se, as it also stands in violation of the rights against self-incrimination and to due process of law. The right against self-incrimination derives from the right to defend oneself and from the equality of all before the law (the naive as well as the clever liars). Both of these in turn derive from a recognition of equal autonomy and dignity for all individuals in the eyes of the legal system. The rights against self-incrimination and to due process imply, among other things, that a suspect may have an attorney present when being interrogated by police or prosecutors. When police obtain a confession by guile from a suspect without an attorney present, they violate due process. But the abuse would be far greater if the lawyer himself were to coax incriminating information from his client and then use it against him. This would make a mockery of all other protections relating to these rights fundamental to our legal system. Hence the duty of confidentiality for a lawyer must be at least as strong as these other central procedural rights.

Regarding the instrumental wrong of breaking confidences, the adversary system cannot function if clients no longer trust their lawyers and are no longer willing to be open and candid with them. Lawyers are able to defend clients, including innocent ones, effectively only if they are able to learn in advance all the relevant facts, both incriminating and exculpatory. Clients are not always capable of judging into which of these categories certain facts fall. Scared but innocent defendants will hurt their defenses by not revealing what they consider to be incriminating, unless they can be certain that their lawyers will not use information against them in less than zealous presentation of their cases. If lawyers withdraw from cases on moral grounds after receiving information from their clients, the clients will be penalized for being candid, and they will seek other attorneys from whom they will withhold the information in question. These lawyers will then be less able to exercise any positive moral influence in the way of advice.[28]

This reasoning applies to noncriminal clients as well, and it argues for generally keeping in confidence client intentions for future acts as well as admissions of past acts. There is perhaps less of a duty in relation to the former, since harmful acts can often be prevented by revelation, and due process is not as much at stake regarding liability for acts not yet committed. The Code certainly draws this distinction between past crimes and future intentions sharply. But the argument for confidentiality that appeals to encouragement for clients to disclose, and to the positive influence that lawyers can then have upon them, applies even more directly to disclosure of future intentions by the clients.

The final argument for the principle of full advocacy, closely related to the first, again emphasizes the limited role of attorneys in the broad legal and social structure. This argument is once more democratic in spirit, but rests upon the lawyer's relation to other officials in the system, rather than to clients as lacking expert legal knowledge. Here appeal is to division of power, checks and balances. When lawyers refuse on moral grounds to pursue that to which clients have legal rights, they substitute their own moral judgment for that of legislators, judges and juries, those entrusted by the citizenry to determine the scope of legal rights according to moral criteria. By deciding which legal rights could be exercised by their clients and which could not, lawyers would assume the power to determine the scope of legal rights themselves. An oligarchy of lawyers would substitute itself for a system of democratically determined legal rights.[29] Since we do not desire such a professional elitist form of social control, we should recognize rights of citizens to pursue objectives and have legal cases decided as the law provides, rather than as lawyers see fit. Just as a judge would eliminate the force of legislative decision by deciding each case on its perceived moral merits, so lawyers, it seems, would have the same effect by limiting their clients' objectives according to their own moral lights. By reasoning parallel to that accepted in the previous chapter, it can be argued, then, that it is not the lawyer's role to determine the extent of legal rights. He should not limit the implementation of such rights by effectively limiting pursuit of objectives recognized as legal by refusing expert assistance. Nor is it the lawyer's role to judge his client. The former is the role of legislators, the latter of judges and juries. When lawyers refuse to pursue their clients' interests or requests within the bounds of law, they are in effect circumventing the legislative and judicial processes.[30]

Thus the lawyer's position must be strongly differentiated: he lacks the authority to thwart his client's objectives according to his own moral conscience. The only limits to the client's pursuit of those objectives must be institutional or legal, in order to maintain a government of laws and not of lawyers. So goes this final and most forceful argument for the principle of full advocacy.

Counterarguments to the Code's Principle

The arguments of the preceding section should not be fully convincing. To see why, it will be useful to preface specific criticisms by an indication of the form of counterargument, recalling some general considerations that relate to institutional obligations. It is worth reiterating that, since justification for all action must be ultimately moral (at least moral permissibility is a necessary condition for the justification of any action), institutional obligations must reduce to moral obligations. When the former amount to strong role differentiation, they nevertheless form a distinct subclass of moral obligations, since they obtain in particular cases somewhat independently of the moral content of the actions they require. Such obligations, as others, exist when their recognition has better moral consequences than does refusing to recognize them. Institutional duties with genuine normative force exist when they are necessary to the functioning of an institution in its protection of moral rights first, and production of collective good second.

It is necessary then in evaluating institutional obligations to look through them to the moral ends they are to serve and moral rights they are to protect, to see whether honoring them in specific situations furthers those ends and rights. We must also emphasize in this discussion that procedural legal rights exist to protect certain moral rights. The question regarding the arguments of the previous section is whether they establish that moral rights and welfare considerations are better satisfied when lawyers pursue their clients' legal rights in neglect of considerations that otherwise would be morally crucial. One set of arguments, for example, emphasized the moral autonomy of clients. In evaluating these arguments according to this criterion, we must consider not only rights of clients, but of all those affected by their actions.

THE TRUTH-FINDING FUNCTION

With this criterion of moral evaluation in mind, we may assess more closely the arguments of the preceding section. Let us begin with the virtues of the adversary system in relation to the lawyer's role within it. Regarding the supposed virtue of adversary proceedings for discovering the facts or ascertaining applicable law, I very much doubt that this is a virtue at all.

Certainly in all other areas in which we attempt to discover the truth or formulate theories we prefer a body of impartial and disinterested inquirers to the formation of opposing advocates, each of whom advances a particular view with the intentional neglect of all evidence damaging to that view.

It is true that initial biases of judge and jury may be overcome by forceful presentation of the opposing side. This is the virtue of adversariness in relation to the truth-finding function emphasized in the brief argument of the Code. It is also true that in other areas of inquiry we seek out opposing views to initial hypotheses, if the former have been impartially formed. But in the legal context the benefit of opposing views is more than offset by the fact that lawyers not only neglect to emphasize evidence supportive of the other side—they keep it from the court. The lawyer is not actively to suppress material evidence, e.g. he may not take possession of a murder weapon and hide it. But neither is he to reveal to the court facts learned from whatever source that may be detrimental to his client's cause. According to the Code, he must reveal adverse law, but not fact. This distinction presumably relates to the duty of confidentiality, often pertinent in regard to the facts but not law. But the negative effect of suppression of either type on the probability of decision on the legal merits is the same. Indeed suppression of fact is the more damaging to the truth-finding function. If we compare again legal trial with scientific inquiry, not only has partisan advocacy little place in science, but suppression of evidence (rather than alternative explanation of it) would be considered an absolute outrage there. Surely in the legal context as well such a practice of suppressing relevant facts of which the opposing attorney, and hence the judge and jury, are unaware cannot be maximally conducive to ascertaining the truth of the matter in court (whether or not this practice is justified on other grounds). Thus a principle of full advocacy is not most conducive to finding the truth in a criminal trial.

In the noncriminal context the threat to rational decision is

far worse than mere suppression of evidence in trials. Here
there are numerous tactics open to the lawyer, the sole purpose
of which is to thwart settlement of the issue in contention on
the legal (let alone moral) merits. These tactics are not only
open to the zealous advocate, but seemingly required by a
principle of full advocacy, a principle that requires the lawyer
to exhaust legal weapons in his client's behalf. We have noted
that the Code prohibits actions whose sole purpose is delay,
and also prohibits threat of criminal charges in a civil context.
But the former prohibition is empty when combined, as it is,
with a principle of zealousness that makes it a duty to exhaust
legal procedure and raise every argument for which some legal
pretense can be made, whether or not the lawyer believes it
could prevail on the legal merits. Thus, in behalf of a potential
plaintiff, the lawyer can threaten civil suit that would be
prohibitively expensive for an adversary to defend, even were
he successful. In behalf of a defendant or potential defendant,
the lawyer can effect costly delay by filing requests for
discovery or for hearings, by raising technical objections,
calling numerous expert witnesses who repeat testimony,
raising counterclaims, filing numerous motions, depositions,
etc.

All of these are common tactics in behalf of corporate
clients; none are brought before disciplinary boards or even
questioned by the Committee on Professional Responsibility.
We need not document here abuses by corporate lawyers.
These are amply described elsewhere: for example a case
involving pricing practices by Nabisco lasting 28 years; a case
on deceptive advertising by Geritol lasting 10 years; one on
peanut butter labeling, 12 years.[31] Anyone who has read
Dickens' *Bleak House* knows that such tactics have been part
of the lawyering repertory for many years. And of course
delaying tactics are not the only ones in which the intention
and result are to thwart decision or settlement of conflict on
legal merits. Lawyers regularly coach witnesses on testimony,
entrap opposing witnesses and prevent them from testifying

coherently, advise corporate clients to clean files periodically before they become evidence, etc. Even such matters as dress and demeanor in court, as well as jury selection, are known by lawyers to affect trial outcomes, while lacking any relevance to the legal merits.

The point here is that zealous advocacy will always require the lawyer to take advantage of such procedures that exist in the law for other purposes (or, where lawyers are zealous lobbyists for their clients and can themselves help to create such loopholes, for those very purposes). Even morally required procedural safeguards in the law can be used to distort, suppress the truth, delay, intimidate or wear down the opposition financially or psychologically, and generally prevent a fair outcome based upon legal or moral merits. Hemming in the principle of zealous advocacy with specific prohibitions, as does the Code (albeit sparingly), cannot significantly alter such opportunity for legal intimidation, except by effectively substituting a completely different fundamental principle of lawyer conduct. Such a principle would have to require the lawyer to aim directly at a legally correct or morally fair outcome, rather than having him rely on the adversary process to achieve one.

The adversary process with full advocacy cannot be most conducive to truth-finding or decision on strict legal merits when one side, the side that knows it is on the short end of the truth or the law, is systematically involved in thwarting those outcomes. This is not to imply that everyone must always aim directly to do what is most moral according to his own lights. One can in certain circumstances defer to the moral or factual judgment of others in seeking justice or truth. We saw in the case of judges that it may be right in some situations to subordinate moral judgment to law. But the most effective way to truth or strict application of law cannot be through deception, suppression of fact, or intimidation, whether these are practiced by only one or both sides to a dispute. And full advocacy entails the use of such tactics when they effectively further a client's cause.

PROTECTION OF MORAL RIGHTS

THE CRIMINAL CONTEXT   It can be replied at this point that the virtue of the adversary system lies not in its superiority to other methods of seeking truth, or in its maximizing the probability of decision on strict legal merits, but rather in the maximum protection it affords to possibly innocent defendants. Only one argument for full advocacy appealed to the truth- (or law-) finding functions of adversary proceedings. Others emphasized the autonomy of the client against the power of the collectivity and his right to pursue objectives within legal limits. This protection of individual dignity and autonomy, even at the expense of collective public welfare, is pervasive in our legal system, as that institution reflects our deeper rights based moral framework. Individual client advocacy can be seen as only one aspect of it. The criminal system, for example, is predicated on the principle that it is worse to violate the right of the innocent not to be convicted and punished than it is to let the guilty go free. Therein lies the justification for rules of evidence, for the doctrine of guilt beyond reasonable doubt, and for the many procedural safeguards we grant to those accused, including the right to be judged by juries and judges rather than by lawyers.

Some have questioned whether the sacrifice of public safety sometimes involved in always giving the benefit of doubt to accused criminals and in protecting them against various forms of evidence collection is worth it. From a moral point of view, I believe it is. First, it *is* worse to punish an innocent man than to release a guilty one, even if the guilty one then victimizes another innocent person. This follows from the stricter obligations imposed by negative rights not to be harmed than by positive rights to protection or aid. Harming a specific individual is an affront to his autonomy and dignity as a person; it expresses a lack of concern for his interests and personal integrity. Furthermore, when the harm consists in sending someone to jail without due procedural cautions, it is a severe harm indeed, more so if the person is innocent and feels justifiable resentment. Failing to take maximal measures to protect unspecified members of the public is not as great a wrong. This difference in itself would justify the asymmetries in our system between rules intended to protect the innocent and those designed to facilitate conviction of the guilty. We may add to this difference the point that even the guilty themselves deserve to be treated as persons and do not forfeit all rights by their criminal activity. Certain forms of evidence collection would violate the rights even of one who committed a serious crime, more so if the crime were not serious. This point in itself does not justify all the procedural safeguards we employ; some are intended mainly to protect the innocent. But it adds to their force.

These two considerations together generally justify a criminal defense attorney's putting the state to the full test by raising every available defense. There is also a serious moral problem in the justification of many forms of punishment typically imposed upon conviction.[32] The principle of advocacy is therefore most at home in such contexts, in which the accused individual, often of unfortunate background, stands alone against the prosecutorial powers of the state. Yet even in the criminal law context, if it is the moral right of the innocent, or possibly innocent, that underlies many of the legal rights in question, then the argument regarding the lawyer's role in guaranteeing maximum protection of this right seems at least partially inapplicable in the case in which the lawyer knows beyond any doubt that the client is guilty. It is true that it is not the lawyer's role to ascertain the guilt or innocence of those accused, and that he is not obligated to do so. It is also true that he must take his role as protector and spokeman for the possibly innocent seriously. But this does not entail, when he knows with certainty of the guilt of his client or potential client, that he is absolved of all responsibility for setting an extremely dangerous criminal free, or that he should use all possible legal tactics to secure acquittal. The gravity of the crime and probability of repetition, as well as the nature of the defense tactic and the harm it might directly impose on others, at least appear to be relevant factors in assessing those tactics that might be required or permissible.

There are cases in which a guilty person should be set free and when his lawyer should pursue this objective with full zeal. One such case is when the crime committed was not serious and the client's procedural rights have been violated by the police. Acquittal may then be necessary to protect future (possibly innocent) suspects. Another such case is that in which the punishment is not morally deserved even by one guilty of the crime in question. My only claim here is that some tactics that might be justified to gain acquittal for someone who might be innocent will not be justified in the situation of known guilt. Although lack of full zeal might be a betrayal of client trust and due process in all such cases, *these wrongs are not absolute,* but must be weighed against the harm that will be caused to others by the proposed tactics. The rape example is one case in which this argument obviously applies, and there are others, although they certainly will not be the rule in the criminal defense context. In such cases the guilty simply do not have a moral right to every conceivable legal tactic by their lawyers to convince the court that they are innocent, and the principle of full advocacy breaks down. The question remains (for the next section) whether we can specify a rule that will single out only such cases for exception, without endangering possible innocent defendants.

The lack of procedural safeguards for clients in lawyer-client interviews and exchanges makes it proper that lawyers themselves cannot convict. It also raises the epistemic standards of knowledge beyond even the lack of reasonable doubt that applies to jurors. Fallibility in the judgment of the lawyer must be given serious weight here. The only question is whether it justifies an iron clad rule of full advocacy whatever the effects on the interests of others, and whatever the extent of the lawyer's certain knowledge. Knowledge of conclusively incriminating facts or admission of guilt can be distinguished from opinion on the moral merits. There are cases in which skepticism on the part of the lawyer is impossible. In such cases the goal of maximum protection for the innocent, which defines the normal role of the criminal lawyer in the adversary system, does not apply. Lawyers are not, therefore, justified in using all those tactics to secure acquittal, including presentation of false testimony, harmfully aggressive cross examination, or impeachment of testimony of truthful witnesses, that they might be justified in using to prevent conviction of an innocent client. If a lawyer knows with certainty that his client is guilty of a serious crime, then his convincing a jury of the client's innocence by hiding conclusively incriminating facts, presenting false testimony, or breaking truthful witnesses appears to thwart the moral purpose of the legal system rather than further it.

I am not claiming that a lawyer ought never to do these things. Sometimes the protection of procedural rights for the innocent, or a morally objectionable degree of potential punishment, or a breach of confidence must be weighed in determining the proper course. But on the other side is the potential evil from setting a dangerous criminal free, the wrong done to the truthful witness, etc. Even in criminal cases, then, there will be situations in which the principle of full advocacy, and the emphasis upon purely legal rather than moral limits, will be too simplistic and out of line with the moral justification of advocacy in the normal case. This justification relates primarily to protection of the innocent; and it is not clear that significantly more innocent persons would fail to be adequately represented were lawyers to apply moral principles directly in cases of clients known with certainty to be guilty.

THE NONCRIMINAL CONTEXT   The protection of the possibly innocent against the full power of the state does not apply in the noncriminal context. The noble image of the attorney for the defense standing alone with his indigent client against a hostile world, or against the power of police and prosecutor out for conviction, fades quickly in relation to the corporate spokesman, whose client continuously exploits an unrepresented, disorganized and ignorant public. There is some recognition in the Code, as we saw, of the different functions the modern lawyer has come to play. The criminal prosecutor, for example, is not to play as much of an adversarial role as the defense attorney. He must, for example, disclose adverse fact as well as law. The lawyer as advisor obviously is not to construe the law always in his client's favor, as he does when defending in court. As advisor he may offer moral advice and may withdraw if it is not taken, as he may not as criminal defense attorney if this would damage his client's chances of acquittal. But these recognized differences are limited and narrow, and it is clear that the Code extends the adversary model from the criminal to the civil context. As others have noted,[33] the Code extends the adversary model as well from the trial context to the many other roles of the present day lawyer—negotiator, draftsman, spokesman, lobbyist, etc. In fact, as we also saw, some of the limitations upon adversariness applicable to the trial context are relaxed by the Code outside it: the lawyer need not reveal adverse law, for example, when negotiating.

In the context of corporate law it is not a matter of an individual against the state, or of two individuals involved in a dispute with minimal effects on others. Some such disputes are well settled by any contest to which the principals agree, and the outcome of which they are willing to accept. The corporate context entails numerous disanalogies with such personal conflicts and with criminal defense, differences not adequately acknowledged in the adversary model of the Code. Rather than defending a client in court against a charge of past wrongdoing, the lawyer on retainer will be an integral part of a continuous policy and pattern of conduct. The traditional notion of detachment of the lawyer from his client and cause will tend to break down here, as not only single lawyers, but whole firms, become linked to certain types of corporate interest through specialization and a desire to avoid conflicts of interest (a major and much exaggerated preoccupation of the Code). When a lawyer is on retainer, his advice will be required continuously, and also his participation in negotiating, drafting documents, etc. The distinctions pressed in the Code between the lawyer's attitude toward past conduct of his client and his relation to the client's future intentions, and between an original decision to accept a client (which is entirely up to the lawyer or firm) and what he must do for the client once he decides to represent him, also tend to be obliterated in the situation of a continuing retainer from a corporation. Even the limits imposed by law will be less certain and firm in the corporate sphere, since the lawyer, especially if he is a Washington lawyer, is likely to be a lobbyist also for the industry he represents. This means that the limits of applicable law may be bounds the lawyer himself helped to broaden and weaken.

If, then, the lawyer is party to an ongoing policy and pattern of client decision, if he is engaged not only in advising the client as to the requirements of law, but also in helping to shape and effectuate business decisions, and if he acts as lobbyist and spokesman for his client's self-interested point of view, then he can hardly dissociate himself entirely from the moral consequences of client policy and conduct. In contrast to personal legal disputes, harm to unrepresented third parties is likely to be far more widespread in relation to objectionable conduct by corporations not yet brought under sufficient legal control. A lawyer here cannot rely upon opposing advocates to counter his pressing a position that he finds personally objectionable. The lawyer who lobbies in the back halls of Congress, in restaurants, clubs and bars, for weakened cigarette warnings, auto safety or pollution control standards, or drug industry regulations certainly cannot assume that the opposing side will be vigorously represented in these nonadversarial settings. If a principle of strong advocacy without moral responsibility obtains here, then legal ethics in this context can never rise above the level of business ethics in practice, a level from which the view is rarely panoramic. Without legal endorsement, business managers themselves might balk at assuming certain self-interested positions that might be ardently pressed by the lawyer at one level further removed from a sense of responsibility for consequences. This outcome seems a far cry from the ideal of fully testing the state's proof against a possibly innocent defendant in a criminal trial.

(1) Client Autonomy and the Distribution of Legal Resources. The counterargument to the principle of full advocacy in civil contexts is thus stronger than its counterpart in the criminal trial situation, given an appreciation of the moral justification for the institutional procedures and legal rights in question. In the civil, and especially the corporate, sphere, the strong benefit of doubt accorded the accused and possibly innocent defendant, which argues most persuasively for strong advocacy there, is of no relevance. The argument for the principle of full advocacy here can appeal only to some notion of autonomy to pursue self-interest within the law, and to a right to equal access to legal expertise. Here the claim was that the adversary system functions to provide access to expert advocates so that no one is unfairly taken advantage of by others with greater expertise and capability of manipulating the legal system to their own ends. That each individual or corporation can employ a legal expert to protect his or its interest is to ensure that no one is unfairly manipulated for lack of such expertise. Again the moral purpose of the system is to maintain a structure of institutional rights that will guarantee fair treatment and protection of moral rights for all within the system. If each can have access to his own legal expert, who will apply his expertise in the interest of the client alone, then those who possess such expertise will have no unfair advantage in the social and economic arena over those who do not. So goes the argument for full advocacy here.

But if this democratic and liberal ideal of equal access and individual autonomy motivates the extension of the principle of advocacy beyond its natural home in the criminal trial context, then the moral consequences of its extended operation make a mockery of its professed intent. For the entire argument here presupposes that a fair and equal distribution of legal resources results from the system of advocacy for hire. More strongly, the argument not only presupposes this result, it appeals to it as the principal reason for maintaining the system as we know it. Given use of the adversarial tactics described above, the main purpose of which is to prevent decision on moral or legal merits, the outcome of adversarial opposition is only accidentally just at best. In an adversarial situation with equally competent lawyers on both sides and equal resources at their disposal, and with litigation and decision by trial as an imminent possibility, the outcome might be just at least on legal criteria, despite the motive of the side with the weaker case to delay, obfuscate, etc. But the probability of the outcome's being determined on the merits reduces when, in addition to the lack of moral constraints, the excesses on one side cannot be offset by an equally zealous and competent advocate on the other. Indeed, this is the reasoning behind the call for zealousness, to offset any advantage of those with opposing interests. But in a context of vastly unequal distribution of talent, as that which results from our free enterprise system of lawyer service, a principle of strong advocacy only magnifies the inequalities. In the corporate context, it is not just a matter of capital resources, but of continuing superior organization that results in a near monopolization of legal expertise by certain interests.

The Code pays lipservice to the rights of all, including "unpopular clients," to competent legal representation. As we saw, it also presupposes the realization of these rights in supporting a principle of full advocacy. But at the same time it leaves it entirely up to each lawyer whether to accept any particular client. In this case the individual prerogative nullifies the collective obligation of lawyers. Specialization and strict rules against possible conflicts of interest add to the maldistribution. The Bar's sins on this matter are not merely ones of omission and good intention. There were in addition the scandalously self-serving campaigns against advertising, legal clinics and group financed legal services, as well as strong support for minimum fee schedules. It is still primarily the prohibitively expensive cost of legal service that gives the rich and organized such an overwhelming advantage, despite the recent growth of public interest law. Admittedly this obvious fact about the unequal distribution of legal services is not an argument in itself against strong advocacy. But it certainly renders highly suspect any democratic argument for the principle that appeals to removing disadvantages from ignorance of law. Democratically motivated arguments for a system that results in so markedly anti-democratic results must be dismissed, at least in the present social context.

While distributive injustice exacerbates the moral faults of extreme advocacy, it might be possible to distribute legal services more equally without abandoning that principle. Indeed some public interest lawyers are suspicious of any call for reduced advocacy at a time when the disadvantaged are just beginning to find advocates for their interests.[34] But given that the poor continue to be under-represented in relation to corporate interests, for example, this argument against fully zealous advocacy retains its force. More important, even if the balance shifted further toward equal legal representation, indeed even if various groups and economic interests commanded absolutely equal attention and advocacy from the collective Bar, the problem of distribution for the principle of full advocacy would not disappear. There will remain specific situations in which advocacy of narrow selfish interests without moral constraint can harm those with inadequate representation or no representation at all, individual consumers or children for example.

Even when advocates represent both sides to a dispute, as long as winning remains the sole motivation, the outcome may depend more upon the relative skills of the lawyers to exploit vulnerabilities in the other side, vulnerabilities that may be economic, psychological or professional, than upon the moral or legal dimensions of the dispute. These micro-maldistributions in specific cases constitute a problem endemic to the operation of a principle of full advocacy, as the problem of gross distribution by ability to pay does not. The latter could be corrected (perhaps only by fundamental changes in our social and economic structure); the former cannot, as long as lawyers aim only to win or to serve their clients' interests. The monopolization of legal expertise by practicing attorneys, and the distribution of such expertise among those in the legal profession, will therefore always argue more for the protection of the unrepresented or under-represented against serious harm from lawyers' actions than for zealous advocacy of clients' interests in total disregard for that harm.

To the claim that the moral autonomy of the client is at stake in his ability to find a strong legal advocate for his interests, several further replies are in order. First, just as in practice the ideal of lawyer detachment from client point of view is subverted by the present organization and operation of the legal system (specialization of firms), so may be the ideal of client autonomy. The client may in fact lose his own sense of moral responsibility when he sees his most partisan interests warmly embraced and given institutional respectability by his lawyer. Certainly the many technicalities and rituals of legal maneuvering tend to alienate all but the most sophisticated corporate clients from participation in the achievement of their own supposed legal objectives. The encounter with a special professional ethic seemingly oblivious to ordinary notions of moral responsibility can add to that sense of moral alienation.[35] If the client were required instead to justify his objective to his lawyer, or at least to claim a moral right to pursue it in highly questionable cases, this might restore a sense of moral responsibility and autonomy rather than squash it. To be morally autonomous is to assume moral responsibility for one's own actions, not simply to act out of narrow self-interest. Moral rights create space for individual values and the development of autonomy in this sense as well. Features of the legal system that lessen the sense of moral responsibility might diminish the sense of autonomy within the system too, for clients as well as lawyers. Extreme partisanship is one such feature.

I have emphasized earlier that the individual does have a prerogative to prefer his own interests and the interests of those close to him over that of strangers. He may pursue private objectives at the expense of greater collective welfare. The granting of such individual prerogative against the aggregate welfare of collectives is necessary to the development of distinct healthy individual personalities, indeed of genuine persons. For the same reason, and because of the fact that certain interests are central to individual expression and development, we grant persons moral rights that override aggregate utility considerations. If one has a moral, and not merely legal, right to speak freely, then he may do so even when others are offended by what he says, and when the consequent disutilities outweigh any utilities that might result from his saying it. If one has a moral right to her legitimately owned property, then it is not adequate justification for taking it from her that others might benefit from it more.

One argument for the principle of full advocacy viewed the lawyer's role as that of helping the individual client to achieve the same personal prerogative of private interest within the framework of the legal system.[36] But the appeal to autonomy here as a support for the principle loses whatever remaining force it has when the autonomy of those affected by clients' objectives is taken into account, and not just that of clients themselves. The crucial fact ignored in this argument is that the domain of individual prerogative must be limited by that same domain as it is staked out for other individuals. It consists precisely in those patterns of conduct and objectives that individuals have moral rights to pursue. The domain of individual autonomy is adequately protected precisely by the recognition of moral rights; but in order for it to remain intact for each individual, each must also accept at least negative rights of others as constraints upon his actions. This point is almost too familiar to mention, except that it is notably neglected in the exclusive emphasis upon client interest in the accepted view of proper legal practice.

For this reason the domain of clients' moral rights is clearly not congruent with that of all and any objectives they may wish to pursue, even with those requiring only legal tactics on the part of their lawyers. Whatever validity there is to the appeal to autonomy in the argument for full advocacy, it clearly must be balanced against the degree of immorality in particular clients' purposes or demands and the consequences of their realizing their objectives. It cannot justify a principle of doing whatever the client demands as long as it is not clearly illegal. The ideal to which the argument appeals is itself defeated in cases in which legal expertise is used to deprive someone of that to which he has a moral right. It once again appears that a deeper apprecia-tion of the moral rationale of the system in which the lawyer functions reveals the principle of full advocacy to be too strong. Defense of the moral autonomy of the client cannot extend to his violation of the moral rights of others, i.e. to his invasion of their proper domains of individual sovereignty.

Extension of this notion of individual autonomy to the corporate context is in any case problematic. Just whose autonomy is supposed to be at stake in this area? Not the executives', for they are to act only in the interest of the stockholders. But the autonomous action of the stockholders themselves is not at stake either, for they play little or no role in corporate decision-making anyway. Even if we can swallow that it is the autonomy of the corporation itself of which we speak here, surely *its* freedom and personal prerogative cannot justify ignoring moral rights of real (rather than fictitious legal) persons. (Do we protect corporate moral rights in order to develop healthy and creatively valuing corporations as well as individuals?)

(2) The Collective Effect of Moral Restraint by Lawyers. It might be replied still that the issue here is not whether it is right for the client, individual or corporate, to pursue objectives that violate moral rights of others. We can readily agree that it is not. The issue is rather whether lawyers should be given authority to prevent clients from pursuing such objectives according to the lawyers' moral perceptions. It might be emphasized that if persons, including corporate persons, are to be restrained in their conduct, this should be by legal authority

and not by personal decisions of lawyers. The argument once more emerges that only legal bounds can be properly imposed; within them the lawyer cannot impose his own moral limits by denying clients the freedom to choose and act on their own initiative. Such denial appears to substitute a government of lawyers for a government of law.

As an initial step in continuing the counterargument we can point out that the lawyer is not coercively forbidding the client to act in morally objectionable ways; he is simply refusing to take part himself in achieving client objectives at the expense of moral rights of others. And, after all, the moral autonomy of the lawyer himself is at stake. If he must do whatever the client demands or desires in continuing to represent him, then the lawyer is relinquishing all moral control over his own actions to the client. Aside from the effects of this denial of responsibility upon the social framework, and upon the foremost goal of protecting moral rights within that framework, we may wonder what kind of people professionals can be if they matter-of factly ignore moral rights of others not to suffer harm. In the case of judges, as noted, they can view the necessity of enforcing law sometimes in opposition to specific moral rights in terms of the need for a stable legal system to maintain those values for which moral rights themselves are recognized. But can a lawyer advancing a corrupt corporate cause against defenseless consumers really take himself to be serving the deeper moral good?

Even this last question might yet be answered affirmatively by one who feared the collective results of allowing lawyers full moral veto of client decisions, or of ascribing full moral responsibility to lawyers for their roles in achieving objectionable client objectives. It remains true that we would not want an oligarchy of lawyers to replace the legislative and judicial structure in determining the scope of exercisable legal rights. The question is whether that odious form of de facto government would result from lawyers' adhering to normal moral principle in regard to matters within the law. The major fallacy in this argument from the previous section is the implicit assumption that lawyers act as a corporate body to determine collectively how clients may act. In fact they do not form such a body. They do not vote on how cases should be pursued, but rather act as individuals whose moral opinions may differ among themselves. They do not collectively prevent clients from pursuing objectives held by consensus to be immoral, but rather may refuse individually to aid in the pursuit of objectives judged to violate moral rights. If an individual lawyer refuses to do for a client that which he feels the client has no right to do, the client can always seek another lawyer. For the client to be refused by all available lawyers (assuming there are several) who judge his objective by their normal moral principles, his purpose would have to be blatantly immoral on normal criteria. (Whether a lawyer represents the only legal service or expertise in a particular area may then be a relevant consideration as to whether he should substitute his moral conscience for legal guidelines. The smaller the number of available lawyers, the more certain he must be that his client has no moral right to his aid in the course of conduct in question.)

We would be correct to mistrust an oligarchy of lawyers more than we mistrust the present system of legislatively and judicially determined legal rights to operate always for the protection of moral rights. But we are not wrong to oppose the moral sense of individual citizens, lawyers included, to the general rules of legislators in deciding whether to act or aid others in acting in ways perceived to be morally abhorrent. We may again contrast the position of lawyers in this regard from that of judges as a positive illustration of strong role differentiation. In the case of judges, it is the effect of their decisions upon the law itself, the requirement that the law be consistent and predictable, and the fact that judges would indeed circumvent the entire legislative process were they to decide all cases according to their perceptions of the moral merits, that make it better for them to defer to legal criteria for decisions (except in extreme cases). The position of lawyers is not analogous. Their individual decisions to aid or not to aid their clients' objectives on moral grounds lack "gravitational force;" they need not influence other lawyers' decisions on the same or similar matters. Nor do their individual decisions tend to alter the structure of legal rights or the system of legal sanctions. Because they do not act as a corporate body, their clients will not be barred from pursuing objectives when lawyers act directly on moral principle, except when the objectives so blatantly violate moral rights that no one can aid in their pursuit in good conscience in the absence of institutional blinders.

But, it might be replied, while individual lawyers cannot appreciably affect the exercisability of legal rights, and while they do not act in concert in applying moral restraints to clients' behavior, the cumulative effect of their interposing their own moral judgments might be to leave politically unpopular clients and causes unrepresented. If, for example, the vast majority of the Bar was conservatively oriented in the 1950s, and if they had accepted the idea of refusing to aid clients whose causes they found objectionable, then those accused of being Communists would have found the availability of competent legal representation more scarce than it was. There is no question that such politically unpopular clients, including also Nazis and members of the Klan, have a right to legal representation and to protection of their other constitutional rights. If reduced advocacy resulted in violation of such rights, it would be more difficult to support. But to this reply, often made to calls for reduced advocacy on the part of lawyers, there is an obvious counterpoint. It is that lawyers themselves can distinguish between representing unpopular, even morally objectionable clients, and aiding clients, whoever they are, to achieve specific objectives in violation of moral rights of others.

No one would claim that large corporations should go unrepresented (as if there were any danger of that). The question is not one of who should be legally represented, but of how they should be represented. There is all the difference in the world, for example, between aiding Nazis to achieve all their aims, and aiding them by protecting their constitutional rights. Surely lawyers trained to draw fine distinctions can perceive that not very fine one. Even if unpopular clients are those thought to be generally harmful to others or to the social system, this distinction remains between future specific immoral objectives and patterns of conduct on the one hand, and rights that should be protected despite past conduct on the other. For any client, the right not to be at an unfair disadvantage for lack of legal expertise does not extend to a right to take unfair advantage of others through tactics of a skillful lawyer.

The argument that lawyers who adopt unilateral restraints place their clients at a disadvantage in a system in which all tend to act in a strictly partisan way must be dismissed as well. It is not applicable in situations in which lawyers can take unfair advantage of adversaries' vulnerabilities, can violate their moral rights, or avoid settlement of disputes on legal or moral merits. Not to press such unfair advantage does not place clients at a disadvantage to weaker adversaries who might do so if they could. In any case the claim of equal right to do wrong is morally perverse. It could, if allowed, justify any escalation of limited wrongdoing. Thus the collective effect of lawyers' adhering to ordinary moral constraints is not to disadvantage unfairly some proportion of those they might serve. Since lawyers do not collectively determine whether to honor specific legal rights, the individual lawyer is simply maintaining his own autonomy, rather than subverting that of a client, when he refuses legal aid on moral grounds. He is not deciding for the client when he refuses assistance, unless all other lawyers refuse as well. In the latter case we may well suspect that the immorality of the client's purpose outweights the value of allowing him the autonomy of pursuing it.

Thus we cannot argue from the value of autonomous decisions by clients that lawyers must relinquish their own autonomous moral responsibility for legal decisions, even for those within the bounds of current legal practice or tactics. Just as we may dismiss arguments that rest on claims of equal right to do wrong, so we may be suspicious of the imposition of institutional blinders on grounds that individuals are incapable of judging blatantly immoral courses of conduct, at least when the decisions of the individuals in question lack direct institutional effects beyond the specific situations in which they are made. Institutional blinders, such as that imposed by the principle of full advocacy, diminish the moral autonomy and sense of responsibility of professionals and may do so for clients as well. At least in this case they do not seem necessary to protect the rights and autonomy of all nonprofessionals involved.

My argument has departed from the Code in two ways regarding the relation between the individual actions of lawyers and the collective effect of those actions. The Code ascribes a collective responsibility to represent all clients in legal need, and yet reserves the individual right of each lawyer to refuse clients as he sees fit. Given the economic realities, this individual prerogative nullifies the supposed collective obligation. It results in an unfair distribution of legal assistance that exacerbates the problem of full advocacy. Tactics that can be used to avoid just outcomes operate systematically to favor the rich and organized. On the other hand, supporters of a principle of full advocacy seem to fear that individual decisions by lawyers to refuse fully zealous pursuit of certain client demands on moral grounds will collectively leave these clients at an unfair disadvantage. I have denied this. Lawyers are not to refuse to represent clients of whom they morally disapprove; they are only to refrain from violating moral rights in their clients' behalf. Given this limited restriction, and the diversity of moral views among lawyers themselves, the moral constraint prevents unfair disadvantage within the legal system rather than causing it.

CONFIDENTIALITY   There remains from the previous section only the argument regarding confidentiality. This argument condemned the failure to be as zealous as possible in pursuit of a client's objectives as a betrayal of trust or breach of confidence. The two wrongs claimed here are the frustration of the client's expectation for full advocacy, and, in some cases, the use of information supplied by the client under an assumption of confidentiality to his detriment. These wrongs are both intrinsic and instrumental, the latter in that clients will receive adequate representation only if they can trust their lawyers not to hold knowledge of incriminating facts against them, and in that lawyers can exert positive moral influence upon their clients only if they can learn of their intentions. In reply it may be noted first that, while breaking a promise or trust is wrong, it is not an absolute wrong, but must be weighed against the possible violation of other more important rights than the right to have a promise kept.

Even the Code's fanatic defense of confidentiality recognizes this limitation in relation to revelations of intentions to commit future crimes (and in relation to the cardinal sin of not paying a lawyer's fee). The distinction in regard to the duty of confidentiality between past and future acts is not as sharp as the Code would have us believe.[37] Maintenance of confidence regarding knowledge of future intentions would equally encourage disclosure and give lawyers more opportunity for moral influence. That the Code does not accept this argument here is not because it applies less well to revelation of future intention, but because serious harm can sometimes be prevented by such revelation. This can hold true of revelation of past acts too, as is illustrated in our sample case 4, in which another man is serving time in prison for a client's past crime. The distinction therefore does not justify the hard and fast rule implicit in the Code. The main point here, however, lies in the recognition that the wrong in any breach of confidence or trust must sometimes be weighed against more serious wrongs.

The second point on this matter, is that an expectation to be aided in an immoral objective carries less weight. If I have promised a friend to aid him in some immoral end, say to murder his enemy, or less extremely to cheat an adversary out of something he deserves, then the fact that I later refuse the aid does not entail that I have wronged my friend. I should never have made the promise in the first place, knowing that the fulfillment of it would have morally objectionable results; and, having made it, I should not now fulfill it. My friend or a third party might reasonably complain at my having made the promise, but not at my having failed to keep it. In the legal context, by analogy, if clients have any legitimate complaints when their lawyers refuse to use immoral means to their immoral ends, the complaints can be only that they should not have been led to believe that a principle of full advocacy applied in the first place, not that the lawyers refused to act on that principle. The principle must be antecedently fair, or at least not grossly unfair in application, in order for an expectation that it be honored to carry moral weight in favor of honoring it. It cannot be right to help achieve or acquire for a client what he does not deserve at the expense of moral rights of others solely on the ground that he has expected and trusted you to do so. Even if the refusal is based upon knowledge learned from a client under an understanding that it would not be held against him, the lawyer cannot be blamed for refusing to harm others in his client's behalf. If you tell me that an action I was to perform for you will seriously harm another person, trusting fully that your revelation will not affect my loyalty to your objective, I cannot be faulted for then refusing to act in your behalf.

Third, there is a breach of trust only if the client is led to believe that the lawyer is willing to violate the moral rights of others in pursuit of his interests. Refusal to fully advocate immoral objectives or utilize objectionable tactics is a breach of trust only if the client reveals the objectionable aspects of his intentions with the understanding that this will not negatively affect his lawyer's zealousness. A simple disclaimer at the beginning could avoid completely the intrinsic wrong of a breach of trust later. It can be replied to this point that such a disclaimer would discourage clients from being open with their lawyers. Fear of consequences might prevent innocent criminal suspects from revealing incriminating facts of which the lawyer must be informed to defend adequately. In the noncriminal context the lawyer might be prevented from exerting a positive moral influence if he does not learn of client intentions.

Thus the most plausible argument here in favor of the contested principle appeals to the goal of adequate representation and the necessity of willingness on the part of clients to reveal all. If the client knows that certain revelations will result in reduced advocacy in his behalf, he will choose to remain silent. His silence may be damaging to his legitimate interests or to those of others, if it is a question of a future act from which he might be dissuaded. In the criminal context a lawyer's allowing knowledge gained from the client to operate against him by weakening his defense appears to be in violation of principles of due process and the right against self-incrimination. This violation too can be mitigated by the lawyer's informing the client in advance that knowledge of guilt may cause him to refrain from using certain tactics to secure acquittal that he might have otherwise used.

Would such disclaimers have morally disastrous effects? They might cause guilty clients to try to hide their guilt or to omit certain incriminating facts in their accounts to their lawyers. But if a client is guilty, then it is not so troubling that he might want to hide this from his lawyer. If he is innocent, the lawyer should still be able to convince him that it is best for his lawyer to know all incriminating facts in advance in order to defend him effectively. Part of the convincing can consist in the lawyer's assurance that he will assume innocence in the absence of indubitable knowledge of guilt. As for the argument that in non-criminal contexts lawyers will be unable to exert positive moral influence upon clients without knowledge of their intentions and objectives, it seems to me that this influence is rather minimized when clients know that their attorneys are committed to aid in their morally objectionable aims. Refusal to aid can itself be a far stronger influence and show of disapproval. It is true that the lawyer can exert this influence only if he learns of his client's intentions. But the client might reveal them if he requires the lawyer's aid even without any guarantee of obtaining it. In any case a promise of complicity is too high a price to pay for knowledge of wrongdoing.

Thus the arguments of Section A, the most plausible I can think of or extract from the Code, fail to support adequately the principle of full advocacy. They fail to show that the moral ends of the legal system require that lawyers willingly violate moral rights or ignore otherwise morally relevant considerations in pursuit of their clients' interests.

The Principle of Moral Right

We must now make explicit the alternative principle for lawyer conduct implicit in the criticisms of the principle of full advocacy in the previous section. It will then remain to specify its implications for our various test cases, see whether these implications are intuitively more plausible than those of its rival principle, and consider possible objections to this suggested alternative framework. I have criticized the tactics required by fully zealous advocacy, tactics independent of and often inimical to an outcome on the moral or legal merits. The distributive effects of the operation of the Code's principle, and the harm caused by adherence to it to under-represented innocent parties, also came under attack. Rejection of full advocacy, advocacy constrained only by certain specific legal limits, leaves us with a choice between three alternative principles. (There may of course be others, but I consider only the one I defend and what I take to be its most plausible alternatives.)

ALTERNATIVE PRINCIPLES

First, the lawyer could be required to advance his client's cause only through means compatible with settlement of the conflict on the legal merits. He would then forego those tactics that are not strictly illegal, but that function in the circumstances to delay, impose prohibitive expenses on adversaries, or force settlement based upon ignorance of law or fact. Such tactics could be prohibited without permitting the lawyer to restrain his client further according to his purely moral judgment. The lawyer could still pursue whatever his client might be legally entitled to under some favorable construction of the law, without engaging in maneuvers or arguments the primary purpose of which is to win despite the balance of legal right.

A second possible principle would require a lawyer to aid his clients in achieving all and only that to which they have moral rights. This would call upon lawyers to exercise independent judgment in refusing to violate moral rights of others even in the pursuit of that to which clients might be legally entitled. It also might call upon them to exceed legal bounds in order to realize moral rights of their clients.

A third principle, one that grants lawyers yet more moral authority, would have them aid clients only in doing what is moral to do. This principle is different from and stronger than the second because of a general feature of moral rights mentioned earlier, namely that a person may have a right to do some things that it would be wrong for him to do in specific circumstances. A right to speak freely entails the right to make offensive statements even in circumstances in which it might be wrong to exercise that right by making them. A moral right to property entails the right to keep everything that one legitimately owns, even when it would be wrong not to give some of it away. Our sample case in which a mother wants to disinherit her son for morally bad reasons furnishes an example in which the implication the third principle differs from that of the second. Here, if the parent has a moral right to her money, then she also has the right to spend or leave it as or to whom she pleases, whether or not she does so for frivolous or bad reasons. According to the second principle, then, the lawyer should not prevent the exercise of this right or refuse to aid in its exercise, even if the parent's reasons for disinheriting her son are morally objectionable. Of all the alternatives only the third principle would have the lawyer refuse to aid in this case on grounds that the mother would be morally wrong to exercise her right in this way.

It might be thought that the position of the lawyer as representative of the legal system to the public requires that he adopt the first principle, the principle of legal right as we may call it, if not the principle of full advocacy. How can the public be expected to respect the law, it might be asked, if even lawyers do not accept it as the proper guideline for behavior and settlement of social conflict? Then too there are the arguments regarding client autonomy within the legal system and the right to have conduct restrained only by properly elected or appointed officials of the system. It might be agreed that tactics which prevent the law from determining the outcome of a case contradict the system itself. Such tactics should be foregone by lawyers as representatives of the system. But by the same token it can be argued that lawyers should not take it upon themselves to contradict or extend beyond the rules of the system in which they operate.

Nevertheless, I want to recommend the second alternative, the principle of moral right, as the one morally best for lawyers to adopt. We can see why if we once again compare principles on some of our test cases. We may consider three for purposes of comparison here: case 5, in which a couple wants to fabricate evidence for an amicable divorce; case 8, in which a mother on welfare has unreported income and requires her lawyer to ignore this in filing for divorce, if she is not to lose the welfare and face a possible jail term; and case 2, in which a woman seeks to have her child, whom she has abused, returned to her. In the first case involving the desired divorce, the principle of legal right would have the lawyer play no part in fabricating evidence or perpetrating a fraud upon the court; whereas the principle of moral right, assuming that the childless couple has every right to separate and be free to remarry or pursue other relationships, would allow the lawyer to advise them so as to realize their aim. Faced with such an archaic and objectionable law, it seems to me that only a fanatic on the subject of obedience to law would find either the lawyer's or the couple's action objectionable if they pursued their moral right.

In the case involving the welfare recipient, the strict application of law would again have an unjust result, a jail sentence for the struggling mother and failure to provide for the basic needs of her children. Again the principle of legal right would prohibit the lawyer from preventing this outcome or else leave the woman unrepresented in the divorce hearing. In this circumstance I think that a lawyer might be excused who refused to become involved at the risk of his career by knowingly submitting false documents to the court. But my own view is that doing so in this case would be a morally praiseworthy act. We have a case here in which the law must draw some line on outside income, but in which any line it draws will cause injustice on one side or the other if followed by all to the letter. This is simply one instance of a general problem that makes action by private citizens on independent moral criteria preferable to servile obedience to law.

The law is a blunt social instrument. It is necessary as a last resort for settling disputes and controlling behavior, as well as to provide a framework in which commerce and economic interaction can occur smoothly. But legal rights can never be made perfectly congruent with generally recognized moral rights, not even by well-intentioned legislators acting for the public good rather than for political interests. As noted in the Introduction, moral rights form too fine a grid to be captured by general rules. Furthermore, the law cannot hope to control or regulate all behavior in violation of such rights: some attempts at control would be so costly in moral terms as to make the cure worse than the disease. For this reason law can never be a substitute for good moral sense of citizens, lawyers included. I contrasted above the position of lawyers with that of judges, who must give more weight to law in order for it to have its proper, indeed any, force and effect. The public refusal of judges to enforce a generally just law on moral grounds might cause those subject to it to disregard its demands in other circumstances when these demands are reasonable. Lawyers, on the other hand, are private citizens in this regard. Their individual decisions to exceed the bounds of law in some cases, and to accept constraints more stringent and narrow than law imposes in others, lack effects upon the legal system outside these specific cases.

Even for judges the weight given to law is not absolute. In the case of the mother's wanting her abused child returned, for example, if the precedent were to give such mothers a second chance after a brief waiting period, a judge might nevertheless make an exception if he thought it was in the child's interest. But since most judges would defer to the standard legal practice in the matter, and since there are special reasons for their doing so, the question is whether lawyers can leave it to the system to prevent unjust harm in such cases. I believe not. The lawyer cannot himself determine the outcome; if his judgment is eccentric, the client can simply seek another lawyer. But his refusal to violate a perceived moral right or cause serious harm to another is important for maintaining his own personal integrity, as a possible influence restraining the client from doing what he himself recognizes as wrong, and as part of a diverse collective input into the social decision-making process.

I believe that the examples cited themselves answer the claims that moral action by lawyers invades the autonomy of clients or lowers respect for law. In the cases of the divorce and the welfare recipient, the moral autonomy of the clients involved, the realization of their moral rights, depends precisely upon their lawyers' overlooking the precise bounds of law. It is true that in other cases, such as that of the abused child, the lawyer's moral judgment might restrain him, and his client if she continues to employ him, within narrower bounds than those imposed by law. But we can see that there is no guarantee that the strict observance of legal right would maximize freedom or autonomy of clients more than adherence to the principle of moral right. In any case it was argued before that the proper domain of autonomy not only for clients, but for those affected by their actions, consists in those moral rights intuitively granted them. As for respect for law and the legal system, I should assume that it would be lowered more by the spectacle of lawyers mechanically observing its letter and causing injustice thereby, than by their exercising independent moral judgment in such cases.

Ultimately, where one comes down on the choice between the principles of moral right and legal right may depend upon one's opinion as to whether the moral judgments of individual lawyers in specific cases are likely to be more congruent with the proper specification of moral rights than are legal rights, as expressed in general rules developed through the political and legal process. I have argued that the law is necessarily a morally blunt instrument, but that judges, except in extreme cases, must defer to its authority in rendering decisions. On the other side it is common to find as a defense not only of a principle of legal right, but of the more extreme principle of full advocacy, a combination of moral skepticism and professed faith in the legal process. The legal system is held to define rules for dispute-settling as well as we can define them. The outcome according to such rules is said to be, if not absolutely definitive of right, at least more so than the intuitive judgments of individual lawyers.

This argument has more force in defense of the principle of legal right than it did earlier, when it was supposed to excuse tactics designed to intimidate and take advantage of vulnerabilities totally irrelevant to the legal merits of the case at hand. But even here the argument depends upon the definition of moral rights as a matter of pure procedural justice,[38] and upon the claim that our political and legal system embody procedural rules as fair as we can make them. The latter is first of all false. We often see unfair advantages built into the law by legislators who cater to special interests. But even if the second condition obtained, the first does not. Determining whether a moral right would be violated by proposed courses of conduct often need not await the outcome of a legal process in regard to the issue. Awaiting a flip of a coin to determine who has the right to a first move in a game, paradigm of pure procedural justice, is not analogous. The right in the game is a matter of pure procedural justice, because there is no independent criterion for who has it, and because we know that a coin flip is perfectly fair in itself. But moral rights in general are not so dependent on legal processes. If they were, we would have no grounds for criticizing the law or the results it imposes in specific cases. Yet we all can recognize cases in which the law, even as it is likely to be applied by judges after adversarial proceedings, will operate to enforce injustice or deprive parties of their moral rights. I speak not only of the more spectacular illustrations like legally enforced segregation, but also of more everyday examples such as the three sample cases discussed afford.

Can we seriously maintain that a lawyer could not predict in case 2 that the little boy would be harmed again by his mother (if the indications are that he would), and that it would be wrong to prevent this from happening, until hearing the judge's ruling as to whether the law requires his return? Or that a couple has a right to part only if one of them commits adultery, if that is what the law says? A right-wing libertarian with a fanatically strong idea of property rights might wonder whether the welfare recipient's children have rights not to starve, but most of us would not morally fault a lawyer who helped prevent this from happening. It is only in such clear cases, those in which the lawyer clearly perceives an opposing moral right (recognizing that others may nevertheless differ with his perception), that the principle of moral rights has bite in opposition to the other principles.

There is a striking resemblance, as we shall see, between this argument against the principle of moral right for lawyers and an argument in the context of business ethics that corporate managers must pursue maximal profits within legal limits, without worrying about broader social responsibilities. Both are "invisible hand" arguments. Both combine a suspicious (because self-serving) moral agnosticism with a faith in "the system," in the one case legal, in the other economic, to produce morally optimal results from morally neutral (or worse, perverse) intentions. Both must be rejected for similar reasons, primarily because moral rights cannot be identified with those claims that prevail in the free-for-all operation of these systems. We did not define moral rights in the Introduction as claims that receive recognition in the legal process, but offered a different criterion. They were defined as claims arising from interests so vital to individual integrity that we do not allow aggregations of lesser interests across different persons to override them. The suggested criterion for recognizing such claims as rights appealed to judgments of contractors in an initial position of equality (without knowledge of social position and without special interests).

According to this criterion we may test opposition to the principle of moral right by asking whether such contractors, or we ourselves stripped of our special interests, would agree to having our moral rights violated by lawyers so that they might do the same to others in our behalf in other circumstances. If the answer is negative, as it must be if we value rights in the first place, then the opposition is misguided and the principle of moral right is the correct one. Of course we must also ask ourselves whether we are willing to allow lawyers to refuse to aid us in objectives that they perceive to violate moral rights of others, and whether the protection of our moral rights against other potential clients is worth the possibility of such refusal. Here, assuming that lawyers will differ among themselves on borderline cases and that several lawyers are available, I believe the answer is affirmative. We may compare again the situation of judges in relation to this test. If we ask whether contractors adopting moral principles to establish the framework for the social system would agree that certain of their moral rights might sometimes be sacrificed for a stable system of law, for which judicial decision according to legal criteria is necessary, the answer appears again affirmative. The difference is that full advocacy in violation of perceived moral rights is not necessary for a stable legal system. In most countries with stable legal systems this principle does not govern legal practice; whereas judicial decision by law is, I take it, standard in all such systems.

Given the contractarian test for the identification of moral rights, we might say that their definition is a matter of pure procedural justice, since they can be identified as whatever claims emerge intact from this hypothetical process. But this would not be quite right either, since the validity of this criterion itself depends on its ability to capture our independent recognitions of moral rights in situations in which we ourselves are disinterested. The crucial point is that, whichever general criterion we accept, and whichever moral rights we recognize, we will not take these to be strictly congruent with the set of legal rights determined by the political and judicial process. One reason for the lack of congruence is the necessary generality of law. Another derives from the special interests that will enter into the political process, no matter how well we establish its framework. No contemporary philosopher I know of defines moral rights in purely legal terms. Doing so would rob us of the ability to identify unjust laws and legal systems. The claim that the principle of moral right is empty, because moral rights cannot be identified independently of the legal process itself, is therefore false. We have identified them as claims that override collective utilities, as these claims would be recognized by disinterested equal agents.

This is not to say that lawyers will agree on the precise specification of moral rights. I suspect that there would be at least as much disagreement in this area as over questions of legal right. But it is precisely that diversity that renders lawyers' independent judgments and behavior based upon them a constructive input into the social system, rather than a collective univocal restraint upon clients, amounting to a de facto separate government.

The primary way in which the principle advocated here differs from a principle of legal right is in requiring the lawyer to forego legal actions that he clearly recognizes to violate moral rights. This restriction, although not empty, would be limited in practice. Lawyers need not constantly act as judges toward their clients. A criminal defendant, for example, may well have a moral right to a fully vigorous defense, despite his initially apparent guilt before the law. The differences between trial and nontrial, and between criminal and noncriminal, contexts, emphasized in the criticism of the Code for extending the full advocacy model beyond its natural setting, do not demand different basic principles of conduct. The principle of moral right itself would imply strong advocacy where called for on moral grounds, and not otherwise.

The principle of moral right differs from that of legal right in being sometimes more restrictive of lawyer conduct and sometimes more permissive in regard to legal tactics. As we saw, it might on rare occasions call upon the lawyer to exceed the bounds of law itself, although, as any other citizen, he would have to risk the penalty for doing so. On other occasions he might be required to take advantage of vulnerabilities irrelevant to legal merits, when an important right of a client, such as the right to liberty of a (possibly) innocent criminal defendant, is at stake. Here, although the results may be the same, my principle differs from that of full advocacy as well, in demanding that opposing rights and interests be weighed, so that a right of a witness or adversary is overridden only when that of the client is more important or fundamental. In cases in which the lawyer does not clearly perceive where the moral right lies, he can give the benefit of doubt to his client, and all the principles would agree.

While I take the principle of moral right to be preferable to that of legal right for the reasons given, both principles would agree in opposing that of full advocacy in all the sample cases not yet discussed in this section. In the case of the wine producer (1), if the substance in the wine presents a serious health risk as determined by adequate impartial testing, then the producer has no right to inflict this risk on unsuspecting consumers, and the principle of moral right would prohibit a lawyer who perceived the situation in this way from aiding the client in marketing the wine. Likewise the principle of legal right would prohibit tactics designed to thwart or delay the proper legal order. In the rape case (3), both principles would prohibit taking advantage of vulnerabilities irrelevant to the legal or moral merits. Similarly in case 4, involving the client who confesses to a murder for which another man was convicted, the client has neither a legal nor a moral right to have the other man serve the life sentence for him. The wrong involved in breaking confidentiality, hardly of the same import as another's life, will be overridden. In the case of the appliance corporation with the defective part, the company will have neither a legal nor moral right to avoid reimbursement, and the lawyer should not advise its managers to do so. Case 7, involving the negligent auto mechanic, presents another example of a vulnerability, this time on the part of the opposing attorney, irrelevant to the legal or moral merits. There seems to be no reason why Lawyer G should be permitted to take advantage of it in settlement negotiation, when he would not be permitted to do so in court.

Full advocacy must be rejected not only on the moral grounds that suggest the principle of moral right, but even on its own terms. For many of the arguments calling upon lawyers to subordinate their independent judgments to those emergent in the legal process support a principle of legal right rather than full advocacy. Tactics utilized to prevent an outcome determined by legal merits, but required under a rule of full advocacy within the law, simply cannot be defended by appeal to the moral superiority of the legal system over individual judgment. While full advocacy therefore ranks low among alternative rules for lawyer conduct, the principle at the extreme other end of the scale, which calls upon lawyers to aid clients to achieve only what the lawyers consider morally right, can be rejected with equal ease. We have seen that rights are recognized in order to stake out an area of individual autonomy and interest that will not be overridden by aggregate utility considerations relating to less important interests. If rights are recognized primarily to stake out an area of autonomy in individual choice and action, and if a necessary feature of rights is that they allow choice even when some options for exercising them would be wrong, then there is no reason to permit lawyers to prevent others from exercising their moral rights on grounds of disapproval of that exercise.

The existence of a moral right implies that it is wrong for

others to prevent its exercise, and there is no reason to exempt lawyers from this injunction. Genuine moral rights and the ability to exercise them must be protected even when pressing their claims is not the right thing to do. The principle of aiding only morally praiseworthy objectives would indeed give lawyers too much moral authority, in allowing them to prevent, or at least delay, the exercise of moral rights. The recognition of such rights entails that no one but their bearers have rights to decide when they may be exercised. The existence of a legal right, on the other hand, does not imply in itself that it would be wrong of others to deny its claim or prevent its exercise. It implies only that it would be wrong, other things being equal, for those charged with enforcing the law not to enforce the legal right. Legal rights have more general normative force only when they can be translated into their moral counterparts.

One who wished to defend the more extreme moral principle might raise a point here to which I appealed in an earlier context. It is true once more that lawyers cannot singly prevent others from acting by refusing aid—other lawyers might be available. But since lawyers are in a unique position to assist people in exercising those moral rights that require legal expertise, rights to make certain kinds of agreements or bequests for example, and since the existence of moral rights implies that their exercise should be facilitated by those in a special position to do so, I believe that lawyers have a duty to assist in such cases. Thus the principle of moral right is once more preferable to an alternative, this time one more restrictive. In case 9 Lawyer I should draw up the new will even though he objects to its terms.

CONCLUSION: DIFFICULTIES AND DEFENSES

The principle defended here is certainly not without its difficulties. Lawyers would certainly complain at the prospect of its adoption that the economic motive for clients to enlist their services would be reduced. The system of legal expertise for hire could not survive if those hired did not then prefer the interests of their clients to claims of outsiders. The principle of moral right does not, however, obliterate client advocacy. It merely brings it into our common moral framework. Lawyers of course are to continue to prefer their clients' legitimate interests, legitimacy being bounded only by the clear moral rights of others. There is much room for partisanship within these limits; indeed room for personal preference is again a general feature of a rights based moral framework. The lawyer can indeed be as a friend to his client.[39] But this model is misapplied in a context of full advocacy, since the partisanship of friends cannot extend to the violation of rights of strangers. Advocacy means that the position of lawyers is weakly role differentiated, as is any position to which special contractual obligations attach. The obligation to prefer and pursue the legitimate legal interests of their clients arises within our common moral framework as an instance of the general obligation to keep promises or contracts made. Given its place in that framework, it is limited in cases of conflicts with other rights.

Despite room for partisanship, advocacy, and role differentiation permitted by the principle of moral right, it remains true that the acceptance of purely moral restraints by ethical attorneys will widen the opportunities for the unscrupulous to attract certain high paying clients, who desire their interests to be pursued beyond legitimate moral boundaries. But that iniquity sometimes pays, that moral restrictions sometimes require genuine sacrifice, has always been true, notwithstanding the spectacular attempts of some philosophers to reconcile the moral point of view with that of self-interest.

A more serious problem for the principle from a moral, if not practical, viewpoint concerns its enforceability. Since the implication for the conduct of particular lawyers of the restriction against violating rights depends upon their individual moral perceptions and identifications of moral rights of others, it will not be possible to tell with certainty whether they are violating the principle, that is violating rights that they perceive to be rights. I have admitted that there will be sincere disagreement over the existence of such rights in particular cases. This means that it will not be possible to enforce the principle in its full generality, since lawyers can always claim that their moral perception did in fact guide their action. This problem of legal enforcement should not be considered fatal to the adoption of the principle, however. First, a major point here has been that legal obligation can never be made perfectly congruent with moral obligation. Our subject is how lawyers ought to act, not whether they can be forced by law to act as they should. Second, given the minimal level of disciplinary enforcement of the truly moral provisions of the present Code, even complete nonenforceability of an alternative fundamental framework would not be much of a comparative disadvantage. Third, the principle of moral right could be incorporated in spirit into the basic canons and ethical considerations of a new code (if indeed a new code is required once the idea of a special professional ethic distinct from common morality and common decency is abandoned). The principle can motivate changes in the disciplinary rules without itself being incorporated as a disciplinary rule. The principle of full advocacy is, after all, itself only implicit in the rules. It is not in itself easily enforceable either, since lawyers can always claim that they were doing their best for their clients.

The most serious problem for the suggested principle still relates to its granting and requiring a much larger place for the independent moral judgment of client demands by lawyers. It must stand or fall on that ground. Responses to arguments against such moral discretion pointed out first that lawyers act independently and cannot therefore single-handedly prevent clients from pursuing legal objectives. Clients who are convinced of the rightness of their actions can always seek other lawyers. It was pointed out second that the principle operates to deter lawyers only from aiding in the violation of clearly perceived rights. Hence its acceptability does not rest upon the acceptance of the particular contractarian criterion for identifying moral rights that was suggested earlier (or upon any such general criterion). Disagreements that may exist over the scope of moral rights will generate disagreements on specific implications of the principle in particular cases. They will not nullify the preferability of this principle over that of full advocacy, even if the latter is more mechanical in application.

It must be admitted also that the moral perceptions of lawyers may be mistaken even when they take them to be clear. They might overestimate the moral case for the other side and refuse to aid clients without objectively sufficient reason. Clients will then be forced to seek other lawyers, perhaps at additional expense and cost in time. But given the strong economic motive to satisfy clients, given a historical tendency toward moral skepticism and respect for law, and especially given the call to resolve doubts below a certain intensity in favor of the clients, the greater danger will still lie on the side of failing to protect moral rights of others.

Positive points in favor of our principle appeal first to those moral rights that are violated when lawyers put on their institutional blinders, when they narrow their moral vision to client demands. Clients themselves might be deterred from courses of conduct they would be ashamed to pursue were they not given institutional respectability through the tacit endorsement of their lawyers. That adoption of a principle results in fewer violations of fundamental moral rights than does its alternative is perhaps the strongest argument that can be given in its favor. Of only slightly less importance is that ascription of full moral responsibility to lawyers allows them to retain the moral integrity as professionals to which they should aspire as persons. Dilution of responsibility always has its moral price, and the stakes must be high to justify it. Total client satisfaction does not meet that standard.

Thus we may prefer the principle of moral right while admitting that it is less mechanical in application than that of full advocacy. Indeed it fails to give pat legalistic answers in many of the morally complex situations in which lawyers are likely to find themselves. All may depend upon the broader moral context in which the rights in question, sometimes in competition, must be weighed. In the case of the judge about to assign probation under the mistaken belief that the convicted client had no criminal record, while the lawyer's current legal duty may be specified precisely as that of maintaining confidentiality while avoiding perjury, direct assessment of his moral duty depends upon such varied and complex factors as the danger posed by the criminal to others, the fairness of the likely sentence if the truth is revealed to the judge, the wrong involved in misleading the court, that involved in breaching the trust of the client, etc. On such questions as a lawyer's allowing false testimony to be presented, or to stand once presented, or his impeaching the testimony of an adverse witness known to be truthful, the moral wrongs involved must be weighed against the moral right of the client. If the client is presumed to be innocent in a criminal proceeding, his right to be acquitted normally prevails over the wrong involved in misleading the court on some piece of information or challenging the word of some witness. In a noncriminal proceeding, on the other hand, the damage done to a truthful witness's reputation or mental condition from a badgering cross examination might outweigh the interests or moral rights of the client in the case.

In such morally charged contexts the lawyer, like anyone else, must simply be sensitive to the opposing moral claims and considerations. The legality of attacking an opposing witness and the illegality of allowing false testimony, the sole relevant considerations under the principle of full advocacy within limits of law, seem to me to be relatively minor considerations in these situations, in light of the ability to look through the legal guidelines to the moral rights at stake. If my counterarguments to the imposition of institutional blinders are sound, it is the moral calculation that directly determines what a lawyer ought to do. Here as elsewhere those means permissible to achieve specific ends will vary with the relative strength of rights to achieve those ends, and with the strength of opposing rights. This calculation applies to tactics designed to delay or prevent application of law, as well as to those designed to facilitate it. Of course where legal right is congruent with moral right, as it normally should be, or where the two do not clearly conflict, the law ought to prevail in settlement of the dispute.

The relative ease of application of the principle of full advocacy and the simplified moral universe that this principle creates for the practicing lawyer may be prominent reasons why lawyers have been so ready to accept it as the fundamental rule of legal ethics.[40] Then too there is the economic motive of satisfying the demands of those who pay for legal services. The reputation for satisfying their interests attracts future potential clients as well. Of course to point to such obvious nonmoral motivation is not to evaluate the arguments in favor of the presently accepted principle, but it does nullify any presumption in its favor to be derived from its widespread acceptance within the legal profession.

A final consideration here relates not to justice or the immediate satisfaction of moral rights, but to social tranquility. A stable social framework provides the setting in which individuals can pursue their own ends and exercise their rights. Provision of a stable system of law provided the justification for strong role differentiation for judges, at the expense sometimes of the immediate satisfaction of moral rights of litigants. Here it can be argued that the stability of the legal system depends upon the willingness of citizens to settle their disputes within it, at least as a last nonviolent resort. It might perhaps be argued further that persons are more willing to submit disputes to legal settlement when they know that a legal expert will be advocating their side with full zeal. Especially the side on the short end of the legal or moral merits might be less willing to use the courts without a strong legal advocate.

I think that we can simply admit this last point and yet count it as a further point in favor of a principle of lawyer restraint, rather than full advocacy. The tremendous amount of litigation in our society and the length of legal procedures are not signs of health and tranquility. To reduce this volume, to return the courts to places of last rather than first resort, would be a boon to society. Especially in the corporate sphere I believe this volume could be reduced if managers could no longer count on the cleverness of their lawyers, rather than the merits of their causes, to prevail. For those with genuine grievances the courts will remain a viable resort as long as they retain power to enforce their decisions. For others, moral turpitude worked through the legal system itself is perhaps a greater evil than the threat of lawlessness that motivates this last argument.

In reaching a final verdict on the demand for full advocacy, it should be clear that a strong burden of proof rests with those who would defend it. This, we have said, is always the case with defenses of strong role differentiation. The demand here is that lawyers ignore normally crucial considerations for determining morally proper conduct, in order to pursue single-mindedly their clients' interests. The initial liberal assumption regarding the problem of authority and responsibility is always that each individual has the right and duty to act on his own moral perception. This premise accords with the central value of individual autonomy in a rights based moral system. We have added to that general presumption here another regarding the social framework: that individual autonomy generates creative input into the political system and the process of molding law itself. This presumption of direct responsibility can be overridden, as we have seen, when these same considerations of individual integrity demand doing so. But if moral perceptions are to be overruled, if moral rights are to be ignored or overridden, it can be only for the protection of more important moral rights. If institutional rights, such as a right to full advocacy, are to claim this status, it can be only because they are instrumentally necessary for the protection of more fundamental noninstitutional rights.

The other justification for strong role differentiation, that of protecting intrinsically valuable intimate relationships, expressed through identification with and preference for the interests of the other person, does not apply in this institutional context. A lawyer-client relation is not assumed because of its intrinsic value. A lawyer prefers his client's interest not out of affection, but because he is paid to do so, and because of the extrinsic institutional ends that the role of legal advocate is to serve. In any case, a lawyer would have to be not merely a "legal friend," but a legal spouse or parent, to prefer his client's interests to the moral rights of others for the sake of the relationship itself.[41] Such a relationship with one's clients would be reason to seek the help of another professional, one in mental health care. Except in the context of such intimate relations, it should be emphasized that one cannot morally perform an action for another that the other person would not be justified in doing for himself.

Thus the case for the principle of full advocacy has not been adequately made on either ground. We must assume that positions are not strongly role differentiated unless it is decisively shown that they are; and this has not been shown for lawyers. If the best arguments for the principles of full advocacy and legal right fail, then, I believe, the principle of moral right wins by default. For this is not some alternative institutional blinder, but represents the direct application of normal moral reasoning to the lawyer's conduct. It grants to lawyers the same ability to see through institutional rules and procedures to the moral ends they are to serve, and to act in accordance with those ends when observance of the rules would not serve them, that I believe we must grant to all citizens. The principle of full advocacy rests upon the assumptions that it is always good for people to be aided in exercising their legal rights, and that lawyers cannot presume to judge the law in deciding how to act. Both assumptions are false. The removal of this pervasive institutional blinder would render the conduct of lawyers more in accord with moral principle. It would encourage lawyers to be more morally responsible and sensitive in their professional roles. At present they protect the lives and freedoms of many guiltless clients. But by extending the same model of zealousness to contexts with important moral distinctions, they continue to incur the same suspicion from laymen that we find reflected in literature from Plato to Shakespeare to Dickens.

4

Medical Ethics: The Goal of Health and the Rights of Patients

The practice of medicine generates a diverse set of moral problems. Many, while complex and of crucial social importance, can be approached in an obvious way by the straightforward application of general moral theory. Rights to medical care and the allocation of scarce medical resources, for example, fall directly within a broader theory of distributive justice and of rights in relation to needs. Similarly, one's position on the question of medical experimentation with human subjects will depend only upon one's general position with regard to individual rights against the collective welfare. If individuals have negative rights not to be harmed or physically tampered with for the pleasure or benefit of others, then experimentation without consent is ruled out. This conclusion regarding the medical issue is directly implied by a right with application elsewhere as well. The same is true for most issues addressed in texts on medical ethics. Even the questions of abortion and infanticide, philosophically interesting because of the metaphysical issues raised, reduces to weighing universally recognized rights (to life or self-defense for example) against one another once those metaphysical issues are decided. Once we decide whether fetuses and newborns are persons with rights to life, whether they meet criteria according to which we would recognize alien beings, for example, as having such rights, and once we decide whether parents have responsibility to keep their children alive at significant expense to themselves, questions again not specific to medicine, these difficult issues can be settled.

I shall not address such interesting issues further in this chapter. I shall turn immediately instead to the more fundamental question for medical ethics of strong role differentiation for doctors, a variant of the question we have been addressing throughout the earlier chapters. We want to know here whether central medical norms can override rights of others, here patients, that would otherwise obtain.

The Hippocratic Principle

While the central professional norm for judges requires them to render legally correct decisions, and while lawyers typically construe their fundamental professional aim as that of aiding clients to exercise legal rights or achieve legal objectives, the best candidate for a strongly differentiated professional norm in medicine is that embodied in the Hippocratic tradition as "doing no harm" to patients. This is interpreted in modern terms as the duty to maintain the health, or prevent disease, disability or death for the patient. In yet other terms the duty is to provide that treatment with the best chance of cure and least overall risk of harmful effects.

Notice that this norm appeals to patients' (health) needs, rather than to their desires or rights, in contrast to the accepted principle of conduct for lawyers. Perhaps because legal clients, especially corporate clients, are expected to have a better understanding of legal objectives and tactics than do patients of medical conditions or treatments, perhaps because legal clients are not expected to be in as fragile a state of mind as are medical patients, lawyers typically view themselves as pursuing clients' rights or wishes, while doctors see themselves as ministering to patients' needs. For this reason the central question for the medical norm is whether it can override rights of patients themselves that would otherwise obtain; while the question for lawyers was whether they can justifiably ignore normally relevant moral rights of others in pursuit of their clients' legal objectives. On rare occasions a doctor's providing treatment to a (potential) patient might conflict with other social interests, for example if Hitler had come to a doctor (other than a loyal Nazi) for care. But far more frequent and important are cases in which patients' medical needs appear to conflict with certain of their own rights. For this reason also strong role differentiation for doctors in relation to the medical norm represents an augmentation of their authority to decide courses of action on perceived moral grounds of overall benefit and harm, rather than a limitation of responsibility as in the cases of lawyers pursuing client interests and judges rendering legally correct decisions.

In the case of doctors the question is whether they have the authority to make decisions for others that they would lack as nonprofessionals. The goal of providing optimal health treatment may be seen to conflict in some circumstances with the otherwise overriding duties to tell the patient the truth about his condition or to allow him to make decisions vitally affecting his own interests. Again the assumption of the profession itself appears to be that the doctor's role is strongly differentiated in this sense. The Principles of Medical Ethics of the American Medical Association leaves the question of informing the patient of his own condition up to the professional judgment of the physician, presumably in relation to the objective of maintaining or improving the health or well-being of the patient.[1] I shall concentrate upon these issues of truth telling and informed consent to treatment in the remainder of this chapter. They exemplify our fundamental issue because the initially obvious answer to the question of who should make decisions or have access to information vital to the interests of primarily one person is that person himself.[2]

Rights are recognized, we have said, partially to permit individuals control over their own futures. Regarding decisions vital to the interests of only particular individuals, there are three main reasons why such decisions should normally be left to the individuals themselves, two want-regarding and one ideal-regarding. First is the presumption of their being the best judges of their own interests, which may depend upon personal value orderings known only to them. There is often a temptation for others to impose their own values and preferences, but this would be less likely to produce satisfaction for the individuals concerned. The second reason is the independent value to self-determination, at least in regard to important decisions (in medical contexts decisions may involve life and death alternatives, affect the completion of major life projects, or affect bodily integrity). Persons desire the right or freedom to make their own choices, and satisfaction of this desire is important in itself. In addition, maximal freedom for individuals to develop their own projects, to make the pivotal choices that define them and to act to realize them, allows for the development of unique creative personalities, who become sources of new value in the goods they create and that they and others enjoy.

Resentment as well as overall harm is therefore generally greater when caused by a wrong, even if well-meaning, decision of another than when caused to oneself. There is greater chance that the other person will fail to realize one's own values in making the decision, and, when this happens, additional resentment that one was not permitted the freedom to decide. Thus, since individuals normally have rights to make decisions affecting the course of their lives and their lives alone, doctors who claim authority to make medical decisions for them that fall into this self-regarding category are claiming special authority. The normally existing right to self-determination implies several more specific rights in the medical context. These include the right to be told the truth about one's condition, and the right to accept or refuse or withdraw from treatment on the basis of adequate information regarding alternatives, risks and uncertainties. If doctors are permitted or required by the principle of providing optimal treatment, cure or health maintenance for patients sometimes to withhold truth or decide on their own what therapeutic measures to employ, then the Hippocratic principle overrides important rights to self-determination that would otherwise obtain, and the practice of medicine is strongly role differentiated.

This is clear enough in the case of informed consent to therapy; it should be equally clear in the case of withholding truth, from terminally ill patients for example. The right violated or overridden when truth is withheld in medical contexts is not some claim to the truth per se, but this same right to self-determination, to control over decisions vital to the course of one's life. In fact, it seems on the face of it that there is a continuum of medical issues in which this right figures prominently. These range from the question of consent to being used as a subject in an experiment designed primarily to benefit others, to consent to treatment intended as benefit to the patient himself, to disclosure of information about the patient's condition. In the first case, that of medical experimentation, if the consent of subjects is required (as everyone these days admits it is), this is partly because the duty not to harm is stronger than the duty to provide benefits. Hence if there is any risk of harm at all to subjects, they cannot be used without consent, even if potential benefits to others is great. But consent is required also because the right to self-determination figures independently of calculations of harms and benefits. Thus a person normally ought not to be used without his consent to benefit others even if he is not materially harmed. This same right clearly opposes administration of treatment to patients without their consent for their own benefit. It opposes as well lying to patients about their illnesses in order to save them distress.

What is at least prima facie wrong with lying in such cases is that it shifts power to decide future courses of action away from the person to whom the lie is told.[3] A person who is misinformed about his own physical condition may not complete certain projects or perform certain actions that he would choose to perform in full knowledge. If a person is terminally ill and does not know it, for example, he may fail to arrange his affairs, prepare himself for death, or may miss opportunities to complete projects or seek certain experiences always put off before. Being lied to can reduce or prevent from coming into view options that would otherwise be live. Hence it is analogous to the use of force, perhaps more coercive than the use of force in that there is not the same chance to resist when the barrier is ignorance. The right to know the truth in this context then derives from the right to make for oneself important decisions relating primarily to one's own welfare and to the course of one's life. If the doctor's authority is to be augmented beyond that of any nonprofessional, allowing him to override these important rights in contexts in which this is necessary to prevent serious harm to the patient's health, then his position appears to meet in a dramatic way our criteria for strong role differentiation.

THE CASE FOR MEDICAL PATERNALISM

Since the primary rights in potential conflict with the presumed fundamental norm of medical ethics are rights of patients themselves, and since the norm seeks to serve the health needs of patients themselves, arguments in favor of strong role differentiation in this context are clearly paternalistic. We may define paternalism as the overriding or restricting of rights or freedoms of individuals for their own good. It can be justified even for competent adults in contexts in which they can be assumed to act otherwise against their own interests, values, or true preferences. Individuals might act in such self-defeating ways from ignorance of the consequences of their actions, from failure to weigh the probabilities of various consequences correctly, or from irrational barriers to the operation of normal short-term motivations. Paternalistic measures may be invoked when either the individual in question, or any rational person with adequate knowledge of the situation, would choose a certain course of conduct, and yet this course is not taken by the individual solely because of ignorance, carelessness, fear, depression, or other uncontroversially irrational motives.[4]

PARADIGM CASES   It will be useful in evaluating arguments for strong role differentiation for doctors to look first at criteria for justified paternalism in nonmedical cases, in order to see then if they are met in the medical context. In approaching the controversial case of withholding truth from patients, we may begin with simpler paradigm cases in which paternalistic behavior is uncontroversially permissible or required. We can derive a rule from these cases for the justification of such conduct and then apply the rule to decide this fundamental question of medical ethics.

The easiest cases to justify are those in which a person is acting against even his immediate desires out of ignorance: Dick desires to take a train to New York, is about to board the train for Boston on the other side of the platform, and, without time to warn him, he can only be grabbed and shoved in the other direction. Coercing him in this way is paternalistic, since it overrides his right of free movement for his own good. 'His own good' is uncontroversial in interpretation in this easiest case. It is defined by his own clearly stated immediate and long-range preferences (the two are not in conflict here). Somewhat more difficult are cases in which persons voluntarily act in ways inconsistent with their long-range preferences: Jane does not desire to be seriously injured or to increase greatly her chances of serious injury for trivial reasons; yet, out of carelessness, or just because she considers it a nuisance and fails to apply statistical probabilities to her own case, she does not wear a helmet when riding a motorcycle. Here it might be claimed that, while her action is voluntary in relation to trivial short-term desires, it is nevertheless not fully voluntary in a deeper sense. But to make this claim we must be certain of the person's long-range preferences, of the fact that her action is inconsistent with these preferences (or else uncontroversially inconsistent with the preferences of any rational person). We must predict that the person herself is likely to be grateful in the long run for the additional coercive motivation. In this example we may assume these criteria to be met. For rational people, not wearing a helmet is not an essential feature in the enjoyment of riding a motorcycle, even if people ride them primarily for the thrill rather than for the transportation. The chances are far greater that a rider will at some time fall or be knocked off the cycle and be thankful for having a helment than that one will prefer serious head injury to the inconvenience of wearing protection that can prevent such injury. Therefore we may justifiably assume that a person not wearing a helmet is not acting in light of her own true long-range values and preferences.

As the claim that the individual's action is not truly voluntary or consistent with his preferences or values becomes more controversial, additional criteria for justified paternalism must come into play. They become necessary to outweigh the two considerations mentioned earlier: the presumption that individuals know their own preferences best (that interference will be more often mistaken than not), and that there is an important independent value to self-determination or individual freedom and control (the latter being true both because persons value freedom and because such freedom is necessary to the development of genuinely individual persons). The additional criteria necessary for justifying paternalism in more controversial cases relate to the potential harm to the person from the action in question: it must be relatively certain, severe, and irreversible (relative to the degree of coercion contemplated). These further criteria are satisfied as well in the case of motorcycle helmets, because the action coerced is only a minor nuisance in comparison to the severity of potential harm and the degree of risk.

It is important for the course of the later argument to point out that these additional criteria relating to the harm that may result from self-regarding actions need not be viewed in terms of a simple opposition between allowing freedom of action and preventing harm. It is not simply that we can override a person's autonomy when in our opinion the potential harm to him from allowing autonomous decision outweighs the value of his freedom. His right to self-determination, fundamental to individuality itself, bars such offsetting calculations. The magnitude of harm is rather to be conceived as *evidence* that the person is not acting in accord with *his own* values and preferences, that he is not acting autonomously in the deepest sense. A rights-based moral theory of the type I am assuming as the framework for this study will view the autonomy of the individual as more fundamental than the particular goods he enjoys or harms he may suffer. The autonomous individual is the source of value for those other goods he enjoys and so not to be sacrificed for the sake of them. The point here is that cases of justified paternalism, even where the agent's immediate or short-term preferences are overridden, need not be viewed as reversing that order of priority.

Criteria for justified paternalism are also clearly satisfied in certain medical contexts, to return to the immediate issue at hand. State control over physician licensing and the requirement that prescriptions be obtained for many kinds of drugs are medical cases in point. Licensing physicians prevents some quacks from harming other persons, but also limits these persons' freedom of choice for their own good. Hence it is paternalistic. We may assume that no rational person would want to be treated by a quack or to take drugs that are merely harmful, but that many people would do so in the absence of controls out of ignorance or irrational hopes or fears. While controls impose costs and bother upon people that may be considerable in the case of having to see a doctor to obtain medication, these are relatively minimal in comparison to the certainty, severity and irreversibility of the harm that would result from drugs chosen by laymen without medical assistance. Such controls are therefore justified, despite the fact that in some rare cases persons might benefit from seeing those who could not obtain licenses or from choosing drugs themselves. We can assume that without controls mistakes would be made more often than not, that serious harm would almost certainly result, and that people really desire to avoid such harm even given additional costs.

There is another sense too in which paternalistic measures here should not be viewed as prevention of exclusively self-regarding harm by restriction of truly autonomous actions. The harm against which laymen are to be protected in these cases, while deriving partly from their own actions in choosing physicians or drugs, can be seen also as imposed by others in the absence of controls. It results from the deception practiced by unqualified physicians and unscrupulous drug manufacturers. Hence controls, rather than interfering with autonomous choice by laymen, help to prevent deceptive acts of others that block truly free choice.[5] This is not to say that some drugs now requiring prescriptions could not be safely sold over the counter at reduced cost, or that doctors have not abused their effective control over entrance to the profession by restraining supply in relation to demand, maintaining support for exorbitant prices. Perhaps controls could be imposed in some other way than by licensing under professional supervision. This issue is beyond our scope here. The point for us is that some such restraints appear to be necessary. Whichever form they take, they will be paternalistic, justifiably so, in their relation to free patient choice.

We have now defined criteria for justified paternalism from considering certain relatively easy examples or paradigm cases. The principal criterion is that an individual be acting against *his own* predominant long-range value preferences, or that a strong likelihood exist that he will so act if not prevented. Where either clause is controversial, we judge their truth by the likelihood and seriousness of the harm to the person risked by his probable action. It must be the case that this harm would be judged clearly worse from the point of view of the person himself than not being able to do what we prevent him from doing by interfering. Only if the interference is in accord with the person's real desires in this way is it justified. Our question now is whether these criteria are met in the more controversial medical cases we are considering, those of doctors' withholding truth or deciding upon courses of treatment on their own to prevent serious harm to the health of their patients.

APPLICATION OF THE CRITERIA TO MEDICAL PRACTICE   The argument that the criteria for justified paternalism are satisfied in these more controversial medical cases begins from the premise that the doctor is more likely to know the course of treatment optimal for improving overall health or prolonging life than is his patient. The patient will be comparatively ignorant of his present condition, alternative treatments, and risks, even when the doctor makes a reasonable attempt to educate him on these matters. More important, he is apt to be emotional and fearful, inclined to hold out false hope for less painful treatments with little real chance of cure, or to despair of the chance for cure when that might still be real. In such situations it again could be claimed, as in the examples from the previous subsection, that patient choice in any event would not be truly voluntary. A person is likely to act according to his true long-range values only when his decision is calm, unpressured, and informed or knowledgeable. A seriously ill person is unlikely to satisfy these conditions for free choice. Choice unhindered by others is nevertheless not truly free when determined by internal factors, among them fear, ignorance, or other irrational motivation, which result in choice at variance with the individual's deeper preferences. In such circumstances interference is not to be criticized as restrictive of freedom.

The second premise states that those who consult doctors really desire to be cured above all else. Health and the prolonging of life may be assumed (according to this argument) to have priority among values for any rational person, since they are necessary conditions for the realization of almost every other personal value. While such universally necessary means ought to have priority in personal value orderings, persons may again fail to act on such orderings out of despair or false hope, or simply lack of knowledge, all irrational barriers to genuinely voluntary choice. When they fail to act rationally in medical contexts, the harm may well be serious, probable and irreversible. Hence another criterion for justified paternalism appears to be met; we have another sign that the probable outcome in these circumstances of unhindered choice is not truly desired, hence the choice not truly voluntary.

While it is possible that a doctor's prognosis might be mistaken, this can be argued to support further rather than weaken the argument for paternalism. For if the doctor is mistaken, this will infect the patient's decision-making process as well, since his appreciation of the situation can only fall short of that of his source of information. Furthermore, bad prognoses may tend to be self-fulfilling when revealed, even if their initial probability of realization is slight. A positive psychological attitude on the part of the patient often enhances chances for cure even when they are slight; and a negative attitude, which might be incurred from a mistaken prognosis or from fear of an outcome with otherwise low probability, might increase that probability. In any case it can be argued that a bad prognosis is more likely to depress the patient needlessly than to serve a positive medical purpose if revealed. The doctor will most likely be able to convince the patient to accept the treatment deemed best by the doctor even after all risks are revealed. The ability to so convince might well be conceived as part of medical competence to provide optimal treatment. If the doctor knows that he can do so in any case, why needlessly worry or depress the patient with discussion of risks that are remote, or at least more remote or less serious than those connected with alternative treatments? Their revelation is unlikely to affect the final decision, but far more likely to harm the patient. It therefore would appear cruel for the doctor not to assume responsibility for the decision or for remaining silent on certain of its determining factors.

Thus all the criteria for justified paternalism might appear to be met in the more controversial cases as well. The analogies with our earlier examples appear to support overriding the patient's right to decide on the basis of the truth by the fundamental medical principle of providing optimal care and treatment. Let us apply this argument more specifically first to the question of decision regarding treatment, for example whether to operate or not in a case of diagnosed cancer. Take the case in which breast cancer is diagnosed and radical surgery is thought to afford the best chance for cure, while less radical surgery with chemotherapy or radiation offers less chance.[6] Time may well be of the essence. The patient could be expected to value cure above all else; but, if informed that the chance of cure is only fifty per cent at best, may opt for inoptimal treatment, seek out those who might provide it, or simply delay out of false hope, fear, despair, or initial over-reaction to the thought of altered appearance. Why should the doctor then inform the patient of this percentage and of the alternatives, rather than forcefully insisting upon the radical surgery as the only good chance for recovery? After all, having the operation is clearly the rational course to take, the one that maximizes chances for the outcome that the patient herself truly desires. Only present fears or short-range more trivial values could overwhelm this choice's being made in any case. Why give such irrational causes a chance to come into play when this could well result in mortal harm?

Rational persons, it might be argued, would value cure above all else in this circumstance, hence would choose the course of treatment with the best predicted chance of this result. Other choices would be prompted only by fear or irrational motivation, hence not truly voluntary in the sense of being in accord with what could be presumed to be anyone's deeper preference orderings (death from cancer must surely be near the bottom). Hence information regarding alternatives with lower chances of cure, that could only increase chances of those alternatives being irrationally chosen, can be withheld without negatively affecting the voluntariness of the choice. If only one choice is truly rational and voluntary anyway, only one in accord with the patient's own calmer preferences, why not ensure that choice? And, if that choice is likely to be made even if the risks and alternatives are fully described, why depress the patient with such information needlessly? So must many doctors reason who fail to inform patients fully of alternative treatments in contexts judged medically to call for surgery.

It might be counter-argued here that withholding truth or information because disclosure might result in choice of the wrong treatment itself implies that the patient has the right to choose the treatment.[7] If the patient did not have this option, the doctor could simply inform and still choose the treatment he deemed best. To grant the patient this right and then withhold the information that alone would allow her truly to exercise it appears to be inconsistent. I believe there is some force to this counterargument, but still several possible replies. First, it might be denied that the patient has the right to choose for herself, but admitted that physical coercion after full disclosure of alternatives would be far less practicable than persuasion through manipulation of information. Second, as mentioned, there is in some cases reason not to fully inform independent of the predicted effect on choice of treatment: the information may depress the patient and lessen the chance for recovery even with otherwise proper treatment.

Rights to make decisions, and indeed rights in general, are recognized in order to allow individuals to assert interests and be protected from harm even against the collective welfare. But when recognition of a right or refusal to limit one results only in harm or increased chances of harm to the person whose right is in question, doing so seems to lack rationale. It is true that we claimed also an ideal-regarding reason for recognizing rights, having to do with the development of unique individual personalities. But pressing this reason at the expense of fundamental interests like life and health seems perverse, suggesting a kind of fire and brimstone morality in disregard of true individual welfare. A seriously ill person may not be in a rational enough frame of mind to make those medical choices in his own best interest, and may endanger his life or health by trying to do so.

The argument may be applied as well to the case of with-holding truth when no other medical decisions remain to be made, when the question is what to tell the terminally ill patient for example. Here recognition of an absolute right of the patient is likely to result in needless mental suffering and even in some cases hasten death. The dying patient is likely to realize at a certain point that he is dying without having to be informed. If he does realize it, blunt and open discussion of the fact may nevertheless be depressing. What appear to be pointless deceptive games played out between patients and relatives in avoiding such discussion may actually express delicate defense mechanisms whose solace may be destroyed by the doctor's intrusion. When the doctor has no reason to predict such detrimental effects, then perhaps he ought to inform. But why do so when this is certain to cause needless additional suffering or harm. To do so appears not only wrong, but cruel.

We certainly are justified in lying to a person in order to prevent serious harm to another. If I must lie to someone in order to save the life of another whom the first person might kill if told the truth (even if the killing would be noninten-tional), there is no doubt at all that I should tell the lie or withhold the information. Rights to be told the truth are not absolute, but, like all rights, must be ordered in relation to others. If I may lie to one person to save another from harm, why not then when the life of the person himself might be threatened or seriously worsened by the truth, as it might be in the medical contexts we are considering? Why should the fact that only one person is involved, that only the person himself is likely to be harmed by the truth, alter the duty to deceive or withhold information in order to prevent the more serious harm? If it is replied that when only one person is involved, that person is likely to know the best course of action for himself, the answer is that in medical contexts this claim appears to be false. The doctor is likely to be better informed than the patient about his condition and the optimal treatments for it.

Thus there are two situations in which the doctor's duty not to harm his patient's health or shorten his life might appear to override otherwise obtaining rights of the patient to the full truth. One is where the truth will cause direct harm—depression or loss of continued will to live. The other is where informing may be instrumentally harmful in leading to the choice of the wrong treatment or none at all. Given that information divulged to the patient may be harmful or damaging to his health, may interfere with other aspects of optimal or successful treatment, it is natural to construe what the doctor tells the patient as an aspect of the treatment itself. As such it would be subject to the same risk-benefit analysis as other aspects. Doctors must constantly balance uncertain benefits and risks in trying to provide treatment that will maximize probability of cure with least damaging side effects. Questions regarding optimal treatment are questions for medical expertise. Since psychological harm must figure in the doctor's calculations if he is properly sensitive, since it may contribute as well to physical deterioration, and since what he says to a patient may cause such harm, it seems that the doctor must construe what he *says* to a patient as on a par with what he *does* to him, assuming full responsibility for any harm that may result. Certainly many doctors do so conceive of questions of disclosure. A clear example of this assimilation to questions regarding treatment is the following:

From the foregoing it should be self-evident that what is imparted to a patient about his illness should be planned with the same care and executed with the same skill that are demanded by any potentially therapeutic measure. Like the transfusion of blood, the dispensing of certain information must be distinctly indicated, the amount given consonant with the needs of the recipient, and the type chosen with the view of avoiding untoward reactions.[8]

When the patient places himself in the care of a physician, he expects the best and least harmful treatment, and the physician's fundamental duty, seemingly overriding all others in the medical context, must be to provide such treatment. Indeed the terminology itself, "under a physician's care," suggests acceptance of the paternalistic model of strong role differentiation. To care for someone is to provide first and foremost for that person's welfare.[9] The doctor ministers to his patient's needs, not to his immediate preferences. If this were not the case, doctors would be justified in prescribing whatever drugs their patients requested. That a person needs care suggests that, at least for the time being, he is not capable of being physically autonomous; and given the close connection of physical with mental state, the emotional stress that accompanies serious illness, it is natural to view the patient as relinquishing autonomy over medical decisions to the expert for his own good. Being under a physician's care entails a different relationship from that involved in merely seeking another person's advice.

There are of course different medical contexts in which physicians may act in different capacities. In this respect the legal profession is analogous. A person may seek a lawyer's advice on some point of law and may seek different lawyers' advice on the same legal matter. But once a client has chosen a lawyer and decided to go to trial on some serious matter, the lawyer must assume responsibility for certain key trial strategies and tactics. A client might veto certain proposed moves, but the lawyer's principal responsibility at that point is to enlist the client's cooperation in presenting the most effective case (within those moral constraints described in the previous chapter). Similarly, it might be held, there are medical contexts in which a patient might seek a physician's advice on some minor problem, or might seek the advice of different physicians on how to proceed in regard to some more serious condition. But once he has chosen to become the patient of a particular physician, once he has placed himself under that doctor's care for a particular condition, the doctor must assume primary responsibility for decisions relating to ongoing treatment. His primary responsibility again is to enlist the patient's cooperation in providing optimal treatment, not to detail painstakingly every conceivable alternative and risk. It seems that the doctor at least sometimes can more effectively further the patient's fundamental interest in recovery for which he is hired by taking over, or at least limiting, decisions crucial to that interest. This means making decisions in virtue of professional expertise that might otherwise be left to individuals themselves as a matter of right. And that in turn entails strong role differentiation for doctors, a special augmentation of their authority to act on their own moral perceptions, indeed a different and more paternalistic moral framework than that applicable to the conduct of nonprofessionals.

This completes the argument for strong role differentiation according to the Hippocratic principle. The next section will show it to be unsound.

Refutation of Medical Paternalism

There are two ways to attack an argument in favor of paternalistic measures (while accepting our criteria for justified paternalism). One is to argue that honoring rather than overriding the right of the person will not in fact harm him. The other is to admit that the satisfaction of the person's right may harm in some way, but argue that the harm does not merit exception to the right, all things considered. The first is principally an empirical, the second a moral counter-argument.

The latter is not a perfectly clear-cut distinction, either in general or in application to the question of paternalism. For one thing, the most inclusive notion of harm is relative to the values and preferences of the particular individual. (This point will be important in the argument to follow.) A person is harmed when a state of affairs below a certain level on his preference scale is realized rather than one higher up. Our notion of harm derives what objectivity it has from two sources, again one principally empirical and the other more purely moral. The first is the fact that certain states of affairs are such that the vast majority of us would wish to avoid them in almost all conceivable contexts: physical injury, hastened death, or depression itself for example. It is an empirical question whether these states of affairs result from certain courses of conduct, hence, when they are predicted results, principally an empirical question whether harm ensues. The second source of a concept of harm independent of individual differences in subjective preferences is ideal-regarding: when the development of an individual capable of freely and creatively formulating and acting to realize central life projects is blocked, that person is harmed, whether or not he realizes it, and whether or not any of his present desires are frustrated.

The first argument against paternalistic interference holds that allowing an individual free choice is not most likely to result in harm taken in its objective sense. The second argument is somewhat more complex. It admits likely harm in the objective sense—worsened health, depression, or even hastened death in the examples we are considering—but holds that even greater harm to the individual is likely to ensue from the interference, harm in the more inclusive sense that takes account of his whole range of value orderings and the independent value of his integrity as an individual. In this latter situation there is one sense in which the individual is likely to suffer harm no matter what others do, since a state of affairs will be realized that he would wish to avoid, other things being equal, a state of affairs well below the neutral level in his preference orderings. But from the point of view of others, they impose harm only by interfering, since only that action results in a state of affairs lower on his scale of preferences than would otherwise be realized. In this sense harm is a relative notion, first because it is relative to subjective value orderings, and second because it is imposed only when a situation *worse* that what would otherwise occur is caused. We appeal to this second more inclusive notion in the second type of argument against paternalism.

EMPIRICAL ARGUMENTS

Returning to the medical context, other philosophers have recently questioned the degree of truth in the empirical premise that patients are likely to be harmed when doctors fully inform them. Sissela Bok, for example, has noted that in general it appears to be false that patients do not really want bad news, cannot accept or understand it, or are harmed by it. Yet she does not deny that information can sometimes harm patients, can cause depression, prolong illness, or even hasten death; and she explicitly allows for concealment when this can be shown in terminal cases.[10] Allen Buchanan questions the ability of the doctor to make a competent judgment on the probability of harm to the patient, a judgment that would require both psychiactric expertise and intimate knowledge of the patient himself. Doctors are not generally trained to judge long-term psychological reactions, and even if they were, they would require detailed psychological histories of patients in order to apply this expertise in particular cases. As medical practices tend to become more impersonal, certainly a trend in recent years, such intimate knowledge of patients, even on a nontheoretical level, will normally be lacking. Physicians would then have to rely upon loose generalizations, based on prior impressions of other patients and folklore from colleagues, in order to predict the effect of information on particular patients.

Buchanan appears to consider this point sufficient to refute the argument for paternalism, eschewing appeal to paitents' rights.[11] But unless we begin with a strong presumption of a right of the patient to the truth, I do not see why the difficulties for the doctor in judging the effect of information on the patient recommends a practice of disclosure. If the decision is to be based upon risk-benefit calculation (as it would be without consideration of rights), then, just as in other decisions regarding treatment, no matter how difficult to make, it seems that the doctor should act on his best estimate. The decision on what to say must be made by him one way or the other; and without a right-based presumption in favor of revealing the truth, its difficulty is no argument for one outcome rather than the other. In fact, the difficulty might count against revelation, since telling the truth is generally more irreversible than concealment or delay.

One could, it is true, attempt to make out a case for full

disclosure on strict risk-benefit grounds, without appeal to rights. As we have seen in earlier chapters, utilitarians can go to great lengths to show that their calculations accord with the intuitive recognition of particular rights. In the case of lying or deceiving, they standardly appeal to certain systematic disutilities that might be projected, e.g. effects upon the agent's trustworthiness and upon the trust that other people are willing to accord him if his lies are discovered. In the doctor's case, he might fear losing patients or losing the faith of patients who continue to consult him, if he is caught in lies or deceptions. A utilitarian could argue further that, even in situations in which these disutilities appear not to figure, this appearance tends to be misleading, and that potential liars should therefore resist the temptation on this ground. One problem with this argument, as pointed out in the chapter on political ethics, is that it is empirically falsified in many situations. It is not always so difficult to foretell the utilitarian effects of deception, at least no more difficult than is any other future-looking moral calculation. In the case of terminally ill patients, for example, by the time they realize that their doctors have been deceiving them, they will be in no condition to communicate this fact to other patients or potential patients, even if such communication were otherwise commonplace. Thus the doctor has little to fear in the way of losing patients or patients' faith from his policy of disclosure or concealment from the terminally ill. He can safely calculate risks and benefits with little regard for such systematic disutilities. Again we have little reason to prefer honoring a right, in this case a right to be told the truth, without appealing to the right itself. The only conclusion that I would draw from the empirical points taken in themselves is that doctors should perhaps be better trained in psychology in order to be better able to judge the effects of disclosure upon patients, not that they should make a practice of full disclosure and of allowing patients full control over decisions on treatment. These conclusions we must reach by a different rights-based route.

I shall then criticize the argument for paternalistic strong role differentiation on the more fundamental moral ground. To do so I shall restrict attention to cases in which there is a definite risk or probability of eventual harm (in the objective sense) to the patient's health from revealing the truth about his condition to him, or from informing him of all risks of alternative treatments and allowing him a fully informed decision. These cases are those in which the high probability of harm can be supported or demonstrated, but in which the patient asks to know the truth. Such cases are not decided by the points of Bok or Buchanan, and they are the crucial ones for the question of strong role differentiation. The issue is whether such projected harm is sufficient to justify concealment. If the patient's normal right to self-determination prevails, then the doctor, in having to honor this right, is acting within the same moral framework as the rest of us. If the doctor acquires the authority to decide for the patient, a normally competent adult, or to withhold the truth about his own condition from him, then he has special professional license to override otherwise obtaining rights, and his position is strongly differentiated.

Before presenting the case against strong role differentiation on this basis, I want to dispense quickly with a possible conceptual objection. One might claim that the justification of medical paternalism would not in itself satisfy the criteria for strong role differentiation as defined. Since paternalism is justified as well in other contexts, the exceptions to the rights in question need not be seen to derive from a special principle unique to medical ethics, but can be held simply to instantiate a generally recognized ground for restricting rights or freedoms. If serious harm to a person himself generally can be counted as overriding evidence that the projected action is contrary to his own true preferences or values, and if this generally justifies paternalistic interference or delegation of authority for decisions to others, if, for example, legislators assume authority to apply coercive sanctions to behavior on these grounds, then the authority to be paternalistic would not uniquely differentiate doctors.

The above may be true in so far as paternalism is sometimes justified in other than medical contexts, but that does not alter the import of the argument for medical paternalism to our perception of the doctor's role. If the argument were sound, the medical profession might still be the only one, or one of only a few, paternalistic in this way. This would differentiate medical ethics sufficiently. I argued earlier that legislators must in fact honor normal moral rights. While paternalistic legislation is sometimes justified, as in the requirement that motorcycle riders wear helmets, such legislation is so relatively small a part of the legislator's concerns, and the amount of coercion justified itself so relatively light, that this does not alter our perception of the legislator's general moral framework. If the paternalist argument were sound in relation to doctors, on the other hand, this would substantially alter the nature of their practice and our perception of their authority over certain areas of our lives. We can therefore view the paternalist argument as expressing the underlying moral purposes that elevate the Hippocratic principle and augment the doctor's authority to ignore systematically rights that would obtain against all but those in the medical profession. The values expressed and elevated are viewed by doctors themselves as central to their role, which again distinguishes this argument from claims of justified paternalism in other contexts. Furthermore, viewing the argument in this way brings out the interesting relations between positions of doctors and those in other professions and social roles. It brings out that doctors tend to assume broader moral responsibility for decisions than laymen, while those in certain other professions tend to assume less. In any case, while I shall not in the end view the doctor's role as strongly differentiated, I do not want to rely upon this terminological point, but rather to refute the argument for overriding patients' rights to further the medical goal of optimal treatment.

THE MORAL ARGUMENT

In order to refute an argument, we of course need to refute only one of its premises. The argument for medical paternalism, stripped to its barest outline, was:

(1) Disclosure of information to the patient will sometimes increase the likelihood of depression and physical deterioration, or result in choice of medically inoptimal treatment.

(2) Disclosure of information is therefore sometimes likely to be detrimental to the patient's health, perhaps even to hasten his death.

(3) Health and prolonged life can be assumed to have priority among preferences for patients who place themselves under physicians' care.

(4) Worsening health or hastening death can therefore be assumed to be contrary to patients' own true value orderings.

(5) Paternalism is therefore justified: doctors may sometimes override patients' prima facie rights to information about risks and treatments or about their own conditions in order to prevent harm to their health.

THE RELATIVITY OF VALUES: HEALTH AND LIFE   The fundamentally faulty premise in the argument for paternalistic role differentiation for doctors is that which assumes that health or prolonged life must take absolute priority in the patient's value orderings. In order for paternalistic interference to be justified, a person must be acting irrationally or inconsistently with his own long-range preferences. The value ordering violated by the action to be prevented must either be known to be that of the person himself, as in the train example, or else be uncontroversially that of any rational person, as in the motorcycle helmet case. But can we assume that health and prolonged life have top priority in any rational ordering? *If* these values could be safely assumed to be always overriding for those who seek medical assistance, then medical expertise would become paramount in decisions regarding treatment, and decisions on disclosure would become assimilated to those within the treatment context. But in fact very few of us act according to such an assumed value ordering. In designing social policy we do not devote all funds or efforts toward minimizing loss of life, on the highways or in hospitals for example.

If our primary goal were always to minimize risk to health and life, we should spend our entire federal budget in health-related areas. Certainly such a suggestion would be ludicrous. We do not in fact grant to individuals rights to minimal risk in their activities or to absolutely optimal health care. From another perspective, if life itself, rather than life of a certain quality with autonomy and dignity, were of ultimate value, then even defensive wars could never be justified. But when the quality of life and the autonomy of an entire nation is threatened from without, defensive war in which many lives are risked and lost is a rational posture. To paraphrase Camus, anything worth living for is worth dying for. To realize or preserve those values that give meaning to life is worth the risk of life itself. Such fundamental values (and autonomy for individuals is certainly among them), necessary within a framework in which life of a certain quality becomes possible, appear to take precedence over the value of mere biological existence.

In personal life too we often engage in risky activities for far less exalted reasons, in fact just for the pleasure or convenience. We work too hard, smoke, exercise too little or too much, eat what we know is bad for us, and continue to do all these things even when informed of their possibly fatal effects. To doctors in their roles as doctors all this may appear irrational, although they no more act always to preserve their own health than do the rest of us. If certain risks to life and health are irrational, others are not. Once more the quality and significance of one's life may take precedence over maximal longevity. Many people when they are sick think of nothing above getting better; but this is not true of all. A person with a heart condition may decide that important unfinished work or projects must take priority over increased risk to his health; and his priority is not uncontroversially irrational. Since people's lives derive meaning and fulfillment from their projects and accomplishments, a person's risking a shortened life for one more fulfilled might well justify actions detrimental to his health.

This question of the meaning and value of life, one of the classic questions of philosophy, is raised directly by our issue in medical ethics. We cannot avoid a brief plunge into such deep waters, if we are to come to grips with the doctor's claim to be justified in acting above all else to protect the life and health of his patients. We have seen that this claim presupposes an ultimate value to life itself, but this is called into question once we begin to ponder life's meaning, the sources of its value and significance beyond mere physical existence. We noted above that in both social policy and individual activity we appear willing to trade near certainty of shorter life for the chance of accomplishments and even small enjoyments. The same value ordering is manifest in our varying attitudes toward different forms of life.[12] Not all biological life is considered sacred: lower forms of animal life, for example certain insects, are held to have little if any value at all. Nor is it simply a matter of human life versus all other forms; we recognize a continuum in which some forms of animal life are due greater respect and even granted rights, against cruel treatment for example. It also seems clear that not only humans could qualify for full scale moral status as persons, i.e. beings with a full battery of moral rights. Extra-terrestrial forms of life might so qualify if they met certain criteria. This suggests that it is on the basis of such criteria that humans too deserve full moral respect, a point of great relevance here. These criteria might include self-motivativation, the ability to have desires and feelings, make plans, enjoy satisfactions and suffer frustrations, and to respect the autonomy and rights of others. Thus the value of life, as this is measured by the respect shown it by other valuing persons, is connected to the fundamental right of self-determination, the ability to create and realize value in activities. Respect for individual lives is connected to respect for individual moral agency.

From the personal point of view as well, life has meaning when it has value for the subject himself; and the value it has derives from the value that the subject finds in his activities and satisfactions. What gives life meaning for the individual are the goals and projects he sets for himself, in terms of which particular means acquire significance and hence derive value. These goals and projects may of course vary in dimension, ranging from life-long plans to immediate desires for pleasurable sensations. They may be more or less biologically determined. Those more so are not necessarily less significant for it, since they are a source of natural enjoyments, from the satisfactions of sating physical appetites to those of interpersonal relations. But such natural enjoyments themselves derive whatever greater significance they may have from their place in longer-term relationships and longer-range goals and projects. The latter stand in various nesting and subordinate relations to each other, giving to life as a whole its timbre and significance for the person whose life it is.

This view is of course sharply in contrast with the predominant religious view, in terms of which an individual life derives ultimate meaning from without, from its place in God's plan and its relation to the afterlife. These radically different orientations toward life entail different stances toward death as well. The religious stance appears to me somewhat schizophrenic: on the one hand the demand to preserve life is nearly absolute, since one is not to choose death before one's appointed time (the influence of the clergy on medical ethics is clear here); on the other hand, the arrival of death cannot be conceived as an unmitigated evil, at least for those religions in which belief in afterlife is central. The common thread is the idea that the manner of death is never to be a matter of individual choice or purely human intervention. This idea reflects the other-worldly perspective from which one's life is not truly one's own, nor its significance one's own creation. The secular stance toward death is less ambivalent. Nevertheless, the evil of death is clearly relative to the quality of life in question on this view.

If living has meaning and value for the individual only in terms of his capacity to plan, act, desire and value, then it follows that when these capacities are lost, the value of continuing to live is lost as well, and death is no longer an evil. For most of us desires are constant and goals and projects follow automatically. But, in terminal illness for example, when significant desires can no longer be fulfilled, and when pain robs its victim of simple enjoyments and even the power of thought, life may lose all positive value for the individual. (Despite their radical differences, the religious and secular views may share implications regarding heroic life-prolonging medical strategies in the context of terminal illness, but from different premises.) In other less drastic circumstances as well the sources of value in life may rationally take precedence over minimizing risks to longevity.

The upshot of these ruminations for our issue in medical ethics is that questions such as whether a person has affairs to be arranged, projects to be completed, or simply desires a peaceful death, will affect the rationality of various courses of treatment, not all of which will be optimal for curing, prolonging life, or avoiding depression. Certainly the rationality of such decisions has an important bearing on the right to be informed of risks or incapacitating side effects of various treatments, or of a terminal disease. Furthermore, where a diseased condition is not likely to be immediately fatal if not optimally treated, different attitudes toward risk itself become significant. The doctor is likely to assume that his own neutral attitude should be that of the patient as well, giving equal weight to all degrees of probability for benefit and harm. He is likely to dismiss other attitudes toward risk as expressions of understandable but irrational fear; but again, there is no uniquely rational attitude under any noncontroversial definition of rationality.

Of course to be neutral toward risks is not to be indifferent towards them. It is rather to be averse toward more serious risks in strict proportion to their increasing seriousness. The latter is to be measured in terms of the disutility attached to a particular outcome discounted by the probability of its occurring or not occurring. More precisely, the risk-neutral agent performs an approximation to a Bayesian calculation. He considers the products of the utilities (positive or negative) of each possible outcome of each alternative action and the probabilities of their occurrence, totals these for each possible action, and then performs the action that maximizes expected utility.[13] But this model, which the doctor is likely to assume when he puts himself paternalistically in his patient's place, amounting to a utilitarian calculation applied to the individual self-regarding agent, is only one model of rational behavior.

The patient may have a different reaction toward risks, and, given his reaction, it may be rational to opt for a less than optimal treatment, if optimality is defined as above, strictly in terms of percentage chance of cure versus chance of harmful side effects or death. The doctor may view the patient's reaction to risk as emotional and irrational, as itself justifying the withholding of information regarding risks of various treatments in order to avoid it. But the reaction may be more deeply engrained in other value orderings; it may reflect values that can be realized except if the worst risk is actualized. It may again reflect, in other words, discontinuities or lexical priorities among outcomes that are not expressed in the normal Bayesian calculation, which takes utilities as in principle continuous. The patient with an important project to complete, for example, may be rationally unwilling to risk even minimal chance of death or prolonged incapacitation, even for a good chance to correct an extremely unpleasant condition, an attitude that is likely to appear irrational to his doctor. We encounter here once more the point about value orderings that resulted (along with ideal-regarding considerations) in the recognition of rights and in the inability of utilitarians to account for them. In the medical context the further point here is that the doctor may be unaware not only of facets of the patient's personal life that affect his assignment of utilities and disutilities to medical outcomes, but also of the discontinuous ways in which these assignments may be affected. What is dismissed as an overly emotional reaction toward risk may not be irrational given the patient's own preferences. He may not even be able to express these preferences well except in light of his reactions to various proposals. Certain patients may indeed react in ways inconsistent with their true long-range preferences, but the doctor will be in no position to know this without approaching full disclosure. If he can estimate harm at all from disclosure, it will only be in the narrow objective sense, insufficient ground on which to base decision.

To doctors in their roles as professionals whose ultimate concern is the health or continued lives of patients, it is natural to elevate these values to ultimate prominence. The death of a patient, inevitable as it is in many cases, may appear as an ultimate defeat to the medical art, as something to be fought by any means, even after life has lost all value and meaning for the patient himself. The argument in the previous section for assuming this value ordering was that health, and certainly life, seem to be necessary conditions for the realization of all other goods or values. But this point, even if true, leaves open the question of whether health and life are of ultimate, or indeed any, intrinsic value, or whether they are valuable *merely* as means. It is plausible to maintain that life itself is not of intrinsic value, since surviving in an irreversible coma seems no better than death. It therefore again appears that it is the quality of life that counts, not simply being alive. Although almost any quality might be preferable to none, it is not irrational to trade off quantity for quality, as in any other good.

Even life with physical health and consciousness may not be of intrinsic value. Consciousness and health may not be sufficient in themselves to make the life worth living, since some states of consciousness are intrinsically good and others bad. Furthermore, if a person has nothing before him but pain and depression, then the instrumental worth of being alive may be reversed. And if prolonging one's life can be accomplished only at the expense of incapacitation or ignorance, perhaps preventing lifelong projects from being completed, then the instrumental value of longer life again seems overbalanced. It is certainly true that normally life itself is of utmost value as necessary for all else of value, and that living longer usually enables one to complete more projects and plans, to satisfy more desires and derive more enjoyments. But this cannot be assumed in the extreme circumstances of severe or terminal illness. Ignorance of how long one has left may block realization of such values, as may treatment with the best chance for cure, if it also risks incapacitation or immediate death.

Nor is avoidance of depression the most important consideration in such circumstances, as a shallow hedonism might assume. Hedonistic theories of value, which seek only to produce pleasure or avoid pain and depression, are easily disproven by our abhorrence at the prospect of a "brave new world," or our unwillingness, were it possible, to be plugged indefinitely into a "pleasure machine." The latter prospect is abhorrent not only from an ideal-regarding viewpoint, but, less obviously, for want-regarding reasons (for most persons) as well. Most people would in fact be unwilling to trade important freedoms and accomplishments for sensuous pleasures, or even for the illusion of greater freedoms and accomplishments. As many philosophers have pointed out, while satisfaction of wants may bring pleasurable sensations, wants are not primarily *for* pleasurable sensations, or even for happiness more broadly construed, per se. Conversely, the avoidance of negative feelings or depression is not uppermost among primary motives. Many people are willing to endure frustration, suffering, and even depression in pursuit of accomplishment, or in order to complete projects once begun. Thus information relevant to such matters, such as medical information about one's own condition or possible adverse effects of various treatments, may well be worth having at the cost of psychological pain or depression.

THE VALUE OF SELF-DETERMINATION   We have so far focused

on the inability of the doctor to assume a particular value ordering for his patient in which health, the prolonging of life, or the avoidance of depression is uppermost. The likelihood of error in this regard makes it probable that the doctor will not know the true interests of his patient as well as the patient himself. He is therefore less likely than the patient himself to make choices in accord with that overall interest, and paternalistic assumption of authority to do so is therefore unjustified. There is in addition another decisive consideration mentioned earlier, namely the independent value of self-determination or freedom of choice. Personal autonomy over important decisions in one's life, the ability to attempt to realize one's own value ordering, is indeed so important that normally no amount of other goods, pleasures or avoidance of personal evils can take precedence. This is why it is wrong to contract oneself into slavery, and another reason why pleasure machines do not seem attractive. Regarding the latter, even if people were willing to forego other goods for a life of constant pleasure, the loss in variety of other values, and in the creativity that can generate new sources of value, would be morally regrettable. The value of self-determination explains also why there is such a strong burden of proof upon those who advocate paternalistic measures, why they must show that the person would otherwise act in a way inconsistent with his own value ordering, that is irrationally. A person's desires are not simply evidence of what is in his interest—they have extra weight.

Especially when decisions are important to the course of our lives, we are unwilling to relinquish them to others, even in exchange for a higher probability of happiness or less risk of suffering. Even if it could be proven, for example, that some scientific method of matching spouses greatly increased chances of compatibility and happiness, we would insist upon retaining our rights over marriage decisions. Given the present rate of success in marriages, it is probable that we could in fact find some better method of matching partners in terms of increasing that success rate. Yet we are willing to forego increased chances of success in order to make our own choices, choices that tend to make us miserable in the long run. The same might be true of career choices, choices of schools, and others central to the course of our lives. Our unwillingness to delegate these crucial decisions to experts or computers, who might stand a better chance of making them correctly (in terms of later satisfactions), is not to be explained simply in terms of our (sometimes mistaken) assumptions that we know best how to satisfy our own interests, or that we personally will choose correctly, even though most other people do not. If our retaining such authority for ourselves is not simply irrational, and I do not believe it is, this can only be because of the great independent value of self-determination. We value the exercise of free choice itself in personally important decisions, no matter what the effects of those decisions upon other satisfactions. The independent value of self-determination in decisions of great personal importance adds also to our reluctance to relinquish medical decisions with crucial effects on our lives to doctors, despite their medical expertise.

Autonomy or self-determination is independently valuable, as argued before, first of all because we value it in itself. But we may again add to this want-regarding or utilitarian reason a second ideal-regarding or perfectionist reason. What has value does so because it is valued by a rational and autonomous person. But autonomy itself is necessary to the development of such valuing individual persons or agents. It is therefore not to be sacrificed to other derivative values. To do so as a rule is to destroy the ground for the latter. Rights in general not only express and protect the central interests of individuals (the raison d'être usually emphasized in their exposition); they also express the dignity and inviolability of individuality itself. For this reason the most fundamental right is the right to control the course of one's life, to make decisions crucial to it, including decisions in life-or-death medical contexts.[14] The other side of the independent value of self-determination from the point of view of the individual is the recognition of him by others, including doctors, as an individual with his own possibly unique set of values and priorities. His dignity demands a right to make personal decisions that express those values.

REFUTATION OF OTHER ARGUMENTS AGAINST INFORMING

These considerations destroy the analogies used in support of the argument for medical paternalism. One such analogy attempted to equate lying to one person in order to prevent more serious harm to another with lying to a person to prevent his causing harm to himself, and the latter with lying to or withholding information from a patient to prevent harm to his health. The criterion that morally distinguishes such cases is whether the person who requests the information has a right to acquire it. To decide this, one has to weigh the individual interests on opposing sides. Normally a person will not have this right when serious harm may befall another from his acquiring the information in question; and normally a person will have the right when the information concerns him alone, and when important decisions vital to the conduct of his life may depend upon the information acquired. Thus lying to prevent harm to a third party and lying to a medical patient about his condition or about alternative treatments cannot in general be equated, and cases in which the former is justified do not help to justify the latter. While rights are recognized in order to benefit individuals, and while we therefore generally do not recognize them if this will cause only harm to their prospective bearers, acknowledging a right of patients to be fully informed is more likely to prevent harm to them in the fullest moral sense.

The second analogy in support of the initial argument was to the legal profession, to the assumption of responsibility by lawyers for courtroom strategies and tactics. The disanalogy between that delegation of authority to lawyers and the assumption by doctors of responsibility for decisions regarding treatments and information given to patients consists in the importance of differences in value orderings among patients.

Such differences, we pointed out, may falsify doctors' assumptions of the absolute priority of health and prolonged life. Trial strategies, on the other hand, generally lack side effects upon clients: the choice of particular strategies and tactics normally has import only as it contributes to winning or losing the trial. Hence clients can be assumed generally to desire those tactics to be chosen that will maximize chances for winning. Choosing tactics for them is not normally a matter of overriding their rights, hence does not amount to strong role differentiation for lawyers. Where such choices do reflect upon the clients themselves, apart from the question of winning or losing their cases, as in opting for pleas of insanity, for the use of morally questionable tactics, or tactics harmful to the interests of persons close to the clients, they should be expected to have a say in the choices. Turning back to informed choices of medical treatments, these are likely to produce side effects that may be more important to the patients themselves than even the degree of medical success of the treatments. The effects, if incapacitating, will relate directly to the quality of the patients' lives. Thus the right to choice in this area is a matter crucial to self-determination. In addition, medical treatment involves invasion of the patient's body, again a violation of a fundamental right in the absence of consent. Once more the analogy with the legal profession breaks down.

A third supposed analogy in the previous section was to other cases of justified paternalism in medicine. I accepted there that licensing of physicians and requirement of prescriptions for many drugs are justified on grounds that laymen would otherwise make choices out of ignorance contrary to their own true preferences. It can now be seen that such cases support the argument for full disclosure to patients by their doctors, rather than supporting the opposing paternalistic position. Nondisclosure results in ignorance that blocks free choice, as would deception by drug companies or unqualified physicians in the absence of controls. Disclosure is therefore required on these very same grounds.

Reiterating the main argument of this section: because it is not patently irrational to decide against a course of treatment with optimal chances of cure or of prolonging life, because neither health nor longevity can be assumed to be of utmost value, and because self-determination is of independent and indeed of more fundamental value, the Hippocratic principle of maximizing benefits to the health of patients cannot override their rights to make decisions or know the truth in medical contexts. Nor do other excuses for withholding information when decisions regarding treatment depend upon it have force in the context of this broader argument. That a patient will not be able to understand his condition, possible courses of treatment, risks and prognoses, that he will be more likely than his doctor to make wrong decisions because of misunderstanding, must be dismissed. Given the argument of this section, the harm that might result to a patient from his own wrong decision is of less moral consequence than that which might result from a wrong decision of his doctor, which the doctor had no right to make in the first place.

The adoption of a rule that bars doctors from withholding information from patients on the basis of judgments that disclosure will result in harm to them may well occasionally result in overall harm to a patient. Some doctors operating under such a rule may forget that even bad news can be divulged kindly and sympathetically; some may tend to be unnecessarily blunt and brutal. But even statements of patients' conditions or of risks associated with treatments that are properly made can occasionally be harmful, all things considered. It is our inability to predict correctly every time that raises the moral issue of authority to act as one sees fit in the first place, the issue with which this book is primarily concerned. That our powers of predicting human reactions and the full consequences of our actions are limited means that we must grant rights and adopt rules that do not operate optimally in every circumstance. The harm that may occasionally result from granting patients rights to medical information concerning them whenever they request it is parallel in this sense to the unnecessary offense sometimes caused when people exercise their rights to free speech. We need not deny that the harm may be genuine in both cases in order to hold that the rights nevertheless ought to be granted. For the harm that results from granting them is less serious (nonaggregatively) than that which would be caused to individuals (and individuality) if we did not grant them. Obviously, if we demand full disclosure from doctors, we cannot hold them morally or legally liable for the distress or harm caused to patients who exercise their rights to information. We can expect them to divulge the information in an intelligible and reasonably humane way, however.

If the right to decide remains with the patient, then it becomes part of a doctor's competence to be able to explain these matters in clear and intelligible terms,[15] just as a lawyer must be able to explain legal rights or lines of defense, or an accountant the financial condition of his client. Regarding decisions about treatments, routine disclosure consists in recommended procedures, projected risks and benefits (including magnitudes of harm and benefit and rough probabilities of their occurring), as well as degrees of uncertainty in these estimates, monetary costs, and alternative treatments with their probable risks and benefits. This explanation should of course be followed by a request for questions. Sometimes arguments against disclosure appeal to the possibility of mistaken diagnosis, but surely the patient can be made to understand the degree of uncertainty of a prognosis or degree of likelihood of a risk. One need not understand the underlying biological causes of a disease in order to be able to grasp the likelihood of recovery and possible side effects of alternative treatments when these are explained. The claim that the demand for full disclosure assumes knowledge or intellectual capacity on the part of the patient comparable to that of the doctor is nonsense. The patient is asked to comprehend only the likely gross effects of a few alternative courses of action. Surely it is presumptuous of a doctor to assume that a normally competent patient's mental capacity is so far below his own that the patient cannot comprehend when told this tiny fraction of what the doctor is expected to remember routinely without even consulting his texts.

It is not credible either that a doctor could fully comprehend the prognosis and yet be unable to explain it in English. If there is an epistemological factor in a doctor's unwillingness to disclose, it more likely relates to an unwillingness to reveal his uncertainties or ignorance. But there is no moral reason to keep these hidden. Whether a very unlikely or uncertain risk need be reported depends upon the importance of its potential effect on the patient and its possible effect upon his decision. That such detailed explanation takes time is also no excuse for withholding it. How much time a doctor should spend in informing depends upon the decision to be made and the centrality of those values likely to be involved.[16] Many patients will not want detailed explanations; if those who do want them require the doctor to see fewer patients, then the answer is to loosen the present restrictions on the number of doctors.

Finally, when a patient asks to know the truth or the possible risks from treatment, his doctor must assume that he really wants the information requested. While a right may be waived or not exercised by the rightholder, in the absence of explicit waiver, he must be assumed to desire to have it honored. Psychological hypothesis regarding possible insincerity is therefore out of place here. There is first of all in this regard a real question whether the doctor has the competence as a psychologist to judge insincerity or hidden motive from subtle intonations in the patient's phrasing of his questions. And for those accustomed to withholding truth, there may be perceptual set to detect such lack of desire despite the questions. After all, discussing possible or actual disaster for the patient may be very unpleasant. Given an expectation on the part of the doctor that a patient would rather avoid such discussion, a genuine uneasiness natural for the patient may be misinterpreted as a hidden desire to be deceived.

Second, when doctors find it legitimate to engage in such psychological speculation, there exists a difference in recourse available to the patient who wants to know the truth versus the one who wants to avoid the anguish of a dire prognosis. If a patient can be assumed not to want the truth despite asking for it, then he is helpless to have his right honored; whereas a person who wants to relegate responsibility to his doctor or avoid hearing bad news can simply indicate this explicitly in advance. (I discuss the honoring of this request below.) Of course, if a patient who does not want to know the worst must request explicitly that such information be withheld, then by doing this he foregoes the possible satisfaction of a good prognosis known to be truthful. But this requirement is necessary to protect the more important right of others to self-determination.

The fact that there is a right to the truth here also destroys the distinction, to which appeal is sometimes made, between lying and simply withholding information. Normally our duty not to lie to people is both broader and stronger than our duty to disclose truthfully whatever information they may request. Lying is an expression of disrespect to the person who is deceived. In many circumstances, however, persons do not have rights to information we possess, and we therefore have the right to remain silent or change the subject when they request it. But when a person does have the right to information, as I have claimed that patients have rights to medical information concerning them, remaining silent has the same moral effect as lying and cannot be distinguished. The former, as the latter, prevents informed decision-making. I have not appealed to the intrinsic wrongness of lying in the course of this argument. It has not been a question of opposing the value of truth or of truth-telling to that of kindness or the minimization of suffering, although many doctors who deceive patients undoubtedly see it that way. Rather, lying to a patient has been seen as shifting the power to make decisions central to his life away from him and toward his doctor. It is his ignorance that debilitates him here, and this ignorance results equally from lack of information as from outright deception. The right violated is that to self-determination, and this is the right now shown to override the Hippocratic principle for doctors, the principle of maximizing benefits and minimizing risks to health or life.

The Principle of Patients' Choice

The principle of patients' rights for which I am arguing does not imply that information ought never to be withheld. I maintain only that when a right to the truth, deriving from a more fundamental right of self-determination, would otherwise obtain, it may not be overridden by the rule to do no harm to patients' health, or to provide the best treatments possible. The principle implied by the dismissal of strong role differentiation does not demand that the truth always be told, but neither does it allow withholding truth whenever its probable effect is harm rather than benefit to the patient's health and happiness. It demands telling the truth or providing information whenever the patient has a right to it that he does not explicitly waive. He will have this right whenever the information is relevant to his control over decisions affecting his life, when the information concerns himself in a way that affects what he does or can do.

Of course if the information relates to the patient's condition at all, then it ought to be open to him in the absence of strong reason to withhold it. Medical records and charts should be routinely open for patients' inspection. It is only when a serious threat to health or psychological well-being is seen to be posed that the question of concealment arises at all. When it does, the right to self-determination, the possible relevance of the information to decisions of the patient, becomes the criterion for whether or not to disclose.

When that right becomes relevant, the doctor cannot argue that he would be able to convince the patient to accept his recommended treatment or procedure even after full disclosure of risks, uncertainties and alternatives, and that disclosure would therefore have no effect on the final decision. Although after the fact, when the doctor has convinced the patient, it may appear that the process of disclosure only caused needless worry or depression, it is precisely the doctor's ability to predict infallibly what choice would be made by the patient that has been called into question. Then too there is independent value to the choice's actually being made by the patient, the person most concerned, even if it does accord with the doctor's recommendation. It is legitimate for a doctor to urge a given course of medical procedure in addition to listing the alternatives, but not to ensure its adoption through coercive or deceptive measures. Likewise in the case of terminal illness, the doctor cannot assume that the patient knows that he is dying without being informed. A patient who suspects the truth may convince himself otherwise on the basis of the doctor's lie or silence, and he may take part in such (self-)deception even when he sincerely wants to know the truth.

The position advocated here is close to that enunciated by the United States Appellate Court in its important decision in Canterbury v. Spence.[17] There too it was held that the requirement of disclosure is relative to the importance of the information to future decisions, including decisions regarding treatment, by the patient. The Court allowed an exception, however, when disclosure is seen to pose a serious threat to health, although the possibility of refusal of therapy thought necessary by the doctor was held insufficient in itself for concealment. The courts in general have been moving toward a strong position on fully informed consent, but inconsistencies remain. Some courts continue to impose a standard of disclosure only according to that predominant in local medical practice.[18] This traditional standard respects the independence of the medical profession and its ethics of placing optimal medical treatment first. The recent trend, however, has been to adopt a standard of disclosure that a "reasonable man" might demand as patient, or else one according to the relevance of the information in question to the patient's decisions. I advocate the latter, but it is important to add that the decisions in question need not be only medical decisions on further treatments. The courts have emphasized the latter, although a case now pending on a doctor's failure to inform a patient about the test for fetal abnormality may extend the legal criterion.

The exception allowed in Canterbury, so-called "therapeutic privilege" to withhold information on the basis of the doctor's projection of direct harm from disclosure, remains standard in legal decisions. This exception to disclosure, even together with its rider on refusal of treatment, creates an ambiguity that I would not allow. My account does not hold threat to health itself sufficient for overriding the right of the patient, when this right would otherwise obtain. If I did allow this exception, it would be difficult to distinguish refusal of treatment from other threats to health. Once decisions whether or not to disclose are placed within a cost-benefit to health framework, once the latter becomes the primary consideration, there is only one moral distinction regarding grounds for concealment between a prediction of deterioration from refusal of treatment and a prediction of deterioration from psychological depression. The difference is that certain forms of treatment without consent constitute invasions of the patient's body—in legal terms, battery. But from the point of view of the patient, those nonmedical decisions he may be prevented from making because of ignorance of his own condition may be of equal or greater importance than decisions on medical treatment. Hence there seems little reason to grant the right to information in the one case but not in the other. We need not attempt to press the distinction. The claim that health can be assumed to be the uppermost consideration in either case is precisely what I have denied.

SAMPLE CASES

The issue of when rights to truth and to make decisions regarding treatment obtain, and when exceptions to the practice of disclosure in the absence of these rights can be made, will be clarified by considering a few sample cases. One author cites a case of an apparently unsuccessful transplant operation in which the doctor delays revealing early signs of rejection.[19]

Such concealment might be justified for a brief period, but not when a decision whether to operate again nears. I mentioned previously the case of diagnosed breast cancer. This might seem to meet the criterion for paternalistic interference, since it could be argued that any rational person would value cure above unaltered appearance. But when it is only increased chance of cure that must be balanced (at the present stage of research there is controversy regarding which treatment affords such increased chance), the patent irrationality of alternatives becomes more difficult to maintain. Given the effect of the decision on the person's life, full disclosure is demanded.

CHOOSING DEATH   What of the well-tried case in which a needed blood transfusion is refused on religious grounds: is not such refusal patently irrational; and, if patently irrational, is this not grounds for paternalistic interference, for administering the transfusion? Here we must distinguish between false belief and irrationality, in the sense of acting against one's own values. Persons who meet at least minimal criteria for rationality have held bizarre religious beliefs. Given the value orderings of those who refuse transfusions, this act is not patently irrational. The fact that these value orderings themselves are based upon bizarre or false beliefs is no grounds for ignoring them in treating the persons in question. If the right to self-determination were contingent upon one's actions being based on beliefs held by others to be true, it would again be fragile indeed. There is once more here an epistemological problem in assuming authority to override the self-regarding decisions of others on grounds that they are based on false belief, namely that those who interfere may hold false beliefs themselves in this and many other cases. Of course false belief *in some sense* must justify paternalistic interference if it is ever to be justified, and our prior arguments have not ruled it out in all cases. I have suggested as a compromise criterion that the belief must be such as to cause the agent to act against his own value ordering in order for interference to be justified. This criterion is in accord with the spirit of the right to self-determination, whereas a broader one would not be. That an action instantiates a value ordering held to be based upon false belief is not then morally sufficient for preventing it, even if it is predicted to seriously harm the agent. The harm must be such that it is not truly worth it *to the agent himself* to risk it for the sake of performing or foregoing the action in question.

While some actions fail to be autonomous because of the agent's false beliefs regarding consequences, i.e. true costs and benefits, others may be autonomous even though grounded ultimately in false belief. Relevant to this distinction is that between beliefs that are more or less value neutral and easily verified to be true or false, and those that are intimately connected to and expressive of the agent's values and not readily verifiable. The latter is not a sharp distinction, but represents a continuum in which the difference is clear enough at the extremes. Beliefs in the second class render problematic the authority to intervene on paternalistic grounds. Since false religious beliefs fall clearly into this class, a doctor cannot justifiably ignore refusal of treatment based upon them. It is not the fact that the beliefs in question are religious that is crucial, but the fact that they are expressive of the agent's autonomous value ordering. Hence the argument on refusal of treatment can be extended to any case in which a subject refuses in full knowledge of the relevant medical variables.

The right to consent to treatment, to which lipservice is often paid, amounts to no right at all without the correlative (identical?) right of refusal. This applies not only to transfusion, but* to refusal of surgery, medication, dialysis, life support systems, to requests that no attempts be made at resuscitation in coronary cases, etc. Nor is there any relevant distinction between refusing to begin treatment and withdrawing from it after having given one's consent. If patients were permitted only to refuse treatment initially, but not to withdraw consent after its inception, their choices would be too limited. A decision to try a certain course of treatment would amount to a binding contract delegating all further authority to the doctor. Such a contract would be contrary to all previous arguments of this section, especially if involuntary. Patients may therefore experiment with different treatments, withdrawing from any that are judged to be no longer worth the costs. Autonomy implies the right to act on values that may appear capricious or perverse to others, at least in so far as self-regarding actions are concerned. Ignorance of the patient is to be remedied by further disclosure by the doctor, not by deceptive coercion.

(1) The analogy with suicide. The cases discussed so far involve only competent patients. Competency is to be measured precisely in terms of the ability to comprehend clearly explained alternatives and risks and to make choices in light of this information in accord with one's own values and true preferences. Whether those values themselves appear rational to others is not in question. Some have compared forced transfusion or other forced life-saving treatment with intervention to prevent suicide, held justified in other contexts. If we may intervene to prevent attempts at suicide from succeeding in other contexts, and if refusal of needed transfusion or other life-saving measures is tantamount as an act of self-destruction to suicide, then why may we not intervene here to require the treatment? In distinguishing these cases there is first a question of whether we can indeed equate refusal of treatment held medically necessary for survival with attempt at suicide. There is a difference of intent that some might hold sufficient to distinguish the cases and our right to intervene in them. In the medical context under consideration there may be no desire to die. The patient may desire to recover without the use of the treatment that is unwanted or forbidden by his religion, however unlikely such recovery might in fact be. He is therefore risking his life by refusing the treatment, but not necessarily committing suicide, even if he should die as a result of the refusal.

If suicide were intrinsically immoral (I do not believe it is), this difference in intent might be sufficient to exempt these acts in medical contexts from condemnation. But I do not want to rely here upon this particular application of the "doctrine of double effect." (This moral principle, popular in Catholic ethics, distinguishes in evaluating acts between what is intended as a means or end, and what is merely a foreseen consequence of an action. The latter is sometimes excused or ignored when it would not be if it were an intended means or end.) In general it seems to me that the more likely an outcome of an action becomes, the less it can be distinguished from an intended consequence of the action. At least persons must be held equally responsible for consequences foreseen but not desired in themselves; and our rights to prevent these outcomes appear to be the same whether or not they are desired or intended by the agents themselves, if they are otherwise morally prohibited. In any case, we do not require this distinction here, since I do not believe that intervention in suicide attempts is always justified. It is not justified in precisely those cases that are most analogous to most cases of refusal of life-saving treatment.

I would hold intervention to prevent suicide to be morally permitted and required only when the desire for death is likely to be only temporary in the case of prevention. Again the desire must not be in accord with the stable long-range preferences of the subject. On these grounds, in the absence of personal knowledge of a subject attempting to commit suicide, for example the total stranger on the ledge of the building or the unconscious patient rushed to the emergency room with an overdose of barbiturates, we are justified, I believe, in coercively preventing the successful act of self-destruction. This is because many such attempts are found to result from temporarily deranged or depressed states, hence not to reflect the fixed resolve that derives from a stable personal ordering of values. Such attempts are not rational from the point of view of the agents themselves, hence not truly autonomous, although they may seem so to them at the time. For self-destruction to be a rational act, one in accord with the person's own values and preferences, it must be so not only in relation to present short-term suffering or depression, but in relation to a whole possible future of goods and evils and possibly altered preferences.[20] In many cases the subject cannot predict or even envisage such altered condition in his present state. He therefore acts in a kind of ignorance of his own total value system, giving unwarranted emphasis to a small time-slice of it.[21] In general it is relevant to the justification of paternalistic interference that the agent will later be grateful for it, after his short-term preferences have shifted in light of new knowledge or experience. (The shift in preference must not have come about through coercion.) This is the case with many suicide attempts in moments of despair. If most in fact fall into this category, then interference is justified in the absence of knowledge that the present case is different. There is also the fact that suicide is irreversible, while a person who is resolved to do so can succeed in a later attempt even if prevented earlier.

This right and duty to intervene to prevent suicide in the absence of personal knowledge of the agent or of the circumstances of his case has limited application in medical contexts. If a person's leg is crushed in an accident and must be amputated immediately in order to save his life, and yet he refuses the amputation, saying that he does not want to live with one leg, doctors can assume that his reaction is one of shock or stress.[22] The amputation should be performed on this assumption. If it is mistaken, if the person's leg has some special significance for him beyond its normal function that causes loss of all value and significance to his life without it, he can act on his resolve to die at a later time. The same is true of patients brought to emergency rooms with overdoses of barbiturates, self-inflicted gunshot wounds, etc. But the case is very different for the terminally ill patient, whose prospects are unlikely to improve or preferences to change in the future, for the patient who refuses transfusion on religious grounds, or for the suicide attempt known to result from long-standing and stable resolve.

If an attempt at suicide is known to derive from a fixed resolve reflecting a stable order of values, then, other things being equal, I do not believe that paternalistic interference is justified, even in this seemingly extreme case. The ceteris paribus clause here refers primarily to the responsibilities the individual may have to family or others dependent on him.

Where the welfare of young children depends upon one's continued existence, for example, one's life may not be one's own to do with as one pleases. But in other cases suicide does not appear to be seriously wrong from the viewpoint of a rights-based moral system. It will not be in violation of any rights; rather interference with certain attempts are in violation of the right of self-determination. It can be argued that we do not truly honor the right of self-determination or autonomy by allowing an act, such as an act of self-destruction, that prevents all future autonomous choice by the agent. Since death ends the capacity for autonomous choice, a desire for suicide seems analogous in this respect to a decision to sell oneself into slavery, a contract that even John Stuart Mill did not feel we should respect. Respecting a person's freedom does not seem to commit us to respecting his choice to do away with it.[23]

But these cases are again disanalogous in important respects. The terminally ill person who chooses to die may be incapable of other significant autonomous choices in the future. It may be precisely the loss of ability to function as an independent agent that motivates this one final act of autonomy in the choice to die. Regarding the refusal of treatment on religious grounds, this may so much express and reflect the most central values of the person that all future acts could have only negative significance for him if the choice is not honored. A contract to become a slave, on the other hand, is always irrational. It is irrational because of the possibility of changing one's mind later. One can obey another as long as one wants to without such a contract. The only effect of a binding agreement of this type would therefore be to violate true preference orderings in the future. Since agreement to violate one's own values or preferences is irrational, paternalistic interference is justified in this case, as Mill held. But the medical cases are different. It was argued above that life itself is not of intrinsic value; hence the desire for suicide is not always irrational, not always in violation of stable preference orderings. It is not contradictory, then, to hold that the right to self-determination sometimes entails a right to self-destruction. If continuing to live holds the certain prospect of an overwhelming balance of pain and misery over happiness, if one can continue to live only in a totally incapacitated state, or only at the expense of the lives or well-being of others, or only by violating one's most cherished principles, then choosing to end one's life may well accord with one's stable order of values and preferences. According to this criterion of rationality, the one that I have held relevant to the issue of paternalism, attempts at suicide in these conditions are not irrational, and interference is therefore unjustified.

The case of refusing transfusion on religious grounds when this is likely to be fatal is an instance in which continuing to live violates most cherished principles. Hence intervention by doctors in that case is analogous to unjustified intervention to prevent suicide, not to justified interference on grounds of temporary derangement. Hence it is itself unjustified. Once more the patient's health, and even life, fail to take precedence over his right to decide. Against this position remaining arguments might appeal to some notion of the "sanctity of life," or to the interest that society has and should express in its individual members. But we have seen that life in itself is not treated as sacred in other contexts of social decision and individual activity. Certainly killing a person is normally the greatest wrong one can commit against him; but this is because it normally constitutes the ultimate denial of self-determination. Killing a person who steadfastly wants to die, for whom dying is in accord with stable preferences and values, if wrong at all, is so either because of its effect on others close to the person, or because it is an instance of a rule too open to mistake and abuse. (More on the latter below.) If we were willing to accept coercion by doctors in order to prevent premature death, we would all be placed on rigidly enforced diets, prohibited from smoking, staying out too late, working too hard, exercising too little or too much, etc.

A variation of the argument from the supposed sanctity of life is an instance of a "slippery slope" or "wedge" argument. This holds that once we treat life lightly in one context, our respect for it in general is diminished. Such lowered respect is presumed dangerous because it opens the door for other takings of life indefensible in themselves. The claim is that once we allow competent individuals to choose their own deaths, once we allow them to die without intervening, we will be tempted to allow burdensome incompetent persons to die as well. And once we allow "passive euthanasia," i.e. death by omission, active euthanasia, that is death by commission, will not be far behind, and then killing that is not euthanasia at all, that is not in the victim's own interest, although claimed to be.

To reply to such arguments, we may ask initially why we should not be able to draw intelligent, morally defensible lines and maintain them. It is one thing to say that a particular rule is too open to error or abuse in practice. That may be a legitimate argument against adopting it. It is quite another thing to say that a rule that is clearly understandable, defensible and applicable in itself will, if adopted, cause its replacement by another worse than the present status quo. The latter argument is itself easily abused and can be used to block any proposed change in policy. It is possible for any change to be carried too far. Unless there is a special reason to believe that pressure for unwarranted movement beyond legitimate change is particularly great at a given time, there is no reason not to institute new rules defensible in themselves. Proponents of the above argument can point out that the horrors of the Nazi program were preceded by demands for different types of euthanasia. Despite the historical accuracy of this claim, there is now no reason to believe that if we allow competent individuals to refuse life-saving treatment in deference to the right of self-determination, we will somehow lose our minds or moral sensibilities and become Nazis. When this right to autonomy, hardly uppermost in the Nazi scheme of things, is clearly maintained as the central consideration, morally different cases become easily distinguished.

Another variation of this argument applies it to doctors themselves. The appeal is to the type of persons we want doctors to be, and to the type of doctors we can expect to develop under the influence of different rules of medical ethics.

This issue regarding the type of persons we expect and desire professionals to be, encountered before in relation to politicians and lawyers, may alter in certain contexts those rules of professional responsibility that would otherwise be morally best. Here it can be claimed that doctors should always be encouraged to treat life as if it were sacred, even if it is not so treated in nonmedical contexts. The doctor's special role in society is to look after health and prolong lives. Even if other values have an equal or higher place in the orderings of many people, it can be argued that these particular values are important enough to warrant protection and ultimate concern from a special segment of the population. If these are the special concerns of doctors, then we might expect that individuals will be better as doctors if they are permitted to place these values first in their professional life, as traditionally they have done under the Hippocratic code of ethics. Therefore, while it may be strictly incorrect to treat all desire for death or suicide as mental illness, as a symptom to be treated along with the other symptoms of the patient's primary disease,[24] it can be argued that it is both natural and beneficial for doctors to do so, to place the value of life first in all conceived orderings. Once doctors are made to take life more lightly, their efforts and dedication in behalf of patients who might wish their lives prolonged are likely to be affected. Or so it might be argued under this second variation of the wedge argument.

If this were true of the level of dedication of physicians to medical practice, it is still doubtful that avoiding this consequence would be worth the violations of patients' rights to self-determination involved in granting to doctors the right to coerce or deceive them. More to the point, there is no reason to believe that strong role differentiation will be of moral benefit to doctors, either as persons or professionally. Regarding the former, the initial presumption is always against strong role differentiation, because of the danger of lowered sensitivity to moral rights that generally obtain. Specifically in regard to doctors, do we really suspect that they become better persons when encouraged to deceive and coerce their patients, even when this is perceived to be for the patients' own greater good? More likely they will tend to be more meddlesome, self-righteous, and at the same time practiced and clever liars if convinced that they have such authority or moral license. From the narrower perspective of medical practice itself, a presumed license to lie, deceive and coerce whenever this is perceived to be to the patient's benefit is more likely to extend such practices into situations in which there is not even prima facie benefit to the patient, for example in the deceptive use of medical students as doctors, in a readiness to prescribe placebos in many situations, or in such seemingly harmless phrases as "This won't hurt a bit!".

It might appear that the previous paragraph applies a slippery slope argument in its appeal to the effect upon the character of doctors of adopting a certain rule of medical ethics. I have claimed that permission to lie and coerce in certain situations may be extended as a propensity into other situations in which it is clearly detrimental, but that allowing patients to refuse or withdraw from treatment, in effect to choose death, will not extend to a generally lowered respect for life. Wherefore the difference? It lies in the fact that the distinction between patients with a fixed resolve to refuse life-saving measures and other patients is clear-cut; the ability to know (when told) into which class patients fall can be uncontroversially assumed. The ability to tell whether deception or coercion will truly benefit patients in the deepest moral sense, however, has been questioned. Assumption of authority in this respect is therefore more likely to generalize beyond the area in which its legitimacy could be seriously advocated. There is no danger of patient choice being extended too far; and patient choice is what I am advocating, not lack of dedication on the part of doctors to their medical art. They can and should be encouraged to be fully dedicated within the framework of patient choice, including choice to refuse medical treatment even when necessary to prolong life.

As for the interest that society has in the lives of its members, surely that interest is minimal for society in general and the average individual, in comparison to what is at stake for the individual himself in his right to self-determination. Most of us, fortunately or not, fail to make contributions so vital to social welfare as to reverse this priority. Hence neither the continued existence of society nor the quality of life within it is threatened by the freedom of the individual patient in this regard. The primary moral function of society is to provide a social framework in which both individuality and noncoercive cooperation can flourish. Of more relevance than the relation between individual and society here is that between the individual patient and those whose lives really are affected by his continued existence, his family and others close to him. The traditional taboo against suicide derived from the religious idea that a person's life is not his own—it is a gift from God to be taken away only according to His will. I admitted above that one's life may not be morally one's own when the lives of dependents are closely linked to it. It may be wrong to take one's life in this situation. We are concerned not so much with the morality of suicide, however, as with the question of authority to intervene; and this may be a case in which a person has a right even though its exercise may sometimes be wrong. The right remains if the authority to intervene is too open to mistake or abuse, as I believe it would be here in the hands of medical professionals. Thus patients may have the right to refuse or withdraw from life-saving treatment even when their doing so wrongly harms their family or others dependent on them. (I believe that degree of dependence is relevant here, however, and young children may make a difference when spouses do not.)

Equally to the point is that the relations between patients and those whose welfare is intimately connected to them cut both ways. One frequently heard argument against permitting patients to refuse life-saving treatment is that such decisions may result from family pressure or from concern to save the family costs and extended hardship. Such pressure upon patients is then presumed to be unfair. But even where this concern is a motivating factor, it is not clear why these choices must be blocked. In other contexts we consider self-destructive acts for the benefit of others to be morally admirable and sometimes at least bordering on obligatory. A solo pilot in danger of crashing into a crowded area, who might make the air strip and survive if he remains on course and risks the lives of many others, would be praised for turning into a deserted forest area in which he has no chance to survive. Such self-destructive acts performed for the sake of others are in fact looked upon more favorably than those performed for self-regarding reasons. The acts of soldiers who sacrifice themselves for their fellow countrymen in war time are considered heroic. No one believes that we should adopt rules to spare people in desperate situations like that of the pilot or soldier the feeling of moral pressure to sacrifice themselves. In the medical context doctors should attempt to verify that refusals of continued life-prolonging treatment by patients are genuinely autonomous. But the patients' steadfast pronouncements must in the end be accepted.

Turning back from acts of self-sacrifice motivated by the desire to spare loved ones to choices of death for self-regarding reasons, while the former may be morally praiseworthy, the latter, I have argued, are at least morally permissible when truly autonomous. We have not found convincing reasons for doctors to assume the authority to intervene coercively to block patients' refusals of treatment, even that necessary to prolong life. The case is totally different when we are dealing with incompetents or with the question of active euthanasia.

(2) *Death imposed by others.* Let us consider the former first, for example the case in which parents attempt to refuse treatment for their children on religious grounds. At stake here is not an individual's right to self-determination, central to the integrity of individuality itself and hence fundamental among rights, but rather the right of parents to make decisions concerning the welfare of their children. There are, I believe, at least three sources for such rights of parents. First is the fact that the responsibility of parents for their children is believed

to be normally most conducive to the welfare of the children. Parents generally know their own children better than others know them, and therefore they are apt to know better what is in their interest. Someone has to be responsible for the interests of children, and it seems natural that those adults who raise and support them, and who care most of them, should have the major responsibility for decisions concerning them. The second source of parent rights is the value of the family unit itself, toward which the relations between parents and children contribute. The family allows for relations of intimacy among adults and children that are both of great intrinsic value and important for the development of healthy and moral individuals.

While these first two sources of parents' rights to make choices on behalf of their children appeal to the interests of the children and to the relations between them and their parents, a third source relates to parents themselves. Certainly adults value highly the chance to help shape the lives of their children in the image of their own values. What small chance we have to escape in part the constraints of mortality derives for very few of us from our work and accomplishments, for many more, from our children. Nevertheless, since children are themselves independent individuals, considerations of their interests must come first in decisions primarily affecting their welfare. It is of course consideration of their interest, of the fact that they would in many cases make decisions inimical to that interest, that justifies paternalism toward children in the first place. Only later in the moral logic do we decide who among adults should make decisions for them. Because this is so, when the interests of children are blatantly violated by their parents' proposed courses of action, society may intervene to protect the children. The parents' right to decision can be overridden.

One may wonder why the epistemological problem central in the discussion of forced transfusions for adults is not decisive here as well. There we raised the question of authority to determine that the religious beliefs of these sects are false, authority to override actions resulting from these beliefs on that ground. Why does that question not arise with equal force in the case of forced transfusions for the children of members of these sects? The answer is that the force of the initial question derives from its relation to the right of self-determination, which is not primarily at issue in the latter case. I myself, and I am sure many others, have no problem in judging the beliefs of these sects false and even bizarre. But I do not take this to be grounds for paternalistic interference with their self-regarding decisions, because of the general problem of granting authority to interfere in the lives of others on grounds of disagreement in belief alone. If such authority were granted generally, that would effectively destroy the right to self-determination. Since this right is not fundamentally at stake in paternalistic decisions regarding children, the primary consideration rather being their welfare, we may override parents' decisions when they are seen to be seriously damaging to their children's interests. There are two further limitations upon this claim in our context. The first is that the damage must be potentially drastic, if we are to respect the family as the social unit for raising children. The second is that doctors themselves are not to be granted authority to override parents generally. The courts are the proper source of overriding decision. Doctors are responsible for petitioning their rulings, and in emergencies medical personnel may have to act on their own out of necessity. The latter responsibilities do not represent special authority for doctors, but simply the duty shared by all to report and prevent even well-meaning parental abuse of their children.

I would grant to parents a more absolute right to decide matters of life and death for their children in the case of severely defective newborns. Since, if such children live, their parents must bear the strain and sacrifice of providing any kind of decent life for them, it is also up to the parents to measure the prospects regarding the quality of future life for these children as well as their own willingness to sacrifice. Normally in cases of decisions made in behalf of others their welfare must be placed first. Normally it is not the place of anyone to judge the quality of life for others and to make decisions for them on the basis of such judgments alone. This has been a major theme of this chapter. In this case, however, parents are permitted in my opinion to give primary weight to their own futures. I place their interests first because I do not believe that newborns meet the criteria for personhood and moral rights to life, criteria having to do with agency and future-oriented concepts and desires (these begin to be acquired in the weeks after birth). The argument in metaphysics and philosophy of mind is too involved to be worth stating fully here, and I have tried to do so elsewhere.[25] Fortunately it is also somewhat beside the point, since there is no question of doctors having ultimate responsibility for decisions in this context. Either life-saving measures are mandatory, or parents have this responsibility, the duty of doctors being limited to that of providing information regarding medical prospects. Hence there is no question of strong role differentiation for doctors in relation to these difficult cases.

Regarding adults who have become incompetent as the result of disease, family members are again the logical choice for decision-makers, although here the criterion for correct choice requires not only a judgment of the patient's welfare, but a judgment as to how he himself would have decided were he still competent. Close family members are normally in the best position to make such judgments. Where members equally related disagree, or where the doctor suspects abuse from self-interest, courts again constitute the proper overriding authorities. The responsibility of doctors in such cases lies in raising the issue, not in assumption of authority themselves to override what would otherwise be rights of the family members.

Although the right to self-determination entails a right to refuse any or all medical treatment, I would draw the line at requests for active euthanasia made by patients to doctors. It might seem plausible, if the previous arguments are accepted, that honoring an autonomous request for a painless and rapid death is a logical extension of respect for the right of self-determination. If active euthanasia is not permitted, and some patients are too debilitated to take their own lives, then these patients are in effect punished by being made to suffer a more prolonged death through no fault of their own. If one is permitted to choose to die by refusing all treatment and even by taking his own life, why should this be made more difficult, prolonged and painful than necessary?

There are several reasons. First, a rule permitting active taking of life in such circumstances would stand too open to abuse, and policing it would be too difficult. Second, the possibility of mistaken diagnosis is not as serious in the case of refusal of treatment (which might not then be fatal) as it would be if euthanasia were readily available. Third, if the choice of death is made too easy, there is less check that the decision is a matter of firm autonomous resolve deriving from a stable preference ordering. Fourth, the psychological effect on doctors of a requirement to kill adult persons would undoubtedly be genuinely deleterious.

While I would then prohibit doctors from actively aiding in euthanasia, I would again make an exception in the case of severely defective newborns, who are not distinguishable in moral status from fetuses. If abortion is permissible, then so is active euthanasia at this stage. But while newborns fail to meet criteria of personhood for the same reason as fetuses, i.e. lack of concepts and of desires that would be violated by acts of euthanasia, they do have sensations that render it wrong to make them suffer. Active euthanasia is therefore preferable in this case to letting die, which may be prolonged and painful for all parties. But this is a very special case, more like abortion than like euthanasia in other contexts. We must in every medical instance consider the rule against killing (genuine) persons as absolute, for the reasons given. Some further cases become very difficult in this area, however. We must distinguish where possible, for example, and permit medication to relieve pain that may also hasten death. Another difficult case would be that in which a parent wished to donate a vital organ to a child who would die without it, when removal of the organ would kill the parent. Here again I believe we must prohibit autonomous choice, since we cannot allow killing for organs to develop as a practice.

Drawing the line at active euthanasia for all cases except newborns is in accord with the principles of ordinary morality. Permitting patients to refuse medical treatment is refusing to grant to doctors extraordinary power to coerce or deceive them. Refusing to allow doctors to take part in active euthanasia or killing of patients for any medical reason is also to refuse to grant them special authority, a license to kill upon request. Hence drawing the line here is consistent with our earlier arguments and with common moral demands. While suicide is in general morally permissible, aiding others to kill themselves is not (although there are exceptions in which it is excusable). The rule for doctors is once more simply a direct implication of our common moral framework.

EXCEPTIONS TO THE DUTY TO DISCLOSE   Let us look lastly at some other types of cases in which authority for medical decisions is assumed by doctors, or in which deception is frequently practiced in medical contexts. Allowing patients to be examined by medical students while believing them to be doctors, a common practice, is ruled out even if no medical decisions are affected, since people have the right to decide knowingly whom to see for medical reasons. The deceptive practice of prescribing placebos is normally wrong, in that it might prevent decisions to seek other advice or treatment, psychiactric if necessary. Here there might be exceptions, however, once more when no potential decision is affected. Veatch cites a case in which an old woman is prescribed sleeping pills after an operation and becomes addicted to them.[26] The doctor and pharmacist cooperate in weaning her from this costly addiction by gradually substituting placebos with no negative effects. Here the paternalistic deception seems justified, since it appears that any rational person would desire to take something harmless and inexpensive, rather than an expensive addictive drug, positive effects being equal.

Such cases are complicated by the question of whether deception itself, as an expression of lack of respect, constitutes harm, and, if so, whether it is harmful only if and when discovered. If a person can be harmed only when he *feels* the harm, then deception not discovered by its victim will not appear to be seriously wrong. It might nevertheless be wrong to make a practice of deception whenever it appears that the victim will not discover it, since the latter assumption might be often mistaken. Second, if such lies are discovered by others this might be damaging to one's reputation as trustworthy. More important, our initial premise here is false. A person might be wronged without being harmed, and might be harmed without knowing of it or feeling it. For example, a slanderous statement about a person that has no effect on his good standing or reputation would wrong him without harming him; and, if it damaged his reputation without his finding out about it, it would harm him without his knowing or feeling it. If it cost him a great amount of money that he found out about only much later, then it seems that the harm occurred at the time of the loss, not only when he learned of it, although the shock of the news might cause further harm later. Thus, to return to the case at hand, the fact that deception is undiscovered by the patient and is likely to remain so does not in itself justify its use, even if it does not violate the right to self-determination by robbing the patient of the knowledge with which to make informed important decisions. Deception is prima facie wrong in showing lack of respect; it is prima facie seriously wrong when the person deceived appears to have a right to the truth in question. In the medical context the patient has a prima facie right to the truth whenever it concerns primarily her condition, even if no decisions depend upon it.

But cases like that of the old woman, in which self-determination or control over future decisions important to the course of her life are not at stake, and in which important benefits can be gained for her by deception or concealment, may well constitute exceptions to the right to know the truth, all things considered. As pointed out before, I have not based this right upon the intrinsic value of truth as opposed to falsity. Certainly in other contexts in which persons explicitly request information, they may not be entitled to it. Whether they are depends first upon how the information relates to other rights, and second how it relates to the distribution of utilities. Once a right is granted or recognized, it may not be overriden by utilities in specific cases. But if recognizing it would regularly cause disutility (in the deepest all-inclusive sense) to the prospective right holder, and if there are no good ideal-regarding reasons for recognizing it relating to the development or maintenance of individual control over plans of life, then it should not be granted in the first place. Such appears to be the case with the old woman's situation and others like it. Here the prima facie right to the truth may be overridden by the clear benefits to her and clear lack of harm in any sense.

Use of placebos appears justified only in the case of withdrawal from medication (perhaps also in experimental studies when subjects have advance knowledge of the nature of the study). In other cases they may block action of the patient to get at the root cause of the problem, perhaps psychological, and may encourage reliance upon medication in other contexts when none is necessary. When used for the opposite purpose of weaning from medication, they accomplish what the rational patient desires and would do himself were it not for his ignorance of the true situation, of the fact that he can really do without the medication. Hence this use blocks only continued action based on ignorance, and it helps to achieve what can be presumed first among relevant preferences of the patient—to be relieved of symptoms for which medication was necessary without continued use of the medication when no longer necessary. Hence our criteria for paternalism are met in this narrow instance. This is only because the patient's right to self-determination is not at issue in this one particular use of placebos.

This right becomes relevant whenever decisions or actions of the patient may depend upon his knowing the truth. Such decisions or actions need not appear momentous from the outsider's (physician's) perspective. In the terminal illness case, for example, it need not be a matter of completing a lifelong project or molding one's life into a final coherent whole. Most lives are not like that; they can be viewed in terms of overall significance only from the outside, in terms of significance for others. It may be a case simply of the patient's wanting to be with loved ones or at home. It is the inability of the doctor to predict what may be important that justifies a strict rule of disclosure, of consistently honoring the right of the patient to information about himself. There can again be exceptions when the doctor has lifelong personal knowledge of his patient and knows his reactions to bad news and his true preferences. But such exceptions, increasingly rare in contemporary medical practice, do not alter the rule or the general point on the question of strong role differentiation based on a paternalist model.

The most obvious exception to the duty to disclose is the case in which the patient explicity waives his right by telling the doctor that he does not want to make the medical decisions or hear any bad news.[27] Here it seems that the right to self-determination implies a right not to be told, rather than a continued right to the truth. It is in general possible to waive or transfer rights, or to choose not to exercise them, and such features are part of their value in increasing personal freedoms. Yet in this case too there are problems and counterarguments. It may be wrong for the person to remain in ignorance of his condition: the future welfare of his spouse or children may depend on his taking adequate steps immediately to provide for them. It is irresponsible of a person in that situation to remain in ignorance. Then too it can be argued more generally that a person is free and moral only when he assumes responsibility for his actions. This assumption of moral responsibility and self-control over one's decisions entails responsibility for finding out all information relevant to them. Refusing to learn information relevant to important decisions is like giving up one's freedom and moral autonomy, and one ought not to do so. Such abdication of responsibility may again appear analogous to a contract to sell oneself into slavery. We accepted above that decisions to give up the status of autonomous agent ought not to be honored.

There are once more crucial disanalogies between these cases, however. In the medical case the patient asks to be spared certain information that would normally be relevant to the actions of most people. But it may not be relevant to remaining decisions of importance to him or to those close to him. He may have already prepared for the worst by setting his affairs in order. It may be that no morally significant actions will be affected by his certain knowledge of imminent death. In the case of decision regarding treatment, he may decide that he wants the therapy that is medically optimal in the doctor's judgment, while being spared details as to remote risks. Such a choice is itself a legitimate exercise of autonomy. The doctor's inability to predict what may remain for the patient to decide, the autonomous request not to be informed, and the suffering caused by disclosure in this context call for the doctor to honor this request.[28]

If the interest of a spouse or family is involved, they may have a right to the truth; but then the doctor ought to inform them and not the patient who asks to remain in the dark. If it would be morally better for the patient to bear the burden with his family, this nevertheless appears to be a case in which a person has a right to do what may be wrong to do. This possibility has been mentioned before as a general feature of rights. In the legal ethics chapter we had an example of a woman with a right to will her money as she liked, whether morally inoptimally or wrongly. Of course that someone does not desire to hear the truth does not in general entail that he has a right to remain in the dark. If someone is being obnoxious and does not want to hear about it, it may be right to tell him anyway, and certainly not in violation of any of his rights. But in the medical case, a person contracts with or hires a doctor and therefore has a right to set the terms. The doctor can refuse to treat him if there are other doctors available and he does not approve of the terms, if for example the doctor prefers full disclosure to all patients. But normally if a patient asks the doctor to choose the most effective treatment without informing him of all risks, the doctor ought to respect this request.

There are of course other morally troublesome possible variations on these cases. The patient may specifically ask that neither he nor his spouse or children be informed if the prognosis is very bad. He may want to spare them as well as himself prolonged anguish. Or the spouse may ask that the patient not be told. Or the doctor might know that if he informs the spouse, the spouse will tell the patient, who has asked not to be informed. In the first case I do not believe that the doctor ought to honor the request. The patient has a right to be spared information if he so requests, but since the information is crucial to the interests of the spouse as well, he has no right to prevent her from having it if she so requests. The spouse's right to self-determination seems to be more at stake in that case than the patient's. In my opinion it overrides the patient's right to privacy as well, since spouses should not keep secret facts about themselves that greatly affect the welfare of their families. Likewise in the second case, the spouse has no right to prevent the doctor from divulging information to the patient if he requests it, since in that case the patient's fundamental right is more at stake. The third case is perhaps the most difficult and refers us back to the problem with the principle of double effect mentioned earlier. The doctor does not intend to inform the patient, who requests not to be told, but only the spouse. Yet, as implied by our objection to that principle, he cannot use this as a blanket excuse in itself should he be certain that the information will be relayed directly. My opinion is that he nevertheless ought to inform the spouse, after trying to convince her to honor the patient's request. The interests of spouses are vitally involved in such cases. In addition it is important that someone in the family be informed so that all decisions affecting its common interests not be made in ignorance or by the doctor exclusively. In fact, given that the doctor cannot assume responsibility for the broad interests of the entire family, the spouse can be kept in the dark only if the patient himself is adequately informed.

Thus there are exceptions to the duty to disclose and to the right to the truth, but these are determined by the relevance of the right to self-determination, and not by the balance of benefits and harms to the patient's health. The right to truth obtains in medical contexts whenever ordinary moral principles imply it, and the Hippocratic principle should not be elevated to strongly differentiate the doctor's role. The doctor has no special authority to make decisions or retain information vital to the interests of the patient or his family. What authority he has to make medical decisions must be explicitly delegated in advance by the patient. The lack of special authority is not meant to imply, however, that the doctor has no specific obligations to his patients, obligations that he does not have to others. Obviously he has a duty to provide health care to those who have contracted for it and to prefer the satisfaction of their health needs to those of others. This does not constitute a special moral framework, but a contractual relation falling under the morality of contracts and promises that applies in many areas of interpersonal relations. He may not violate rights of others. Those who have not been accepted as patients simply have no positive rights against him, except in emergency situations, when the urgency of need creates a moral right against anyone who can render aid without exorbitant personal cost.

There are other more specific obligations as well that attach to the contractual relation between doctor and patient, for example the often discussed duty of confidentiality. Some interpret this duty as if it implied a degree of strong role differentiation, as it would if it obtained when others have apparent rights to medical information about patients. This is not the correct interpretation, however, and not the one prevalent in practice. The contractual relation between patient and doctor, and the patient's right to privacy, both contained within our common moral framework, explain the full force of the duty to keep in confidence information about the patient. Such information, including that obtained in medical examination, is imparted by the patient with the firm understanding that it will not be divulged to others. It is therefore a breach of trust for the doctor to do so. Betraying this trust can also be considered an invasion of privacy, since the information most likely relates to the patient's body or to details of his life that he has a right to keep private. These are backward-looking reasons for the doctor to accept the duty to keep confidences: they look to the understanding with which the information is obtained, to the implicit promise that is a condition of its being given in the first place. There are also forward-looking reasons why confidentiality should be routine in medical practice, chief among them that patients would often be reluctant to seek medical advice or treatment if they could not do so under such an understanding.

All these reasons, none of them unique to the medical profession or to professions as a class, all deriving from general features of situations in which private matters are divulged in confidence to others, create a strong duty to confidentiality. In addition, and equally important, those who seek information about patients often have no independent right to it, not even prima facie right. Where they do have such rights or apparent rights, where for example there is danger of epidemic, or evidence of planned violence or child abuse, or of extremely hazardous driving, the claims of others to be spared unnecessary harm must be balanced against the duty of confidentiality to the patient, as in any other case in which such prima facie rights and duties come into conflict. In the cases just mentioned, I believe that the imminent danger to others outweighs the breach of trust to the patient. Since such cases are exceptions, they are unlikely to affect whether patients with serious diseases consult physicians. They do show that the right to confidentiality in medical contexts has no extraordinary weight and gives the doctor no license to ignore rights of others. Conflicts are to be settled by the application of ordinary moral principle, and so there is no question of special moral authority attaching to medical expertise in this area either.

THE PRESENT STATE OF MEDICAL ETHICS

The recent trend in legal cases, writings in medical ethics, and pronouncements of official bodies in the medical field has been toward increased support for informed consent and truth-telling. It is typical, however, as we saw in the position of Sissela Bok and that of recent courts, to make exception to truth-telling when there is a strong presumption of ensuing harm to the patient's health or state of mind. The 1964 Helsinki declaration of the World Medical Association supporting a doctrine of informed consent adds the rider "consistent with patient psychology."[29] Alan Donagan, in a recent paper that strongly advocates informed consent to treatment, writes:

Nobody questions that good medical practice may require a physician to be reticent in discussing a patient's condition with him, if telling the truth may disturb the patient needlessly and perhaps jeopardize his recovery.[30]

This chapter falsifies that negative generalization, exceeding previous writings in refusing to elevate the Hippocratic principle over a right to the truth when necessary for the fundamental right to self-determination.

As is usual, the A.M.A. lags behind this trend. In their most recent statement on the subject of cessation of life support treatment, the House of Delegates held in 1973 that the patient and/or his family, together with the doctor, may withdraw the use of "extraordinary means" to keep the patient alive when there is "irrefutable evidence that biological death is imminent."[31] This position strongly opposes the letter and spirit of that enunciated here in two related respects. First, there is an implicit attempt in the A.M.A. position to provide an objective criterion for the requirement of treatment, independent of the values of the patient. If death is not imminent, and if the treatment does not involve extraordinary measures, then the implication is that continued treatment that is necessary in the doctor's judgment is required for the patient. Perhaps it is impossible to avoid all tacit appeal to the patient's value ordering here, for if we unpack the sense of 'extraordinary' in the statement, we cannot do so simply in terms of the frequency of the treatment, a major part of its ordinary sense. Rather, extraordinary measures must be those extremely costly in terms of side effect and expense in relation to benefit to the patient. But cost and benefit must be relative to the patient's own resources and values. This is not acknowledged in the statement, however. It may be assumed there that benefit can be measured solely in terms of prolonging life, and cost in terms of physical discomfort and monetary expense.

The second objectionable aspect of this proposed criterion for withdrawal of treatment is its lack of emphasis upon the question of *authority* to decide, as opposed to grounds for decision. From my point of view, more important than the factors taken into account in the decision-making process is the matter of who makes the decision. In the A.M.A. statement non-extraordinary treatment appears to be obligatory for the patient. Furthermore, even if the narrowly defined conditions for cessation of treatment are met, the decision to continue or withdraw appears to be a joint one between patient and doctor, both having an equal say. Completely ignored here is the patient's most fundamental right to self-determination, and the right implied by it to make all decisions crucial to the course of his life. From the perspective of the overriding importance of this right, *no* treatment is obligatory for the patient, and the doctor *never* has the moral authority to make vital decisions for the competent patient, or even for the incompetent patient, except in emergency situations. It is the essentially cost-benefit oriented approach of the A.M.A. criterion for such cases, together with the illusion that true costs and benefits can be objectively determined, that masks the crucial question of the right to decide. This approach is bound to blur the issue of authority for decision, or to elevate the doctor's authority solely on the basis of his medical expertise. My position emphasizes this question of authority first, and so retains the right to decide where it most naturally resides, with the individual most affected by the decision. From this point of view there is no relevant distinction between cessation of treatment once begun and decisions to initiate treatment. The consent of the patient must be continuous and continuously informed.

If most recent writings tend toward my position while falling short of it, actual practice also appears to lag further behind. Recent surveys have shown a sharp discrepancy between doctors' assumptions about patients' desires and their practice in relation to these assumptions on the one hand, and patients' actual desires for information and full disclosure on the other. Many doctors continue to believe that patients want to be spared knowledge of terminal illness or of the risks associated with proposed treatments. But patient surveys have shown that this is overwhelmingly not the case.[32] Despite the move toward fully informed consent and patient choice in the recent literature and court decisions, a 1972 survey of physicians found only 7 per cent who thought that the choice of radical or simple mastectomy should be left to patients after being informed of the options, risks and uncertainties.[31] Such prevalent opinions undoubtedly reflect and are reflected in general practice.

Despite the recent "Patients' Bill of Rights" of the American Hospital Association, life in hospitals as well continues to be filled with needless rituals suggestive of patient passivity, dependence and impotence.[34] The institutional setting is still structured in such a way as to block the exercise of rights at least partially accepted intellectually. Once the decision is made to enter a hospital, there is little suggestion that the doctor is merely offering advice about medications. Patients are rarely permitted even to see their charts; pills are almost literally shoved into their mouths; medications are administered intravenously without the patients' knowledge—until the bills arrive. Nurses often address doctors as gods and patients as children. Often newly admitted patients perfectly capable of walking are taken to their rooms in wheelchairs, an apt symbol of the helpless pose they are made to assume from the time of their entrance into this alien and authoritarian setting.

Medical practice outside hospital settings continues to suggest in subtle ways a paternalistic model also, for example in such seemingly trivial matters as doctors' using first names for patients while continuing to use their titles, in habitual lateness for appointments without excuse, etc. Such ingrained habits of professional practice will be more difficult to alter than intellectual acceptance of the arguments. Office routines can themselves create an aura of professional expertise and authority, conveying the message that a patient's opinions on purely medical decisions are neither required nor sought by those more competent to make these decisions. Such routines subtly prevent patients from exercising rights never consciously relinquished and partially recognized by doctors who self-consciously write on these subjects. Many patients entering the alien world of medical routine are likely to be intimidated into acquiescing with any treatment suggested by the doctor, without knowledge of risks, predicted benefits, or side effects. When this happens, the doctor is assuming authority to make decisions for the patient, authority that he might not defend in self-conscious argument. He is assuming without thought a strongly differentiated position in relation to normally obtaining rights of patients to decide for themselves. In order to prevent such intimidating routine, often not intended as such, undue reliance should not be placed on such recent devices as standard consent or waiver forms. Too often these can function as legalistic evasions of morally right practices. The patient should be made to feel that important medical decisions are his to make. This "affirmative action" is necessary to correct for habits and assumptions that block the exercise of rights never consciously relinquished by patients or denied by doctors in reflective argument.

I attempted in the previous section to summon arguments that best defend an assumption of strong role differentiation for doctors. This assumption, expressed in numerous ways in medical practice, is causally explained less by these arguments that I have rejected than by the long history of group solidarity and professionalism among doctors, at times bordering on religious devotion. Historically, the potential conflict between the Hippocractic principle and the rights of patients perhaps could not be seen. When the medical battle was waged primarily against infectious diseases, the goals of (1) prolonging life, (2) minimizing suffering, (3) preventing or curing illness, and (4) promoting the patient's overall well-being were comfortably congruent. The context of chronic illness is different.[35] Doctors now know that they can no longer assume congruence between goals (1) and (2). Prolonging life in many cases becomes prolonging the natural process of dying; and doing so in those circumstances increases suffering not only for the patient, but for those close to him (not to mention the often outrageous expense). At least at that point it becomes obvious to all that the question of authority to decide is crucial. This question, emphasized throughout this discussion, is less apparent when all these medical goals are congruent not only with each other, but with the overall value orderings of rational persons. Once (1) and (2) come into obvious conflict, personal value orderings become clearly relevant in assigning priority. Prolonging life is not uncontroversially to be placed first, given that the quality of life from the individual's own point of view is what counts.

Now doctors must recognize potential conflicts between goals (3) and (4) as well. I have made much of the point that good health cannot be assumed to take absolute priority in the patient's values. If his overall well-being is defined in terms of his values, as it must be, then treatment that may be optimal in terms of health may not best promote his overall well-being. Costs, time and effort required, side effects, and risks must be measured in terms of his individual priorities. The definition of individual well-being in terms of subjective values does not imply that no criticism of values is possible. A person's values and preferences may be inconsistent, hence self-defeating, or they may conflict with preferences and values of others. But within the limits of consistent and rational orderings there is much room for difference; and from an ideal-regarding viewpoint, such difference appears as a healthy source of diversity in goods that can be enjoyed. Given these differences, the narrower medical ideal (3) and the broader ideal of interpersonal relations (4) cannot be assumed always to coincide. The authority of doctors to impose the former must therefore be limited by respect for individual rights.

In treating patients doctors have extended their notion of harm from the merely physical to include potential psychological harm. Now they must extend it further into a fully moral notion according to which harm consists in preventing an individual's preeminent value from being realized, or in violating a moral right. Once this broader notion of harm is accepted and the right to self-determination is recognized as fundamental, it becomes clear that strong role differentiation on the basis of the Hippocratic principle cannot be justified.

Relinquishing a claim to strong role differentiation for doctors amounts to relinquishing a degree of authority that they have assumed for making decisions for others. I have earlier contrasted this with the case of lawyers. In the case of ethics for lawyers the argument against moral professionalism calls upon them to assume additional moral responsibility, that is responsibility for decisions to pursue objectives of their clients even within the law. It is perhaps easier psychologically to assume greater authority and responsibility than to relinquish it. On the other hand, there are economic motives on the side of deferring responsibility to others, in this case to those who should be responsible for their own decisions. Doctors are less easily charged with malpractice for treatment or lack of it when this is demanded by the patients in knowledge of the risks. The economic motive might be more powerful were it not for the already economically invulnerable position of most physicians. Despite this incentive•then, it may be that deeply ingrained paternalistic attitudes will not change until patients themselves make it clear that they have not relinquished any rights over important decisions to their doctors.

It is important to note that the doctor is not being asked to give up his normal moral responsibility for his own actions. While the patient has the right to full information regarding his own condition and regarding alternative treatments, risks and uncertainties, and the right to accept or decline any treatment, the doctor need not provide treatment or perform services that he finds medically or morally objectionable. He ought not to prescribe against his better judgment, perform abortions if he morally condemns them, etc. Refusing or withdrawing from treatment is the patient's decision alone; but administering treatment must be a matter of mutual consent and cooperation between doctor and patient. The former rather than the latter has been the topic of emphasis in this chapter simply because —and this is different from the context of legal practice—the central issue for doctors falls at the end of the spectrum of moral responsibility where too much rather than too little tends to be assumed.

There is another difference with argument on the same question in the legal context that can be pointed out to highlight finally the structure of the argument against strong role differentiation for doctors. In the legal system the principal aim is justice, which is also the prime consideration morally. The question there was whether a strong adversary-advocacy model best serves this ultimate legal *and* moral aim. If it does, then the issue is settled, since there is only one fundamental value at stake, albeit the one most central in law and ethics. The structure of the argument is different in the medical context. Here our question was not whether strong role differentiation serves the primary medical aim of promoting health, which it does by definition here, but whether this aim itself can be presumed to override other normally obtaining rights. I hope to have shown that it cannot. Doctors must learn to act within the same moral framework as the rest of us, simply because their function, important as it is, does not encompass our most fundamental moral values.

5

Business Ethics: Profits, Utilities and Moral Rights

For several years a debate has been waged in the business journals as to whether or not business managers in their managerial capacities have moral or social responsibilities. Put in these terms, the question is nonsensical. To ascribe moral responsibility to a person is simply to say what he ought to do or should have done all things considered (in a situation in which the consequences of his action are or were morally significant). Moral reasons are simply overriding reasons for action. Such reasons therefore apply to the more significant actions of all of us, those actions that affect the interests of others, whatever our social positions.

But the question rather misleadingly raised in this debate can be rephrased as an instance of the issue that we have taken as central to all professional ethics. Should those in managerial roles assess each decision in ordinary moral terms directly, or should they rather reason first in terms of special business norms? It is again a truism that businessmen ought to act in ways that are cumulatively best from a moral point of view, but a separate and controversial question whether their authority to act on their own perceptions of what is morally best ought to be limited. In business, as in the other professions we have considered, special norms might limit authority to apply usual moral principles directly. Such norms again would be justified ultimately in terms of those moral principles themselves, being conducive to their maximal satisfaction. We recognize this debate, then, as raising the question of strong role differentiation for business managers. By now the balance of negative over positive verdicts on this question is becoming lopsided. The risk of repetition is well worth taking this final time, however, since there is once more within the profession itself, and in this case among certain prominent economists, widespread supposition of an affirmative answer.

We have said that special norms obtain if the institution that defines the professional role, in this case the economic system of free enterprise, serves a vital moral function in society, and if the interposition of the norm are necessary to that function. The occupant of a strongly differentiated position is permitted or required to ignore or weigh less heavily in relation to such norms considerations that would otherwise be morally crucial, considerations relating to the rights of others. His authority to act on his ordinary moral perception is limited. Our question for this chapter is whether the position of corporate manager is strongly differentiated under the norm of profit maximization. Can the business manager ignore what would otherwise be moral responsibilites and obligations in order to pursue maximal monetary gain for his corporation and his constituency, i.e. the stockholders?

We may think of stockholders here as occupying a position relative to managers analogous to the positions of lawyers' clients, doctors' patients, and politicians' constituencies. It is primarily the stockholders' interests that the manager is advancing directly when he attempts to maximize profits, although the interests of employees, including his own interests, are also connected to the financial health of his corporation. In the old days, when all stockholders typically were managers and their knowledge was less specialized, there was somewhat less justification for thinking of business as a profession. But modern managers, who apply highly sophisticated analytic techniques in behalf of a separate body of shareholders as clientele, clearly fit our definition. The argument for strong role differentiation again must show that exclusive pursuit of the interests, in this case material interests, of this clientele is morally optimal for all society.

The principle of maximizing profits is clearly not moral in itself. In fact it appears to be an expression of self-interest often opposed to the moral point of view. Nevertheless, it has been argued by some contemporary economists, descendants of Adam Smith, that pursuit of profits most effectively promotes general welfare while honoring moral rights. Therefore it accords with our most fundamental and general moral criteria, even when pursuit or protection of profits appears to ignore otherwise obtaining moral or social responsibilities. Legal limits are generally recognized. The question is whether businessmen ought to recognize moral obligations beyond requirements of law, when assumption of such obligations is incompatible with maximization of profit. Should managers sacrifice profits for moral reasons not incorporated into law, or can they assume that pursuit of profit within legal limits will tend toward a moral social outcome? Can they trust the invisible hand of the economic marketplace to reconcile their own interests and those of their stockholders with those in apparent conflict?

Recent horror stories in the news about leaking nuclear plants, asbestos filled hair dryers, exploding cars, planes that fall apart, chemical waste dumps, and price gouging by oil companies might appear to render the answer to our question painfully obvious. The unjustified harm so clearly imposed in many of these cases appears in all to result from the nearly maniacal pursuit of profit to the exclusion of all other considerations, including killing people by fire, poison, radiation or other carcinogen. But in all but the last of these cases, dangerous and unethical practices could result from the shortsightedness of managers in relation to the norm of maximum profit, not from the inappropriateness of the norm itself. Such practices may be incompatible with long-range maximal profit, once the public learns of them, as it has in all these instances.

When a corporation blatantly ignores potential harm to the public from the marketing of its product, it can expect not only losses on that product when the harmful defect is discovered, but negative publicity that can affect the sales of its other products as well. The more seriously harmful the defect, the greater the potential effect on future marketing potential. In this way probable harm to the public must be figured as a cost by the corporation. Profit maximization itself therefore motivates minimization of such harm for the far-sighted manager. Where other corporations can gain competitive advantage by avoiding such negative publicity, the losses from it might outweigh in the long run the temporary gains from avoiding the cost of remedying the defect. Thus horror stories such as the Three Mile Island nuclear plant or the DC 10 crashes might result from incompetence, unavoidable human error, or simply unforeseeable accident, rather than from correct application of the norm of profit maximization. Even harm that results from managerial decisions in the name of profit, such as the decision not to remedy the gasoline tanks on Ford Pintos, does not in itself argue against that norm if the decisions are mistaken in relation to it (unless such mistakes are more frequent than correct calculations—in that case the norm might be ideally correct but wrong in practice). Thus citing such cases cannot substitute for careful assessment of the arguments.

These seemingly obvious counterexamples to the case for profit maximization do not settle the issue. The reason is that the market itself acts as a moral constraint by lowering potential profits for corporations whose products or practices harm rather than benefit the consuming public. In the case of oil prices, which may seem excessively high in relation to the recent past, the defense of the profit principle is somewhat different. Ignoring increased costs for foreign crude oil, for which domestic corporations are presumably not responsible (a disputed presumption, however), increased profits to oil companies at this time can be held necessary for proper distribution of present fuel preserves and development of future energy sources. Higher profits first of all motivate and provide capital for futher exploration at a time when known reserves are diminishing. Second, until prices rise above costs of producing oil or other forms of energy from alternative sources such as shale or coal, these alternative sources will not be developed, even though their development might eventually enable costs and prices to level off. Hence once more a case in which pursuit of profit angers the public may actually instantiate the claim that profit maximization maximizes benefits to the public as well.

Support for Profits

While the majority of the public, and apparently the majority of businessmen themselves, regard unrestrained pursuit of profit as unethical, we must assess arguments of certain economists that the commendable moral sense of these people is nevertheless misguided. I want here to assess the entire case for profit maximization within legal limits and expose its weaknesses from a moral point of view. We shall begin from the mythical perfectly free and competitive market, as such analyses always do, and see whether the case for the profit maximization principle can be made there. We can then see whether it can be extended to contemporary market conditions. To avoid all appearance of a straw man issue, I ask not whether pursuit of profit always overrides otherwise obtaining moral considerations, but whether it can ever do so. An affirmative answer to this weaker question would be sufficient to establish the position of business managers as strongly differentiated, and to establish business ethics as a genuinely distinct subdivision of normative moral theory.

THE VIRTUES OF THE FREE MARKET

UTILITARIAN VIRTUES   Arguments in favor of the primacy of the pursuit of profit generally begin by appealing to classic analyses of the role of profit in a purely competitive free market system. In this situation, given fluid resources and labor, and knowledge of prices and product quality on the part of the public, the pursuit of profit, Adam Smith's invisible hand, results in the most efficient collective use and development of economic resources. Efficiency here is defined in terms of satisfying the greatest total of consumer desires at the least cost. The way it is maximized in theory through competition has been known for centuries. Businessmen, motivated by the prospect of profit, produce what has the greatest surplus of value to the public over cost. Public demand for a good or service allows prices in that industry to rise; prices for goods that are relatively scarce in relation to demand are bid upwards. Higher prices and the prospect of higher marginal profit attract more producers to develop supplies or substitutes in order to satisfy high demand, until the marginal value of further production falls to that of other goods. At the equilibrium price and volume of production all goods share the same marginal value. The public gets the quantities it wants at prices it is willing to pay. At the same time goods and services are distributed to those whose demand, measured in terms of willingness to pay, is greatest.

Thus, it is argued, pursuit of profit results in optimal allocation of resources, maximizing the value of output to society as a whole. Whenever production of some new or different product would be worth more to the public than those produced from existing resource allocations, the prospect of higher profit will call forth the capital and labor to produce it, provided that these are fluid, that market research reveals the consumer preference, and that profit maximization is chief among motives. Whenever a producer can cut costs by improving production techniques, he will do so, since he can thereby widen his profit margin, and increase his volume relative to the competition. Any producer who is inefficient will be undersold and will lose his market. Thus the motive to maximize profits achieves efficiency in satisfying demand at a given time and encourages rising productivity through minimizing costs relative to output. This generates economic progress necessary to social progress in satisfying needs and wants. The total pool of goods continues to grow as production techniques are improved under the whip of income retention by individual producers. Profits function in this system as incentives to investors or risk takers and as rewards to firms that use economic resources more efficiently than others.

Thus, it is argued, pursuit of profit in a competitive situation best promotes aggregate social good. Profits measure the surplus of the value to society of goods produced over the value of resources taken from the social pool. If the primary social function of business is to achieve the most efficient allocation and use of resources for satisfying the wants of the public, then degree of profit measures degree of fulfillment of social responsibility.[1] When competition reduces costs, reduces prices relative to costs, and attracts resources to satisfy demand, the market gives the public what it wants most efficiently. Aggregate created wealth is maximized and distributed to those with greatest dollar demand. It is then argued that pursuit of other goals by business managers will hinder the economic enterprise vital to self-defined aggregate social welfare. Any self-imposed restraint upon the goal of maximal corporate income may be self-destructive if it is isolated or, if it is widespread enough, may impose higher costs or fewer goods on the public. Profits of course benefit stockholders and executives; but, if pursuit of profit is at the same time pursuit of maximum value to the public, then managers should be wary of the call to sacrifice self-interest to other values.

NONUTILITARIAN VIRTUES   The defense of placing profit first offered so far is thoroughly utilitarian: it appeals to maximizing satisfaction of aggregate demand or wants. But it can also be argued that pursuit of profit in a free market honors rights of free producers and consumers. Fewer rights will be violated in this system than in alternative economies, since here goods will be produced and distributed through a series of voluntary transactions. Parties enter into contractual relations only when they see the transactions to be to their own benefit. The offer of a sale for profit extends alternatives to consumers rather than restricting freedoms or rights. In order to make a profit, a business must offer an alternative at least as attractive as others will offer to prospective buyers. Free agreements for mutual benefit will violate rights of neither party (assuming that no fraud is involved). But if the businessman tries to place other values over the maximization of profit through the satisfaction of consumer demand, he may in fact diminish alternatives and force consumers to pay for products or features of products that they might not want or be willing to pay for given the choice.

If, for example, automobile manufacturers jointly decide that air bags should be installed for safety reasons, despite increasing unit prices by hundreds of dollars, this will force consumers to pay for something they do not want. At least it will diminish opportunities to purchase a product more to their liking at prices they are more willing to pay. Obviously many parallel examples could be cited. Thus aiming at profits in a free competitive market maximizes satisfaction of wants as well as possibilities for free transactions. It increases alternatives predicted to be preferable to consumers. If limitation of free choice where not necessary to prevent harm to others is unwarranted, then this maximally free economic system appears to be justified not only on utilitarian grounds, but in terms of maximizing opportunities for free choice as well.

LIMITATIONS ON THE AUTHORITY OF MANAGERS

TAXATION OF STOCKHOLDERS   The substitution of the values of the business manager for those of the public, expressed through demand as this creates opportunities for profit, appears to limit choices of both consumers and stockholders. Consider first arguments on the relative authority of managers and stockholders. As Milton Friedman points out, managers are employees of stockholders; they are entrusted with their money for the express purpose of earning a return on it. But if they sacrifice profits in order to aid what they perceive to be moral or social causes, for example by contributing to charity or by exceeding legal requirements for safety or anti-pollution devices not demanded by consumers or included in competitors' products, then they are in effect taxing stockholders without authority to do so.[2] Any sacrifice of profit amounts to an appropriation of funds that could be distributed to stockholders who have a right to demand it. Since managers are their employees, they have a right to set the terms of the employment. It can be presumed that such terms would not include permission to spend a portion of their money on the favorite social causes of the managers. Stockholders probably have their own favorite charitable causes, and in any case have a right to spend or give their own money as they like. Without express approval of corporate contribution or conscience by stockholders, then, managerial decisions to contribute to charity, or even to forego profits for perceived moral reasons, appear to exceed the authority delegated to managers.

It can be argued as well that such assumption of authority is excessive in another sense: it usurps the proper taxing authority of elected government officials. A business manager whose direct application of personally held moral principles makes a difference is spending the money of other persons, money that is not his own, as these other persons would not choose to spend it. His corporation then operates as an extra-governmental institution for selective taxation and public spending. But these functions are better left to the real government. Restraints on private actions to promote the public good should be generated through the political process, embodying principles of majority rule and proper checks and balances. Public officials can be controlled by the electorate and endowed with the resources to determine properly the effects of taxation and public spending upon the general welfare. Businessmen lack the same restraints; they are not appointed on the basis of their ability to tax and spend for social welfare. The morally zealous manager assumes power without the accountability of the electoral process. He also likely lacks the expertise to judge accurately the effects of his presumed moral sacrifice of profits.

Piecemeal decisions of individual managers cannot be based upon accurate prediction of cumulative effects on the economy or on consumer choice. Decisions that negatively affect profits will hurt stockholders, may hurt employees, may misallocate resources away from production with maximum public value, and may be cumulatively damaging to the economy. The point here is that the individual manager is not in a position, as the well-advised government official presumably is, to assess these cumulative effects. His expertise and training are directed precisely toward gauging consumer demand, not toward thwarting it for some hopefully beneficial social result. In imposing his own judgment against projected demand as potential profit, he is opposing the public's judgment of its own interests, and this without adequate projection of the cumulative results of such audacity by himself and other managers. Thus there are good reasons why corporate owners or stockholders do not trust executives to spend their money according to personal moral judgments, why they trust them only to maximize returns through most efficient allocation of resources. Other uses of corporate assets, which may be inconsistent with the values of those who own the assets, are in violation of that trust. They exceed the legitimate delegated authority of executives. Or so argues Friedman.

EFFECT ON CONSUMER CHOICE   Consider next the argument that claims that managerial decisions which sacrifice prospective profits limit consumer choice. When managers seek to maximize profits by maximally satisfying consumer demand, they allow the public to impose its own values upon business through the market mechanism. Whatever moral demands and constraints are dear to the consuming public, they can impose them upon business by buying from corporations that satisfy them. Thus, the argument goes, it is not a question of a manager's being moral or not, but of his deferring to the judgments of consumers. The latter are expressed through demand, as reflected in potential profit. Once more the question of authority, the authority to act on one's own moral perceptions, is brought to the fore; and once more it is distinguished from the question of the rightness or wrongness of the action in question. The distinction again derives from the fallibility of moral judgment, this time in the context of the opposition of the judgments of particular managers to the desires of the consuming public.

When competition exists, consumers need not buy from firms considered to violate the public interest or legitimate moral constaints. Certainly they will not buy products from which they expect harm to exceed benefit to themselves. The market, as reflected in potential profits, appears to be a more sensitive mechanism for satisying a diverse set of values and preferences than would be either imposition of managerial values and moral opinions or centralized political decisions, even if democratically determined.[3] The reason is that the values of any sizeable minority, even if very small relative to the entire population, can create a potential profit for some astute businessman. But these values may not match those independently held by business managers, and the minority may not be sizeable or well-organized enough to affect centralized decisions of government. An argument for deviating from the profit motive beyond obeying legal constraints therefore must be an argument for imposing the independent judgments of business managers upon the consuming public, for substituting the values of a small minority for those of all the various segments of the majority.

Turning more specifically to moral constraints, if a significant segment of the population considers a given moral norm important, the market should operate to impose that norm upon business, or at least to make it worthwhile for some businesses to accept it or operate within its constraints.[4] Consumers can boycott corporations that discriminate against minorities or manufacture napalm (discrimination is inefficient for other reasons too); they can patronize those firms that employ minorities or serve the community in other ways. When such service brings increased consumer loyalty, managers can provide it consistently with profit maximization, in the knowledge that it is consistent with public preference and with stockholder interests. The public's own values are built into the market structure via consumer demand. But if business managers seek to substitute their own moral judgment for the operation of the market, say by adding to a new line of automobiles safety features for which there is no demand rather than more lush interiors for which there is a demand, they either coerce the public into paying for what it does not want, or else lose out to the competition that provides what the public does want. Once again the managers will have exceeded the authority delegated to them by the public to use resources efficiently to satisfy expressed wants, and that delegated by stockholders to compete for returns on their funds.

The case is totally different when moral commitment contributes to long-range profit by according with the public's values as expressed through the market or as imposed by law. Safety or antipollution devices required by law or for which the public is willing to pay, contributions to programs that improve the community environment and thereby improve employee morale, or programs that create effective public relations or advertisement, can all be justified in the name of long-run profit maximization. Here there is no coercion of the public or taxation of stockholders. The businessman stays within his proper bounds as long as he accepts the public's values as expressed through demand curves, rather than imposing his own. These values will themselves impose certain moral constraints and demands, and they will protect the public from harmful products, if corporations truly aim at long-range profit maximization rather than the fast buck. To protect the public against the latter, further restraints are necessary in the form of law, for example against fraud. But in no case, according to this line, should moral judgment of managers beyond law and projected public demand be necessary.

It is not a question then of business managers having a license to be grossly immoral or harmful to consumers. Certainly no serious moral argument could support such license. It is a question only of whose opinion in regard to satisfying wants and needs, realizing values, and honoring free choice should prevail, that of the business manager or that of the consuming public. The manager is under moral restraint to subordinate his opinion of what has maximum value to the opinion of the public as expressed through the market. But this restraint is equivalent to the demand to aim first at maximum long-range profits for his corporation. Harmful products or practices may increase short-term profits if they cut costs; but since they generate bad publicity, they are unlikely to be profitable in the long run. Even if certain practices of this sort would turn out to be overall profitable, they could not be projected in advance to be so as a general rule. Hence they should be screened out by a principle of aiming at maximum long-range profits. Given this moral constraint of the competitive market itself, and the further constraint of law as the outcome of the political process, the primary criterion for business decision must remain profitability, if business is to serve its vital social function rather than usurp that of government or individual free choice. Or so it is argued.

PRICING   The argument on sacrificing profits by failing to set prices at maximal profit levels, say from the commendable desire not to contribute to inflation, is somewhat different from that on product features. In the case of prices, by failing to charge full value, the manager may fail to distribute his goods according to greatest demand. More importantly, he will encourage overconsumption in the present, create more acute shortages of supplies in the future, and fail to encourage the development of more supplies or substitutes to meet real future demand. At least these will be the likely effects if his action succeeds in lowering prices of the good generally by setting off a chain reaction (price war) in the industry. The effects will then be similar to those of government imposed price ceilings. Since demand and supply vary with price, when the price of a product is set artificially low, the amount demanded will exceed the supply available. Since producers continue to produce until the marginal cost of more units equals the price obtainable for them, a low price sets this limit lower and discourages supply while increasing demand. Such lower marginal revenue therefore causes immediate shortages and long-term scarcity of the good in question. Some suppliers will simply be driven out of business, and others will reduce production.

In these situations of rising demand, falling production, and low price, the scarce goods will no longer be distributed by price. This means that they will no longer be rationed according to willingness to pay. If that is not the fairest of all possible systems of distribution, at least willingness to pay is some measure of desire, of the value of the good to the consumer in question. Distribution of goods to those who value them most has some intuitive appeal. Proponents of such market rationing hold that any failure of the criterion of willingness to pay as a measure of relative desire and value is a fault of the initial distribution of wealth, rather than of the method of distributing the goods themselves. In general they hold that such problems in the distribution of wealth should be corrected by direct redistribution, rather than by more fundamental alteration of market mechanisms.[5] In any case the point here is that distribution by willingness to pay a price determined by the market, a price that results when independent small producers attempt to maximize profits, is preferable to methods of distribution that result when prices are limited to artificially low levels. In the latter situations long periods of waiting for the product, e.g. gasoline lines, may become common. Such factors as friendship with suppliers or retailers become relevant. Black markets may arise, and unscrupulous retailers may reap excess profits that rob consumers of any benefits they were to derive from the misguided good intentions of the producers. The only alternative in that situation is government rationing, with all the bureaucratic costs and inefficiency involved in that.

Thus once again well-intentioned sacrifices on the part of managers can have unintended and unfortunate economic effects, effects that derive from failure to conform to market forces. When price and supply are determined by demand and the attempts of independent producers to maximize profits, they reflect marginal social benefit: the value of other goods that the public is willing to forego to purchase the good in question. When producers supply up to the point at which marginal cost equals marginal revenue (the price dictated by the market to small independent producers), resources are employed up to their maximal value for the public. It follows that when prices of goods are held lower than the market will bear, resources best devoted to production of those goods will be diverted elsewhere. This is inefficient; it fails to give the consuming public what it wants. Higher prices would encourage adequate supply, greater conservation of existing supply, and production of substitutes. At lower prices and higher demand the quality of the goods in question is also likely to suffer, since inferior goods can be sold to consumers anxious to have any. All this is not to say, of course, that runaway inflation is a good thing, only that it is not to be controlled by piecemeal decisions of managers to forego profits in the face of high demand. Once again proponents of the free market and of profit maximization would have the government prevent (or perhaps in this case refrain from causing) malfunctions, here by responsible fiscal policy and control over the supply of money.

SACRIFICIAL LAMBS   In this set of arguments for the moral primacy of the profit principle in business there is a final point suggested earlier that requires some expansion. A single firm that sacrifices profits to a moral norm is unlikely in a competitive situation to succeed in imposing that norm. Suppose, for example, that an executive in the automobile industry is convinced that safety in cars is more important than glamour, comfort or speed, but that cost-benefit market analysis clearly reveals that consumer preference runs the other way (up to a certain degree—it is always a question of how much safety at what cost). The competition caters to the demand even though it reflects only carelessness, ignorance or failure to apply probabilities. In these circumstances the executive's firm will not succeed in protecting the true public interest. It is first of all always problematic to assume that interests of others vary from their preferences. We emphasized in the previous chapter the value of allowing people to make their own choices. Only when their short-term preferences are uncontroversially irrational by being incompatible with their longer range desires is it proper to overrule their free choices. In this case it might not be uncontroversially irrational for people to take risks by sacrificing some degree of safety for other values in their automobiles. But the thrust of this consequentialist argument is independent of the validity of this paternalistic assumption in particular cases. When consumers can buy from firms that give them what they freely choose to pay for, the firm that attempts to coerce them by imposing its own values will simply lose out to the competition. In this situation well-motivated paternalism will not work, whether or not is is justified.

Not only may a manager's personal moral norm fail to take effect if opposed by consumer preference, his attempt to impose it may well cause the stockholders to replace him or cause bankruptcy for his firm. Then he will have sacrificed his own interest and that of his family without positive effect, and also that of his employees and that segment of his community dependent on the position of his corporation. Many livelihoods may depend directly or indirectly upon the financial health of the firm. The negative effects of any sacrifice of profits on those persons so dependent are likely to be so severe as to outweigh any moral benefits to the public, especially if the sacrifice of profits fails to impose the manager's moral goal.

When the financial health of the corporation deteriorates, its employees will suffer first and foremost. Even those not laid off may suffer some loss of income or benefits. One moral claim in favor of the free market system is that, when it operates efficiently, each worker or employee is paid (roughly) according to his productivity, as this is measured by the proportionate value of his output toward satisfying public demand. But when profits are sacrificed by managerial decisions, workers may no longer earn the full potential value to the public of their output. In a competitive situation the manager's opposition to the market force of public preference in product features will have little effect except upon those whose welfare is dependent upon the corporation's income. Actions that result in more harm than benefit are morally suspect even if well-intentioned. The imposition of special norms, such as the pursuit of profit principle, that prevent such actions is then supported.

The converse of this argument also seems to follow. That is, the degree to which managers can afford to sacrifice profits to personal moral constraints indicates an unhealthy lack of competition in the industry in question. The luxury of abandoning the profit principle exists only for those who have somehow limited the entry of competitors who can aim to satisfy the public's values and demands.[6] To the degree that competition for profits exists, the attempt by business managers to impose their own moral principles at the expense of profits is unlikely to succeed in affecting what the public buys, but is likely to produce unintended harm to those dependent on their firms. To the degree that managers can succeed in having stockholders and consumers pay for the moral scruples of their firms, they will have exceeded their legitimate delegated authority to give the public what it wants efficiently, and this will indicate an economic fault in their industry. Business should then aim to satisfy the moral demands of the public as these are imposed by law and reflected in long-range profit potential. Their authority to act directly on personal values in managerial decisions should be limited by the profit principle.

Pursuit of profit is essential to the operation of market forces that themselves impose moral restraints upon managers and allow the public to pursue its own values without hindrance.

This completes the initial case for strong role differentiation in business according to the primacy of the profit principle. Subsequent sections will attempt to expose its weaknesses.

Counterarguments

PROFIT MAXIMIZATION VS. THE PUBLIC INTEREST

The arguments outlined in the first section can be attacked initially by showing that profit maximization need not be efficient or maximize satisfaction of consumer wants. To the extent that maximum profits do not guarantee maximal aggregate utility to the public, the norm of profit maximization lacks even purely utilitarian justification. Counterarguments often begin by pointing out that the rider attached to the initial premise regarding market conditions is never perfectly satisfied in practice. Profit maximization is perfectly efficient to the public only when conditions are purely competitive (when each firm is too small to influence prices in the industry single-handedly or to exclude other firms), and when consumers have perfect knowledge of product features, defects, prices, and alternative products. Lack of alternatives under more monopolistic conditions render business decisions inherently coercive in determining what the public must pay for features of products that may be more or less essential and more or less desired. Size generates power over consumers that must be countered by acceptance of moral restraints to the maximization of profits.

NONCOMPETITIVE CONDITIONS   To the extent that the market in a particular industry is noncompetitive, profits might be maximized by lowering quality or supply while raising prices. To the degree that a corporation can determine its own prices and those of the industry rather than taking the price as dictated by the market, it might be able to raise profits by reducing supply and raising the price of its product. It will be able to do so when the demand curve for the product is steeped at an angle greater than 45°, i.e. when demand does not vary sharply with price. A price taker in a more competitive situation cannot do so because he cannot increase the price, hence the total revenue, while reducing supply. With the price fixed by the market, he will continue to produce until his marginal cost equals the price he can obtain for the product. It is only in that situation that the public receives sufficient goods at prices equal to marginal value. With less competition, pursuit of maximal profits may well provide less product at a higher price and thus fail to maximize utility to consumers.

Other pricing practices that are objectionable from the point of view of public utility become possible as well for corporations large enough to dictate prices in an industry or area. "Predatory price cutting" is the practice whereby prices are reduced to drive competition out of business, only to be raised later to recoup losses. Its possibility depends upon costs for new firms to enter or reenter the industry once prices are raised again. Certainly this practice has occurred upon occasion and can maximize profits at the expense of public utility. Large corporations can also price products under a known brand label far above others of identical quality. The excuse for that practice is that it is necessary to cover costs of advertising the known brand. Its utility to the public is a function of the degree to which the advertising provides useful information, as opposed to being deceptive in itself in stimulating desire for the product that is merely more expensive. Other deceptive practices in regard to pricing include raising prices of packaged goods by retaining the price and package while lessening the contents. This does not constitute outright fraud as long as contents are printed on the package, although few consumers would be able to compare earlier packages. Since all such pricing practices in situations that are not fully competitive raise profits at the public's expense, managers in such situations must recognize some restraints to the profit principle if they are to best serve the public interest.

HIDDEN DEFECTS   The examples of deception short of fraud bring us to a second area in which profit maximization may fail to mesh with aggregate public interest, this time relating to product features rather than price. As products become technologically more sophisticated, knowledge of their features will be lacking. To the degree that businesses can succeed in hiding from the public defects that would be costly to remedy, they can maximize profits at the expense of consumers. It is again not always a matter of outright lying or fraud—few businesses would be expected to pay for publicizing every conceivable malfunction or accident involving their products as part of their advertisem nt. When relatively few consumers may be harmed by a defect, when consumption of the product is geographically widespread and knowledge of such harm unlikely to influence future consumption greatly, cost-benefit analysis might well call for ignoring the defect in order to maximize profit. If harm to the few is likely to be serious, then ignoring the defect may be morally objectionable. Free choice and exchange will be utility maximizing and fair only when full information necessary for rational choice is provided. But providing such information, when it relates to defects or potential hazards of a corporation's products, may frighten customers away. The costs of remedying such defects may exceed the costs of lost business from negative publicity if the defects remain generally undetected. But the costs to the public in that case may be greater than the cost of improving the product. Once more moral restraint to protect the consuming public is not compatible with profit maximization.

One might wonder at this point why lack of technical information in this context is held to nullify the preferability of free consumer choice, while in the medical context it was argued that lack of information regarding complex medical matters should not be accepted as an excuse for overriding free choice of treatments by patients. The argument might be pressed by analogy here that costs for removing hazards or improving quality should not be forced upon consumers, that they should rather be able to choose through the power of projected demand whether to incur such costs. One disanalogy here to be emphasized later is that the risks are not limited in this case to individual consumers who might be willing to take them in order to save costs, but may be imposed upon third parties exposed to the products, e.g. dangerous automobiles or chemical wastes. But ignoring this point for the moment, the analogy between the cases calls instead for full disclosure of relevant information to those whose interests are at stake. The initial point in the business context is simply that such disclosure is morally required even though sometimes contrary to projected profit maximization. In both contexts the subject matter might be technical, but in both it can be simplified to specification of risks and costs. Another disanalogy, however, is that in the business case consumers cannot be expected to take an interest in the features of every product they buy comparable to their interest as patients in their medical conditions, even if some of these product features represent significant hazards. When they cannot be expected to spend the time to learn of such product features, there is a stronger case for moving beyond the requirement of full disclosure by corporations to removal of the risks. Both requirements may represent restraints upon profit maximization in the public interest.

EXTERNALITIES   Social costs or harm to the public do not always figure in producers' costs or in projected demand for products. Direct harm from products themselves might be expected to influence demand for them (although, as argued in the previous paragraph, not always enough to make it profitable to prevent the harm); but harm from a production process that does not attach to the product may not influence demand at all. Pollution and waste disposal fall into this category. If such harms are imposed upon neighborhoods in which production is located and not internalized as costs to producers, then production is not maximally efficient to the public. The unfigured costs are often termed "externalities." Even libertarian economists consider them serious shortcomings of unregulated free markets. Externalities, to be more precise, may be either costs imposed by production upon those who derive no benefits from the products, or benefits enjoyed by those who share none of the costs. I have mentioned examples of the former—pollution of all forms. Higher education may provide an example of the latter. When the costs are borne fully by the recipients, the public may nevertheless benefit from the superior services provided by those who have been educated. In both types of cases we have consequences of economic activities not reflected in demand and hence not figured in profit potential. Hence in both there is inefficiency, misallocation of resources in relation to their true net value. When costs are imposed upon the public but not figured by producers (since irrelevant to profit), too many resources will be devoted to overproduction of the product; when unpaid benefits are enjoyed, too few resources will be employed and the good or service will be underprovided.

It is the former case that most interests us here, that in which resources are overused in relation to net value because full costs are not figured in potential profits. In that situation some restraint on the maximization of profit principle for business in the way of refraining from polluting the environment or imposing other neighborhood costs will be a move toward more efficiency to the public. Refraining may not be profit maximizing, since consumers far removed from the neighborhood of production will be unlikely to choose products on the basis of whether or not neighborhood costs are imposed by the producer. Again we see a gap between profit maximization and public utility, a gap that could be filled by direct acceptance of responsibility for avoiding harm to the public even at the expense of profits.

DISTRIBUTION AND DEMAND A fourth counterargument

points out that creating maximum value in terms of satisfying net dollar demand, even when social costs are figured, will not necessarily create maximum aggregate utility to the public. The reason in that dollar demand is as much a function of the existent distribution of wealth and income as it is a reflection of intensity of wants or needs for the goods in question. Distributing goods to those most willing to pay for them is not distributing them to those who want or need them most. Thus their distribution does not maximize aggregate utility or satisfaction unless wealth is distributed equally or the effect of inequalities upon willingness to pay is negligible. For major necessities, unequal distribution will affect not only willingness, but ability to pay. If there is not enough decent housing or medical care to go around, for example, distributing them via a free market will not maximize satisfaction of want, need or value, that is it will not maximize aggregate utility. Those willing or able to pay most will not be those with greatest housing or medical needs. Rights aside, considerations of utility alone would not justify such a method of distribution. If prices are permitted to rise to what the market can bear, important needs and wants, indeed often those most vital and intensely felt, will go unsatisfied. There are many who cannot express their demands through the market. In areas of public decision-making we certainly would not consider it fair to allocate votes according to wealth. Why should we think it fair to allow production and distribution of economic goods to be determined by a system of voting with dollars? Once more moral restraint in setting prices, especially in the case of desperately needed services of professionals, is one way not only to protect rights to these necessities, but to maximize utilities by distributing them to those who need them most or would benefit most from them. It is fine to claim that wealth could be redistributed directly; but the question is whether the profit principle should be used in the present social context and any likely to evolve in the foreseeable future. Once more maximization of profit, or in this case of income of providers of professional services and other necessities, appears incompatible with maximization of utility to the consuming community.

CREATION OF DEMAND Fifth, there is the problem of the relation of consumer preferences to true interests and needs. In the first section I argued that opposing preferences expressed through the market to a different conception of interests is often problematic and objectionable as unwarranted paternalism. But, as Galbraith has argued, when preferences are suspect, when honoring them does not seem to lead to long-range satisfaction or happiness, they become more suspect when largely created by those who benefit from satisfying them.[7] The satisfaction of wants is utility maximizing when the wants are given as data and represent disutilities when unsatisfied. But if the process in question includes the creation of the wants themselves, and if their satisfaction results in greater wants or in other harmful side effects, then the whole process may be objectionable from a utilitarian point of view. As the ancient Greeks realized, contentment may be easier to achieve by eliminating superfluous desires than by creating and attempting to satisfy them.

Certainly for many businesses the goal of profit maximization requires the creation of demand as much as its satisfaction. Advertising and salesmanship are not merely informative. In extreme cases persuasion can amount to coercion, at least in effect, just as nondisclosure can duplicate fraud in its moral effect. Persuasion by advertisement and nondisclosure may amount in effect to coercion and fraud (only the latter are condemned and restricted under libertarian principle) when the context for rational choice is lacking.[8] The advertisement of junk foods on television shows for children, who are highly vulnerable to suggestion, unaware of the harmful side effects, and incapable of obtaining or comprehending information regarding such effects, is an example of an objectionable influence upon "free choice." Here as elsewhere the definition of 'coercion' (as of 'fraud') assumed by libertarian economists is too narrow, and those of 'free choice' and 'free exchange' are too broad. (Other examples include the characterization of the choice of the disadvantaged to live in squalid housing and work at menial low paying jobs as free.) If the libertarian economist were to broaden his concept of coercion, he would most likely apply it first to coercion of consumers by managers who refuse to cater to public demand, or to that of stockholders when earnings are donated to philanthropic causes. The point here is that the assumed equivalence between catering to demand and fulfilling long-range wants and preferences is itself suspect when nonrational means of persuasion are utilized to create the demand. Producers in that situation may not be equal parties to free exchanges, but may have a subtle but definite advantage in effecting the exchanges. In general, we may appeal to the ideal of free bargaining and exchange to capture our intuitions regarding fairness only when the bargaining parties begin from a position of rough equality (which is why contractarian frameworks for stipulating rights build in egalitarian constraints or "veils of ignorance" to eliminate the effects of undeserved advantages). That an exchange is not coerced under threat of physical force does not guarantee that it is free, fair, or utility maximizing for the parties involved.

The fact that a certain set of desires is created by those who then attempt to satisfy them is nevertheless not in itself sufficient ground for condemning the desires or the process that creates them. Such cycles of tastes that are created by those who then feed them are as characteristic of desires for the most exalted aesthetic experience, appreciation of fine opera for example, as they are of the desire for electric gadgets, junk food, or tobacco.[9] We do not condemn teachers of fine music or musicians because the tastes to which they cater must be acquired, and are acquired under their very influence. But this shows only that Galbraith's argument is incomplete, not that it is not enthymemically sound. When we have an *independent* criterion for wants worth fulfilling, then processes can be condemned which create those that fail to satisfy this criterion. One weak criterion that can be adopted from a want-regarding or utilitarian moral theory relates to whether satisfaction of the desires in question increases overall satisfaction in the long run, whether it contributes to fulfilled or worthwhile lives. Desires are irrational when their satisfaction is incompatible with more fundamental or long-range preferences, either because of harmful side effects or because of the creation of more unsatisfied desires. Alcoholism is an example of such irrational desire, the satisfaction of which is harmful overall. Desires for junk food, tobacco and certain kinds of conspicuous consumption are other examples, at least for certain consumers. Processes that create and feed such desires are not utility maximizing, since even the satisfaction of these desires lowers the subject's general level of utility in the long run. The pursuit of profit might well encourage the creation of such wants, especially desires for quickly consumable products. When this occurs, the appearance of efficiency masks a deeper utilitarian inefficiency. The profit motive contributes more to negative than positive utility, creating more unsatisfied than satisfied wants.

It has been argued also against Galbraith that most people are not so influenced by advertisement. They learn to be distrustful of claims made in ads and take them with a grain of salt. (In fact one writer has even suggested that truth in advertising regulations are counterproductive or self-defeating, since they encourage consumers to place more trust in claims of which they should be wary![10]) But while it is true that consumers become resistant to specific product claims of advertisers, it is not at all so clear that they can easily resist the total life style that bombards them constantly in subtle and not so subtle ways in ads for beer, cars, perfume, clothes and whatever else can be conspicuously consumed.[11] The desire for this life style may in turn influence particular desires for products or features of products that are irrational in the above sense and would not arise without this continuous programming. Consumers may desire fast and flashy automobiles more than safe ones; but this may be only because safety cannot be conspicuously consumed or because it does not provide the kind of dashing sexual allure that car advertisers attempt to project onto their products. If this preference is suspect in itself, it certainly appears more so when we recognize its source.

As is obvious in the case of junk food for children, in some industries there is a natural lack of rational restraint on the part of consumers, of which those out for maximum profits can take advantage. Other examples include the funeral and health care industries, in which otherwise rational adults are likely to be in vulnerable states of mind when purchasing products or services. In yet other industries consumers can be influenced to view certain products as symbols of a glamorous life style and desire them on those grounds. Furthermore, the encouragement of a life style of super consumption by numerous advertisers probably results in overproduction of consumable products and underutilization of resources for public goods that are not advertised, not conspicuously consumed, and less immediately enjoyed, for example clean air, water and soil, quality schools, etc. This adds to the effects of externalities mentioned above. The congruence between free market outcome and aggregate utility or social good is once more suspect.

Thus the pursuit of profit is efficient to the public only if it operates under certain moral constraints. Profit maximizing is not efficient or utility maximizing if it results in elimination of competition and hence of optimal prices, supplies and alternative for consumers, in deception regarding product defects or prices, in imposition of neighborhood costs, in the creation and exploitation of irrational desires, or in the neglect of needs and wants of those unable to express demand from lack of wealth.[12] It is likely to result in all of these if maximization of profits is accepted as the principal norm of business ethics. In at least some of these cases restraint can be exercised at the level of managerial decision. More strongly, I will argue below that it will not be effectively imposed in many cases unless voluntarily accepted on moral grounds by business managers.

We have countered also the claim (suggested early in the first section) that immorality in business is never profit maximizing in the long run. Certain immoral practices of a business will hurt its profits, since they will outrage the public, make consumers wary of the products of that business, and reduce demand for those products. Other objectionable practices, such as dishonesty toward suppliers or total callousness toward employees, will be damaging to the production process. The market does impose some moral constraints. But other practices, such as retaining defects in products while hiding them from the public (which is sometimes possible), inadequately servicing products, bribing officials or wholesale buyers, polluting and dumping wastes, creating desires for harmful products, or redlining loans in certain neighborhoods (by banks), might maximize profits while being inefficient to the consuming public.

PROFITS AND RIGHTS

From the point of view of a rights based moral theory, still other practices might be both profit maximizing and efficient in relation to consumers and yet morally questionable. This would be the case if a product were desired (or desired at low cost) by many and yet extremely harmful to relatively few. Nuclear power plants or glamorous yet potentially dangerous automobiles might be examples. In the former case aggregate utility might be maximized through cheap production of electricity, given enough customers who benefit. But is it justified to allow considerations of aggregate utility to outweigh the shortened lives of a few plant workers or neighborhood residents?

Another example in this category relates to work and working conditions. Total exploitation of workers, even if possible, might not be profit maximizing, since production suffers when employee morale sinks too low. But, as Henry Ford discovered long ago, productivity does not vary always with the meaningfulness of work; in fact, in certain contexts it may vary inversely with the interest and possibility for self-realization in work. Nor is consumer demand linked to these variables in working conditions. Profit maximization and efficiency to the consuming public therefore may call sometimes for reducing work to series of simple menial tasks. But the quality of people's lives depends substantially upon the type of work they do and their interest in it. Thus we may ask on moral grounds whether gains in efficiency or aggregate utility, as signaled by increased profit potential, justify reducing work to a menial and dehumanizing level.

Numerous other examples in this category involving workers or neighborhoods of production could be mentioned: questions such as the firing of longtime employees, or the relocation of businesses, in which profit maximization and even aggregate social utility might not be morally decisive. If rights figure in these contexts, then, as argued in previous chapters, aggregate or maximizing considerations drop out from the moral calculation. Whether rights do figure depends upon the importance of the individual interests at stake. Rights against severe harm without consent to risk or opportunity to avoid it, for example, clearly override utilities, and rights to a decent livelihood and to meaningful work may do so as well.

This last category of potentially profit maximizing immorality takes the argument to a new level. Prior paragraphs argued within a utilitarian moral framework: the point was to show how profit maximization may not be efficient in the deeper sense of utility maximization. But the cases just cited appeal to the notion of moral rights as opposed to aggregate utilities. We have defined rights as moral claims to goods or freedoms to act that override considerations of utility. To cite once more the example most dear to the present opposition, the fact that others might benefit more than I from my property does not in itself justify transferring it to them against my wishes, no matter how many might benefit. In the first section, the proponent of profit maximization argued that pursuit of profit in a free competitive market results in maximum efficiency, that is, in optimal allocation of resources for satisfying aggregate demand at least overall cost, and also honors rights and preserves freedoms by extending opportunities for free transactions. One who makes this claim might also argue against some of the initial utilitarian arguments in this section by appealing to rights. The argument that unsatisfied wants and low utility result from distribution by demand in a context of unequal wealth would be countered by appeal to individuals' rights to keep or spend what they earn and to be rewarded in relation to their productivity. Such distribution of rewards is more nearly approximated in a profit oriented free market than in other economies. If unfortunate inequalities result from acquisitions in accordance with rights (on this interpretation rights to free exchange and transfer) then, if they should be remedied at all (here there is disagreement among more or less libertarian philosophies), our first section protagonist would have this accomplished by direct redistribution, rather than by any interference with free market mechanisms. These are crucial both to efficiency and reward of productivity.

MAJORITY PREFERENCE   But appeal to a plausible full theory of rights undoubtedly favors counterarguments to the profit maximization principle. To the argument that business managers have no right to impose their moral opinions on the majority of consumers or upon stockholders, it can be replied that the majority has no right to maximal utility, or the stockholders to maximal profits, in violation of the moral rights of even a small minority. Thus even if the market reveals aggregate public preference for cheap electricity or flashy cars, even if the majority of consumers is willing to take and impose upon others the risks involved in generating electricity by unsafe nuclear reactors, and even if they are unwilling to pay for safety features that might be added to the cars, it is questionable whether they have a right to impose the risks and resulting severe harms on those who are unwilling to accept them. (The case is different if all are willing to take the risks and are equally exposed to them, or if those unwilling are able to avoid them without undue hardship.)

The appeal to the moral norms of the market itself and the

call to allow the public to impose its own norms through the mechanism of demand are also insufficient and in fact hollow. The market reveals both the preferences of consumers (sometimes based on ignorance or deception), as well as their willingness to pay for the protection of rights of others. But whether rights ought to be honored does not depend upon the willingness of the majority to bear the sacrifices involved in honoring them. When buying goods, most consumers are not concerned with whether processes of production impose severe harms or violate rights of others. But the effect of moral norms upon consumer demand is not a measure of the obligations they impose, nor even of their acknowledgment by individuals outside their roles as consumers. The business manager does not have the right to make decisions or retain products or production processes that maim, poison, severely deprive, or contaminate even a few individuals unwilling to take such risks in the name of efficiency to the public or profits to stockholders. In general, as we have seen before, one cannot morally do for others what they would be morally unjustified in doing for themselves. If people are not justified in imposing harms to secure conveniences, then business managers cannot appeal to desires for such conveniences, as reflected in projected demand, to justify imposing risks or harms.

The moral appeal of the market on the consumer side lies in its reflection of the desires of sizeable portions of the public. But that these local majorities or large minorities should not always be permitted to impose their desires upon smaller segments of the population is especially clear from the fact that the market reflects not only their defensible moral norms and their indifferences (regarding others' moral rights), but also their morally objectionable prejudices and fears. Real estate firms, for example, often find it highly unprofitable to attempt to show and sell housing in all White neighborhoods to Blacks. If word gets around that one firm out of several in an area does so, that firm can lose many listings and potential listings. Nevertheless, managers or brokers in such firms should not permit market demand for their services to dictate their decisions (even when such demand clearly reflects the senti-ments and preferences of the overwhelming majority in the neighborhood). They should not pursue maximum profits at the expense of potential Black clients. In many other situations in which moral rights of a minority oppose lesser interests or objectionable preferences of a majority, the latter will often predominate in projections of demand. The profit principle is morally unacceptable in such situations.

INTERNALIZATION OF COSTS   It is not sufficient that businesses internalize costs imposed upon the community or compensate victims of their products or production processes. This might be sufficient in cases like that of strip mining, where the costs of restoring land can be assigned to coal producers, but not when rights of persons against serious harm or risk are involved. In the former case full internalization of external costs is morally sufficient because the harm done the environment can be completely righted with enough corporate investment and commitment. In other cases of environmental ravaging such complete reversal is not possible; and in many cases imposing estimated costs upon the corporations will not be sufficient from a moral point of view. The reason is that cost internaliza-tion, when it is coupled with maximization of profit or net value to the public, still represents purely aggregative calcula-tion. But such purely economic reasoning may be out of place when the harms imposed upon the few are severe. They may not wish to be compensated for having been poisoned or having had their babies deformed, and they have a right to reject that reasoning which holds such compensation sufficient for allowing others to enjoy cheaper chemical products.

The libertarian economist tends to favor two methods of imposing external costs upon corporations. The first is by redefinition of property rights, so that those whose property values are lowered by air or noise pollution, for example, can collect compensation. The space above houses is in effect assigned to the property holders, so that those who invade it with noise or filth must pay to do so. The second method is to impose taxes upon the corporations equal to the total estimated cost to the public and then allow them to continue to operate to maximize profits within this altered framework. The former method is favored when specifiable individuals are adversely affected, for example those who live in the immediate vicinity of an airport or a chemical plant that dumps wastes into the air or water. The advantage of this method is that victims are compensated as well as costs imposed. The latter means of cost internalization is preferable when costs are widespread and imposed more or less evenly throughout the community. An example is air pollution from automobile exhaust. The advantage of taxation over other forms of regulation is that it permits firms who know their own production processes best to alter them in order to avoid the cost (while also avoiding litigation that may be prevalent under the first method). Taxation encourages firms to do so, however, within the limits of genuine costs to the public, as these are added to the other costs of the corporations and balanced against benefits as reflected in income. It therefore appears to be the most efficient way to handle externalities; hence its appeal to economists.

The economic merits of these ways of dealing with externalities also constitute their problems from a moral point of view. For they will reduce the harms imposed only to a level that at the same time maximizes aggregate net benefits to society as a whole. Again we see the purely utilitarian underpinnings of economic ways of thinking; again we may reiterate the ultimate incompatibility of these ways of thinking with moral viewpoints that take rights seriously. Simply attempting to compensate harms or impose charges for them in many cases will be morally insufficient and dangerous in masking their continued immorality. The user of the asbestos filled hair dryer may not be willing to contract cancer and be compensated for it (even if he could prove his case); similarly for the driver of the Pinto that explodes or the infant deformed by chemical waste. Rights are violated precisely when the harms imposed are so severe that we do not allow additions of lesser utilities to override.

While rights cannot be overridden by aggregate utility, they can be and sometimes are overridden by other rights. Thus at certain stages of economic development, when scarcity is still the rule and the means for survival of many people depend upon further growth, expansion of gross output spurred by the profit motive may be a reasonable social goal. But in such a case rights to survival and satisfaction of basic needs are at stake, not mere utility or efficiency. [13] At later stages of relative abundance, as in our society, whatever efficiency is generated by maxmization of profits cannot excuse violations of moral rights in the process. The rights and freedoms exemplified in free market exchange are only a small subclass of those potentially at stake in economic transactions and decisions. [14] If there are, in addition to rights to earn and spend money as one chooses, negative rights not to be severely harmed and positive rights to have basic needs fulfilled, then the latter will not be adequately protected by free market exchange when businessmen place profits first, even when all externalities are internalized.

The profit maximization principle then does not appear to be morally justifiable, except within ordinary moral constraints of honoring rights. It is not a matter of business managers imposing purely subjective opinions upon a majority who hold contrary opinions. When moral rights of the kind I have mentioned are violated, the harms imposed are severe. Such cases are relatively easy to identify. When the profit principle blinder is removed from the eyes of business executives, when consumers outside their roles as consumers are asked, they do not try to justify the imposition of such harms in the name of profit or efficiency. Indeed it is plausible to suppose that neither the public nor the majority of businessmen approve of the maximization of profit principle, not because they are confused about the operation of a free market or ignorant of its virtues, but because a theory of moral rights of the type I am presupposing here captures significant aspects of common sense moral consciousness. Rights against being harmed and to satisfaction of basic needs are seen to override considerations of efficiency or utility. When this theory is taken into account, the position of business manager does not appear to be strongly role differentiated. Profits cannot be placed above moral rights that impose constraints in all areas of nonprofessional behavior as well.

The Role of Law and Consumer Movements

RESTRAINT OF BUSINESS BY LAW

Although the notion of moral rights to which I appealed above is a prominent feature of our common moral framework, it is not prominent in the type of utilitarian theory generally assumed by economists in the background of their appraisals of free market mechanisms. For this reason, while many of the utility related failures of the free market have been noted by economists, the equally serious rights-based objection, perhaps the more obvious to laymen, has not been conspicuous in economic analyses. Perhaps another explanation for this neglect is yet another level of argument left to the proponent of profit maximization for business managers. He can admit the imperfections of the free market in imposing social costs and failing to adequately protect moral rights. Yet he might still argue that these imperfections ought to be remedied by the political process and imposed upon business through law, not left to the personal moral consciences of individual managers.

ADVANTAGES   There are several advantages to having moral constraints imposed by law. First, when social costs or protection of rights at the expense of profits are imposed upon business by law, the burdens are borne fairly by all concerns involved. More strongly, without legal imposition there exists a kind of Hobbesian situation in which the individual corporation that voluntarily accepts these costs or restraints simply places itself at a competitive disadvantage to those that do not accept them. To take the example of pollution, the company that refrains from eliminating wastes in the cheapest way when others continue to do so will have little effect upon overall pollution levels, but will have to price itself out of existence or lower its profit margin, which it may not be able to afford in a competitive industry. In that context, and with that projected result, it seems difficult to maintain that single corporations are morally obligated to accept the cost or restraint in question. But once sanctions are introduced, once all companies are subject by law to heavy taxes or fines for polluting, the desired result can be achieved through the operation of the profit principle itself, and no one will be placed at an unfair disadvantage.

The second advantage of imposing restraints upon business by law via collective political decision echoes a theme of the first section: the political process is a more certain indicator than personal decision by managers that the restraint imposed is genuinely necessary from the point of view of our social morality and that it will operate to protect the public. Once we grant full license to the business manager to introduce into his corporate decisions all moral parameters to which he is personally committed, once these decisions become colored by his favorite social cause, for example, their full effects become uncertain. It is true that the public good does not consist wholly in optimal allocation of economic resources; but it can be argued that such allocation is the particular expertise of the corporate manager in the pursuit of profit for which he is trained. To the extent that immoral or socially disadvantageous practices can be made unprofitable through legal means, we can ensure maximum efficiency within moral bounds through the continued pursuit of profit by business managers. In cases in which it is not morally sufficient that costs be internalized through redefinition of property rights or imposition of taxes, we can prohibit harmful activities absolutely by law. Again this method is more certain in its results and more fair in its distribution of obligations than is reliance upon corporate conscience.

This argument can be applied not only to internalization of social costs and prohibition of harm, but also to correction of other imperfections in the market. Direct redistribution of wealth where necessary, and limitation of the money supply and of government spending, are held preferable to managerial restraint in regard to prices. The redistribution will result in more efficient allocation of present and future resources and supplies, less disruption of the overall economy, and direct benefit to those most in need. If inflation will hurt those who already lack basic goods, then it should be collectively controlled, and the money needs of the individuals in question should be directly met. We can redistribute while leaving the profit motive intact as long as we do not tax away all incentive for additional income. Similarly, when an industry is not competitive, the answer to that problem is not managers with social conscience but action by government to make it more competitive. Again legal action will have more certain and regular desired effects. In general, when moral requirements can be achieved through legal means, so as to alter alternatives that maximize profits while allowing pursuit of profit to continue unhindered, we can honor rights without unduly disrupting efficiency. The conclusion is that we ought to do this, and the reply of our opponent to the argument of the previous section is that the businessman should continue to place profits first within this altered legal and social context. He should do so, it is maintained, for reasons of economic efficiency, while the political process should create the framework in which profit oriented managerial decisions are both efficient and rights preserving.

LIMITATIONS   The premises of this counterargument should convince us that it is best, where possible, to protect the moral rights at issue by means of law. We can admit this while recognizing the price that must be paid. Expansion of government bureaucracy is one cost, but there is a more subtle ethical sacrifice involved. When acceptance of moral restraint is imposed by law or made to accord with self-interest or profit, actions that obey it may not be performed for moral reasons or have moral worth. Moral character, the disposition to do what is right, is more difficult to build and test when fewer challenges to self-interest are permitted. The gravity of this price derives not from some Puritanical value to self-denial itself, but from the need for moral fiber in those situations in which the right course of action genuinely opposes self-interest, even in the long run. Morality cannot be made always congruent with self-interest, and the illusion that it can is dangerous to moral character and action. The additional protection of rights afforded by law and the fairer distribution of burdens make it worth the price in this context, however, to establish a coercive social framework in which prudential or profit oriented incentives or sanctions incline those subject to them to do what is right.

But there is weakness in any Hobbesian argument that attempts to equate rightness with self-interest within such a framework, or, less strongly, to apologize self-interested or profit oriented action within this framework. There will always remain situations, in business many of them, in which sanctions or incentives cannot guarantee congruence between self-interest and rightness. Such situations will remain either because lawmakers are simply ignorant of them, because the costs of attempting to apply the law to them are too great, because those clever enough can evade the force of law, or because those subject to the law can influence legislation. Even when legal property and contract rights are redefined and producers are held strictly liable for harms they cause to innocent consumers and residents, they still may find it cheaper to retain the defects or dangerous methods of waste disposal and compensate victims when necessary. Exactly that kind of reasoning appears to have been involved in the Ford Pinto case. In the example of the real estate broker, it certainly may be more profitable despite the law to discriminate against Black clients, perhaps in ways slightly more subtle than traditionally necessary. This is a case in which the majority of potential customers might well prefer that the law be broken. The reflection of this preference in market demand for the services of the broker differentiates this case from certain others. But the example also illustrates another weakness in exclusive reliance upon law to restrain market forces, the fact that the difficulty of enforcing the law and the costs involved in doing so render it impossible to protect moral rights through this means alone.

The law is a blunt instrument in relation to all morally relevant features of business decisions, even when it is filtered through such regulatory agencies as the Consumer Product Safety Commission or Environmental Protection Agency. And the costs involved in imposing it are often forgotten in Hobbesian arguments of this type. It might be objected that such costs are irrelevant to the argument for profit maximization, since proponents of that principle for business urge willing acceptance of legal limits. They do not argue that the law against fraud, for example, should be broken whenever it is profitable to do so. Indeed they recognize that arguments which link pursuit of profits to utility maximization depend upon managers' "playing within the rules," where the rules in question are those imposed by the legal framework (libertarian complaint of too much legal regulation is of course not uncommon either). Support for the profit maximization principle, when this is coupled with a call to comply voluntarily with law appears to render irrelevant claims that businessmen can maximize profits by ignoring law.

This objection takes us back, however, to arguments of the second chapter that (except in the case of law enforcement officials) an obligation to obey law cannot substitute for primary obligations to honor moral rights, and to arguments of the third chapter that legal rights will never fully duplicate their moral counterparts. There is first of all often a time lag between the imposition of wrongful harm and its prohibition by law. Second, there is the influence of corporate power in the formulation of law, the attempt to weaken regulation in order to continue maximizing profits. Third, it is necessary for the sake of clarity and enforceability of the law to define such concepts as fraud and coercion narrowly within it. But we have seen that the actions of managers can have the effects of these morally objectionable actions without falling within their narrower definitions. These three reasons render it highly unlikely that strict observance of law could ever adequately protect moral rights under a maximization of profit principle.

CONSUMER AGENCIES AND ORGANIZATIONS

Proponents of profit maximization can reply finally that gaps in the present law are partially filled by public and private consumer organizations that arise naturally within a market situation to offset concentrated power within business and protect the values and interests of the public. Such groups can expose defects in products and harmful practices, and their influence can be added to that of legislation in altering the framework in which business managers must project long-range profit. But it remains clear that even this doubly altered framework is insufficient to protect moral rights when profits are placed first. The problems mentioned above apply equally here.

A serious oversight of the "leave it to law" position mentioned briefly above that applies here as well is the fact that the law itself often fails to mirror the public interest precisely because it is shaped by those attempting to maximize profits. If this goal motivates lobbying activities in both Congress and in the regulatory agencies that it establishes, then the law and the agencies established through it will fail to restrain business adequately. Cases of lobbying against protection of consumer rights are too numerous to mention. It is charged, for example, in the present negligent homicide case against Ford Motor Company that the corporation knowingly decided to sacrifice consumers' lives rather than add a protective shield for eleven dollars to the gasoline tanks on Pintos. It then engaged in a vigorous lobbying campaign to delay and weaken regulations on strength of fuel systems in automobiles.[15]

A problem with relying on private agencies to fill the gap is the fact that information provided to consumers by watchdog groups often reaches only those least likely to be duped without it. Relevant also are the small budgets of many of these agencies and the lack of technical expertise routinely at the disposal of businesses. Such groups generally learn of harmful product defects and practices only long after serious harm has occurred in several cases. Even then they lack the funds to do anything about it, as in the case of the EPA and the scandalous practice of chemical waste dumping. Corporations themselves typically know of potentially harmful products and practices before regulatory agencies and watchdog groups do. However, their market analyses may reveal it to be profitable to ignore them until recall is made mandatory or practices forbidden by laws that are enforced. Recall and lawsuits from those harmed may be less costly than initial addition of safety features, remedy of defects, or that purify processes waste. And by the time recall or enforcement occurs, if it does at all, harms will have been suffered and rights violated.

Numerous examples in addition to the Ford case and that of chemical companies come to mind. One which the law has not touched involves selling off drugs deemed unsafe and/or impotent by our Food and Drug Administration in foreign markets that lack the same regulatory restrictions. Certainly this practice is likely to be profit maximizing (or loss minimizing), and this is unlikely to be changed by an altered legal or consumer oriented market framework. Consumers here are unlikely to become very concerned about practices that do not affect them at all, and our laws will not forbid sales of products in foreign markets by corporations located there as well. But the immorality of this practice, the violation of rights of innocent people to be spared such risk and deception, is equally clear.

Morality and Self-interest

The initial argument of the last section seemed to assume that protection of rights by law and their protection by voluntary acceptance of moral responsibility are mutually exclusive. Of course this is not the case. And if the former is insufficient, then the latter must be required as well. Just as the businessman ought not to try to evade justifiable law for the sake of profit, so he should not violate rights against harm or deception in the absence of law. It is not enough to say that such practices should be illegal or that consumer groups should make sure that they will not be profitable. The point is that some practices should be illegal or unprofitable which in fact are neither (and some are wrong but too costly to make illegal). The search for egoistic reasons always to be moral fails here as elsewhere. Morality does sometimes demand sacrifice of self-interest and also of efficiency. We conclude again despite this further appeal to law and the market that the businessman can justifiably pursue profit only subject to ordinary moral constraints imposed by rights, as these represent overriding interests of individuals not to suffer harm, deception, or deprivation.

THE HOBBESIAN ARGUMENT

It remains to answer an earlier argument that also has its prototype in Hobbes. This was the consequentialist argument that when competitors are pursuing self-interest without moral restraint, acceptance of an obligation at the sacrifice of one's interest simply places one at a competitive disadvantage without positive effect. This argument has considerable force in its original Hobbesian context of the state of nature, when survival was said to be at stake and self-sacrifice was to be taken in its most literal sense. It has far less force when what is at stake on the one side is maximal profits for a business and on the other severe harm to or deception of innocent individuals. The lower level employee who stands to lose his job if he blows the whistle on a company practice that is deceptive but not seriously harmful has some excuse for remaining silent. He is entitled perhaps to count his own interest and that of his family on the same scale as that of those duped by the practice (although his complicity and their innocence makes even this questionable, especially if he could find another job). But since this is all he is entitled to from a moral point of view, as the potential harm from the practice increases, the excuse fades. Its force varies with the gravity of the rights being violated and with the severity of sacrifice from noncooperation in the wrongdoing by the employee (with some extra weight for the former). Higher-ups generally lack this type of excuse, since it is less likely that their positions will be at stake.

Even from a purely consequentialist viewpoint, acceptance of this Hobbesian argument appears to be inconsistent. For the consequence of allowing injustice on the ground that others are committing it with personal gain is that any injustice becomes excusable if it is widespread enough. And injustice is likely to be widespread indeed once this excuse is granted. One cannot therefore claim a right to do wrong by complaining that others are benefitting from their wrong actions and that it is an unfair disadvantage when one cannot join in. If there is any force to this complaint, it is that the others should be made to stop, not that anyone who so chooses should be permitted to participate in the wrongdoing. The notion of an equal right to do wrong is simply contradictory.

Hobbes' argument, when removed from the context of the state of nature, in which moral rules cannot be applied at all, needs to be turned on its head. Consider again the case of pollution, in which the argument is most plausible (and yet still unacceptable). There it is claimed that when others are polluting, an individual corporation that refrains is placing itself at a disadvantage without significantly affecting overall pollution levels; and that when others are not eliminating wastes in this way, one corporation's doing so is unlikely to cause major harm to the environment. In both cases the contribution of the single business firm is said to be relatively minimal and therefore inconsequential. To this it can be replied that when others are polluting and the extent of wrongdoing is being used as an excuse for it, one has additional reason to refrain, in order not to contribute to this excuse; and that when others are not polluting, one has an additional duty of fair play to refrain as well. Being a free rider and accepting the benefits of others' restraints while refusing to do one's part is wrong in itself, wrong because it assumes an unfair advantage, resulting in an unfair distribution of burdens and benefits. In regard to the consequences, it is generally not true that the harm caused by actions of single corporations is negligible. It is not the case that those poisoned by the wastes of a particular chemical company would have been otherwise poisoned by some other company, or that those burned by exploding gasoline tanks would have been otherwise burned in some other automobiles. And in any case it is the cumulative effects of accepting the argument at issue that must be considered from a consequentialist viewpoint.

Thus the fact that businesses which refrain from harming or deceiving at the expense of profits place themselves at a competitive disadvantage affords no excuse for the business manager to place profits above ordinary moral rights. Nor, as I argued before, is it an excuse that he acts in behalf of stockholders. Professionals cannot delegate moral responsibility to those for whom they are agents and at the same time accept power to make decisions in their behalf. Stockholders can expect only reasonable returns on their money from business processes within moral constraints, not maximal profits at the expense of moral rights of others. Neither the preference for convenience of the majority of consumers, as expressed through market demand, nor the profits of stockholders can justify violating the rights of a minority. We may appeal again to the general principle than one normally cannot morally do for others what one could not morally do for oneself. Love, for spouses or children for example, might excuse exceptions to this rule. But relations between managers, consumers and stockholders are no more intrinsically valuable loving relationships than are those between lawyers and clients. Strong role differentiation for professionals requires other justification in terms of the instrumental necessity of the norm in question. And that justification, we have seen, is far more difficult to provide.

DEGREE OF ROLE DIFFERENTIATION

CHARITABLE CONTRIBUTIONS   In clarifying the final position that emerges here, it is important to distinguish between the prohibition against violating moral rights and any demand to give aid to charitable or cultural institutions.[16] It would be wrong for a corporate manager to forego paying all dividends in order to aid his favorite worthy cause (needless to say, this is not a major problem in practice for business ethics). But since stockholders are more like bondholders (or, less respectfully, like gamblers) than like laboreres who work hard for their earnings,[17] I do not believe that we need to restrict even corporate contributions of this sort to what will be profitable in the long run. If stockholders were owed not only their shares, but the highest attainable return on them, then all unprofitable philanthropy on the part of business would be ruled out. If I owe someone a certain sum, then the fact that the money might be used for better purposes does not free me from my obligation to repay the entire debt, rather than using it for the better cause. But it has not been shown, although it is often assumed in argument, that stockholders are entitled to maximal returns. As in the context of legal ethics, this premise, where it is not simply assumed, appeals for support to the "understanding" with which stockholders invest their money. Given this understanding or expectation on their part, it is said to be a breach of trust for managers not to aim at maximum profits. But why they are entitled to this expectation, which is never explicitly stated in contract, is not demonstrated. Expectations for profits at the price of injustice are simply not legitimate expectations, as we argued in the chapter on legal ethics. What of expectations for maximal returns short of violating rights? The first question is the extent to which such expectations or desires exist.

There is then another fallacy in the argument from stockholders' rights similar to one encountered in the context of legal ethics. This is the implicit assumption that stockholders (or clients) prefer having their most narrow and partisan self-interests pushed to the extreme. In this instance the assumption is that they desire maximal dividends at the expense of corporate moral responsibility. If anything, the trend in recent years seems to have been more in the direction of stockholders' pressuring managers at meetings to act more responsibly. There was one case in 1961 of a stockholder of Standard Oil of New Jersey who moved to bar corporate philanthropic contributions, but such suggestions have not been generally supported by others. Friedman and his followers argue that, if shareholders want to contribute to charity, they can do so on their own, from their own dividend earnings if they so choose. He holds that they ought to be given the choice of doing so, rather than having their legtimately owned funds expropriated for philanthropic purposes without their consent and often without their knowledge.[18] But it is not as if stockholders separately had the resources to fund projects that organized corporate funds can. We enounter here another version of a fallacious pattern of reasoning apparently common in professional ethics: a fallacy in reasoning from individual actions to their cumulative effects. Corporate organization can be a force for much social good in this context, much of which would remain unfunded by separate shareholders in the absence of knowledge that others were contributing a proportionate amount. A majority of shareholders themselves might therefore wish to participate in such organized contribution. (Regarding the distinction between charitable contribution and restraint from harming or violating rights, we certainly cannot assume that stockholders would approve of the latter as the price of profits.)

There might still be some question whether the majority of stockholders would have the right to commit the minority who might not want to contribute in this fashion. We may also ask whether actual as opposed to assumed consent of stockholders is necessary for justified corporate contribution. But the relevance of both these questions depends upon stockholders' having rights to maximal profits or earnings on their investments. Even if they all would demand maximal returns from managers, their authority to do so has not been established. Of course they are not required to invest their money in any particular corporations. Those who disapprove of charitable contribution can find out in advance whether particular firms engage in this practice and withhold their money from those that do. The conclusion is that if a cause is worthy and present stockholders continue to earn a reasonable return on their money, corporate charitable contribution should not be condemned on the ground that they deserve some higher maximum return. (Of course much contribution is defended on the ground that it is projected to be profit maximizing, in terms of advertisement, good will, or product related research.)

As for the argument that corporate ability to contribute excess profits elsewhere shows lack of healthy competition in the industry, the reply is that this point is irrelevant to the moral status of the contributions. The latter does not create the lack of competitors, and disbursing the earnings to stockholders instead would not bring about a return to conditions of perfect competition. From the standpoint of a single company, rather than that of a whole industry, high earnings might represent efficiency, as the economist argues elsewhere. If it is said that these earnings should be devoted instead to development of still greater efficiency through modernization of equipment, research, etc., the reply is that corporate contribution is generally so limited a percentage of gross income as to be inconsequential to such other uses.

The weaker prohibition against jeopardizing the corporation's financial position through charitable contribution does not amount to strong role differentiation for businessmen, but is simply part of ordinary moral responsibility in handling material assets of others. It does not constitute a special norm for managers that overrides ordinary moral considerations, but simply an application of the property rights of stockholders. We have an instance here of a generally applicable rule that those entrusted with property of others ought not to sacrifice it in ways of which the owners would disapprove (here the rule applies only to the principal funds and a reasonably expected return on them). Nevertheless, this rider makes it clear that the correct position on the social responsibility of business falls between that which calls upon business to cure all social ills and that which excuses it from all ordinary moral responsibility.[19]

CONCLUSION

Given the conceptual framework in which we are operating here, we can say once more that the manager's responsibility to stockholders and employees alike to act for the good of the corporation defines his position as weakly role differentiated. The stronger concept was said to apply when special professional norms override moral considerations that are otherwise crucial, more specifically, moral rights that normally obtain. We have seen that the manager is not to violate moral rights in the interest of his corporation. But neither is he to jeopardize that interest by aiding worthy causes. Such causes and those they represent have no rights to specific contributions, although contribution to them is morally praiseworthy in the absence of conflicting specific obligations. Here the role of manager generates such specific obligations to stockholders and employees. We have defined a position as weakly role differentiated when it systematically involves relatively unique relations to others that define certain obligations to them. The position of corporate manager meets that definition. But since these obligations arise from the direct application of common moral principles to the relations between managers and stockholders, rather than from the existence of special principles unique to the profession, the more interesting stronger concept does not apply.

The power that corporate assets bring to managers requires in addition to obligations to stockholders and employees certain restrictions on the managers' pursuit of their own moral values or political ideals. There is after all some truth to the claim that executives ought not to try to impose their moral views in areas in which they lack expertise and authority.

(Unsound but initially plausible arguments of this type often derive their plausibility from narrower areas in which they do apply.) It would be highly improper, for example, for an executive of a corporation with great economic power in a town in which it is located to use that power to attempt to dictate courses at a local college, political views to be expressed in the local newspaper, dress to be worn on the streets of the town, or the sexual practices of its inhabitants. Such intrusions upon fundamental freedoms would be illegitimate for the business manager for the same reason that they would be illegitimate for the politician, simply because they constitute obstructions to important liberties.

The lack of authority to use corporate powers in these ways should not be confused with a claimed lack of authority to forego profits for moral reasons involving rights, or to make corporate contributions to nonpolitical worthy causes. Such confusion may be responsible for some attacks on the idea of corporate social responsibility. As for the question of whether use of corporate power for self-interested political lobbying is morally objectionable, a full answer would require an essay in political philosophy beyond our scope. Such use of economic clout might be held to constitute excessive influence in violation of the one-person-one-vote ideal. But given acceptance of our political system, in most respects a thoroughgoing pressure group system as opposed to a Rousseauian democracy, corporate lobbying cannot be condemned across the board. We must draw the line only at attempts to block legislation or regulation designed to protect the public from harm imposed by the corporation or its products. Such lobbying is objectionable not because it seeks the corporate self-interest, but because it is part of a larger violation of the duty not to harm.

In denying strong role differentiation for managers, we may again admit that many of the concrete and specific moral problems encountered in business emerge in their full complexity only once we reject the primacy of profit principle. As in the context of legal ethics, rejection of the dominant simplifying norm greatly complicates the moral universe for

business. To take one example, the question of what to do with
an employee of twenty-five years who is no longer performing
competently, simplified if company profits alone are relevant
(although even then employee morale must be considered),
becomes more difficult once additional factors are admitted
into the calculation. As with moral problems in law, we cannot
provide pat answers to such classes of cases under application
of our full set of common moral principles until more details
are known about specific instances. In this case the manager
would have to judge the importance of the position in question, the harm from lack of competence in it to consumers and
to the corporation, the effect upon other employees; also the
effect of forced retirement on the person's life, the available
pension, his other financial resources, whether some token
position can be found for him within the corporation, his
reaction to the offer of such a position, etc.

In many of the cases I cited earlier in the chapter the violation
of moral rights was clear, and the moral prohibition equally
clear once primacy of profit is denied. But many other
examples are more like the one of the employee—cases involving relocation of corporate branches and workers, working conditions, wages, and so on. Once the pursuit of profit
principle is rejected, it can also be pointed out that duties of
benevolence for managers may extend beyond observance of
negative rights. A different kind of case involves products of
good quality that are safe when used properly, but dangerous
when used in negligent ways. Producers ought to try to
minimize the chances of misuse through adequate warning and
perhaps through alteration of features that account for the
possible danger. They ought to do so whether or not it is profit
maximizing, and whether or not adult consumers have rights
to be protected from their own stupidity.

Thus our main conclusion is that the position of the business
manager is not strongly differentiated. He must make decisions within a moral framework defined by principles and
rights applicable with the same force in nonprofessional contexts. Adherence to such principles does not require any

special expertise at judging cumulative economic effects; often it requires only the removal of institutional blinders. This moral framework can be imposed upon business partially through legal and market pressures, as consumers and stockholders come to realize their share of the moral responsibility for protection of their own as well as others' moral rights. But the manager himself must recognize rights as constraints upon profitability, rather than assuming that moral considerations will fall into place within a framework of long-range profit projection.

Not only economists and Hollywood script writers, but many philosophers have spilled much ink trying to show how acting morally must be profitable in the long run, and conversely how evil cannot pay. Business provides some of the many examples in which neither conjunct is true, in which moral demands require sacrifice without expected greater returns to self-interest in the future. We certainly can forgive Adam Smith for taking the remarkable regularities he discovered in the apparently chaotic mesh of self-interested strivings to be a sign of benevolent design, of an invisible hand guiding egotistic individualism toward aggregate social good. But by now the familiar Argument From Design should have been adequately countered by the equally familiar Argument From Evil, the recognition of imperfections in the market that often make its design seem more the work of an evil demon that of a benevolent deity.

As we have seen the incompatibility of self-interest with moral demands, so once more a second incompatibility has been revealed between aggregative and rights based reasoning. It was first suspect whether a free market, even when regulated by law, is utility maximizing. More important, even if it were, it was shown that this would often be at the expense of moral rights. The justification of pursuit of profit in terms of aggregate welfare considerations turns out to be incompatible with the ideal of individualism invoked in the claim that the free market maximizes opportunity for choice. The protection of moral rights basic to the integrity of individuals is required to guarantee maximal choice: when individuals are severely harmed or their basic needs denied, their meaningful choices are curtailed as well.

As always, a strong burden of proof must remain with those who would continue to press the opposing case. Again the final consideration relates to the kind of people we desire professionals, including businessmen, to be. As we have seen in other contexts, acceptance of strong role differentiation involves a moral price, since it encourages occupants of the role in question to become insensitive to the common moral rights of others. It is a price that sometimes must be paid, as in the case of judges, who are obligated to make legally correct decisions even when these run counter to their perceptions of the extra-legal moral factors of the cases. But departure from common moral principle in favor of professional norms would be most dangerous perhaps in the case of business, in which the central norm is linked to personal gain directly, rather than to justice or the immediate good of others, as in law and medicine. Even if the profit maximization principle did most effectively serve the public good or somehow maximize satisfaction of rights, we should be wary of pressing it upon businessmen as superseding direct appeal to common moral principle. It would still be problematic to claim that we should encourage people to place egoistic considerations first, to treat others as commodities, utility vessels, or means to profit, to treat all moral demands as hypothetical imperatives only, as directives toward long-range profit. We cannot expect individuals outside their professional roles to respect norms that place no restraints upon their professional self-interest. The legitimization of pure self-interest and lack of moral restraint by appeal to the marketplace is as dangerous as its legitimization by the anonymity of the mob. Dilution of moral responsibility into a moral division of labor in which everyone claims to be doing for others what he would be ashamed to do for himself, and in which each is at the same time pursuing his own narrow interests, cannot create a morally healthy climate, a climate in which individuals allow adequate moral space for other persons. Here the shift from considerations of maximizing good or rightness to developing moral character only reinforces what was shown before: that the case for strong role differentiation in business according to the maximization of profit principle cannot prevail.

6

Conclusion

We have now played out five variations on the same theme. Only one ended on an affirmative note. Symmetry and balance might have called for several variations on each side. Unfortunately in philosophy we are not free to write the score from scratch, but must follow where the arguments take us. Here, after our initial example of law enforcement, they took us eventually in the same direction each time, although by rather different routes.

Our theme has been the extent to which professionals must operate within different moral frameworks. By 'different' we referred not merely to the unique interpersonal relations defined by professional practices, but, more interestingly, to the appeal to special norms and principles that are taken in professional contexts to override normally relevant moral rights. The argument for strong role differentiation for judges and other enforcement officials was upheld. The norm there requires deference to law and to legally correct decisions. It limits the authority of such officials to act on their own moral perceptions, and so to some degree limits their responsibility for the moral consequences of their legally required decisions. The reasons for this limitation consist in the fallibility of these individuals in predicting the cumulative effects of their decisions upon the law itself; the need for consistency, predictability and stability within the law and legal system; and the need to check their power with that of legislators more subject to the will of the majority.

Legislators and other politicians, it was argued, only appear to have strongly differentiated roles. This appearance is projected from the fact that makers of social policy more often than the rest of us must sacrifice the satisfaction of certain moral rights to that of others. But the orderings that dictate proper social policy in these cases are imposed by our common moral framework, not by norms peculiar to politics. Moral rights could not long survive the latter.

Certain arguments supporting the special norm prevalent in the legal profession, that of strong client advocacy, were analogous to those regarding the proper conduct of judges. Proponents express fear of the cumulative effect of refusal of legal aid on moral grounds, fear that unpopular clients will remain unrepresented and that an oligarchy of lawyers will substitute itself for the system of legislatively and judicially determined legal rights. The autonomy of clients within the legal system therefore seemed to call for full power to exercise legal rights, and that seemed to imply full legal aid from attorneys without their acceptance of direct moral restraints. Here we counterargued that lawyers do not collectively impose their moral views on clients, who are free to seek other lawyers; that they lack systematic effects upon the law; that representation of unpopular clients can be distinguished from representation by objectionable tactics; that the proper domain of individual autonomy is delineated by the system of moral rights itself; that protection of that domain requires respect for those rights by lawyers as well as others; that the law in itself can never adequately protect moral rights if they are not respected on more direct moral grounds; and that full advocacy results in an unfair distribution of legal expertise with undue influence upon outcomes of legal conflicts.

We saw in the next chapter that doctors, unlike lawyers, tend to assume greater rather than lesser authority than normal for decisions primarily involving others. This authority in medical contexts over decisions regarding treatment is presumed justified by the medical expertise and by the calm and objectively detached viewpoint of the doctor. We argued that it nevertheless presupposes a controversial value ordering in which health and longevity are placed above all else by the patient. The possible falsity of this assumption, its failure to correspond to preferences apparent in much of our personal activity and social policy, leaves the criterion for justified paternalism unsatisfied in typical doctor-patient situations. That criterion requires for the justification of interference that the agent otherwise be acting incompatibly with his own long-range stable values and preferences. That this cannot be generally assumed in medical contexts implies that patients must be free to make their own medical decisions, with the doctor's role limited to that of provider of information, advisor, and agent enacting the patient's choices (if these do not violate the doctor's own personal moral beliefs). Truth must be told when it is relevant to such decisions, in light of the supremacy of the rights to self-determination and bodily integrity, fundamental rights indeed within our common framework.

The chapter on business measured the virtues of the profit motive in a free competitive market against the values that appear to be violated by its single-minded pursuit. Profit maximization was seen to be efficient from a broad utilitarian perspective only given certain constraints and ideal conditions. More important, the unhindered operation of the market under the whip of profit and wealth accumulation instantiates certain economic liberties at the expense of moral rights seemingly more important, including rights to be spared unnecessary risk and harm and to have basic needs fulfilled. We pointed out lastly the inadequacy of opposing forces within the competitive social and economic framework, specifically the law and consumer agencies, for fully protecting these vital rights and interests. Business managers, as others, must sacrifice personal, and in this case corporate, self-interest when moral demands require them to do so. Nor can their duties to stockholders, any more than lawyers' duties to clients, excuse their ignoring the rights of innocent third parties, nor their attempts to incorporate these rights into aggregate cost-benefit analyses that must undervalue them in moral terms.

The playing out of these variations, almost invariably ending on the same note, i.e. the reaffirmation of the supremacy of common moral rights, might have been unduly repetitious, were they not so out of tune with assumptions and behavior (often well-intentioned) prevalent within the professions themselves. Then, too, the arguments supportive of the central norms in the different professions were quite distinct from one another, and therefore required separate consideration. I hope to have done them full justice. Undoubtedly there are better arguments to be made for conclusions opposing mine. I have not found them in the literature or in the professional codes themselves. Their statements would be a welcome response to this book, which will become, it is hoped, a chapter in an ongoing public debate.

Given that the arguments in the different areas are distinct, the fact that many led to similar conclusions does not make me fully confident that this would continue to be the case for inquiries into moral foundations of other professions. I have only touched upon several of the major ones, trying to compromise between tedious repetition and length on the one hand, and superficial, insufficient treatment of the foundational question on the other. Unfinished business remains not only because, as acknowledged several times earlier, many of the concrete problems in professional practice emerge in their full complexity only after these foundational questions are answered, and not only because better arguments will be forthcoming from opposing sides, but also because these very foundational issues can be raised with profit for other professions.

Journalists, for example, must grapple with the question of strong role differentiation both in regard to confidentiality of news sources and in regard to printing items harmful to the individuals concerned or to the general reading public. We saw that issues of confidentiality arise for lawyers and doctors as well. I have maintained that their duties in that regard can be understood by appeal both to backward-looking principles relating to privacy and promises (explicit and implicit) and to future-looking consequentialist principles, all contained in our common framework. But confidentiality enters perhaps more centrally into the practice of journalism, and perhaps the duties of journalists in this regard are therefore more stringent. In regard to potentially harmful news stories, there is certainly a real and pressing question whether individual journalists should attempt to estimate directly benefits and harms in this area, or whether their professional duty to report items of interest and importance to the public should be placed first.

Teachers and professors, to cite another example, have a similar problem in relation to research. Scientific research with potentially dangerous technological or social offspring in an obvious case in which the question of professional role differentiation is crucial. We have seen many instances in recent years, from nuclear physics to genetic biology to sociological investigations into the relative intelligence of members of different racial groups. Can professional, in this case academic, license or duty to seek and report the truth in such areas override the potential social harm from the findings no matter how disastrous?

Another area in which teachers encounter the issue of role differentiation is the grading of students. Grades of course do not merely report evaluations of work to the students themselves; they serve the academically superfluous but socially vital function of sorting people for later educational opportunities and careers. Their personal importance to students can therefore be enormous, and their psychological effects sometimes devastating. Nevertheless, the academic norm holds that students should be graded on grounds of the quality of their work alone, that factors normally relevant in interactions with other persons, such as drastic effects of actions on their well-being and life prospects, are to be ignored in grading decisions. This norm not only reflects the academic purpose of grading, but appears necessary to its social function as well. In addition, the competence of teachers to judge relative overall effects, including psychological effects, of grades upon different students can be questioned, as well as their ability to estimate the cumulative effect of their departures from the norm, and, most important, the fairness of their doing so. The norm itself can therefore be well supported by argument similar to that in the case of judges.

Despite this, I believe many teachers do make various allowances in deviating from this norm in grading. I do not hold in general that current professional practice must be given great moral weight, as is obvious from the fact that I have not hesitated to criticize the prevalent norms and practices in other areas. But here is a case in which current practice deviates widely from the professed norm rather than following it. We may wonder whether all those who depart from it should be condemned. First, it can be questioned whether considerations of fairness call for building such factors as effort and prior educational handicaps into the norm itself. Second, we may ask when, if ever, departures from it on broader or more personal consequentialist grounds are justified.

Examples from the different professions can be easily multiplied. My purpose is not to pursue them here. I shall mention only one more class of cases, since they exemplify the issue of authority to act on direct moral perception, the issue with which we have been grappling in different forms, particularly vividly. The nursing profession illustrates the type of case I have in mind, in which one predominant norm calls for deferral to authority of particular other individuals within the professional context. Many obvious questions arise regarding degree of limitation upon the authority of nurses themselves to act in medical contexts, emergency and otherwise. Such issues become acute when those in the subordinate positions disagree with the decisions of those in charge on professional or moral grounds. Similar moral issues directly concerning limitations upon authority and responsibility arise, of course, for those in military service and in such paramilitary organizations as police forces. They arise in fact within any organized hierarchy in which fixed lines of authority are officially recognized. I touched briefly on one example, that of the middle-level business executive. Discussion of other professions would place more emphasis on this issue that surely deserves more treatment than it has received in the philosophical literature.

Such issues for other professions, variations of those we discussed in relation to politics, law, medicine and business, as well as more concrete issues to be approached after settling the question of role differentiation, I shall refrain from pursuing further. The arguments we did pursue were themselves sufficiently similar at least to make clear the nature of the fundamental question and how it might be raised elsewhere. Certain subordinate themes recurred: fallibility in predicting cumulative effects of individual actions based on direct moral perception; autonomy of clients, third parties, and professionals themselves; and checks upon the power of persons in official positions by other officials and laymen. The conclusions drawn relating to both officials within the legal system and other professionals perhaps enable us to predict by analogies and differences (although not with full confidence until specific arguments are examined) how the question will be answered in other areas.

As noted, principles supported in these conclusions differ sharply from the central norms accepted by professionals themselves and from the status they accord to those norms, most strikingly in the case of lawyers. Conclusions so at variance with prevalent practice, itself the result of long historical tradition, might appear cause for embarrassment or apology. It may appear presumptuous to dismiss ethical systems that can claim to embody the combined wisdom of centuries of social development. The principle of lawyer advocacy is a case in point, embedded as it is firmly within our legal and broader social systems.

There are two reasons why neither apology nor even hesitation in opposing these predominant professional norms is necessary. The first is that philosophical criticism is by nature radical, radical in the sense of exposing and questioning the root assumptions of other academic disciplines, of moral systems and social practices. One must evaluate these practices, as I have attempted, by summoning the best reasons that one can to support them, and then by seeing whether these can withstand sustained counterargument. In doing so one cannot grant much weight to the fact that such practices are predominant in a particular society, even if that society happens to be our own (in the case of strong lawyer advocacy, no other society instantiates this norm to the same degree). Appreciation of the historical tradition behind these norms is necessary to causally explaining and understanding their present status, but not to their moral support or lack of it.

The second justification for the boldness of our appraoch is precisely that present professional practices are to be explained more by those historical traditions than by the moral arguments that can be summoned to support them. Our theme has concerned questions of authority and responsibility, limitations and argumentations of the authority of professionals to act on their own direct moral perceptions. Moral theory has rarely distinguished these questions of authority to act from questions regarding the rightness or wrongness of actions on general moral criteria.[1] In the professional context this distinction is crucial, and general moral theory has at least this much to learn from professional ethics. It is clear in practice that assumption of authority as well as disclaimers of responsibility by members of social groups are more linked to political and economic forces, and to the political, economic and social interests of those groups than are opinions on more general questions of right and wrong. The prestige of the professions, their economic and political independence, derive not only from the special expertise of their members, and from their control over acquisition and application of this knowledge, but also from the group solidarity that is reinforced and expressed in special ethics and codes of behavior, set apart from the morality of the common person. The extraordinary authority of the doctor in medical contexts contributes to his prestige on the social ladder; the ability of the lawyer to disclaim responsibility for clients' decisions is to his economic and political advantage, especially in the corporate sphere; the congruence between the self-interest of business managers and the principle of profit maximization goes without saying; and the politician's disdain for moral rights can also be self-serving, as we have seen in recent years.

From the individual professional's point of view the adoption of a special professional ethic can enhance the identification with colleagues that in itself is a source of personal satisfaction and pride. The professional code, like the special technical jargon and ritual dress characteristic of every profession, can be explained as well in these terms as in terms of any moral or pragmatic justification. This internally cohesive function of the special codes is clearly visible in the fact that traditionally they have been as much concerned with etiquette (and with economic protection) as with ethics. Perhaps the least cynical and sinister causal explanation for the nature of these codes, short of attributing their canons to dispassionate consideration and criticism of the moral arguments, would appeal to the understandably single-minded pursuit of goals central to professional practice and service, goals with great social value, like health care and economic production. It is natural for professionals to elevate the primary concerns of their particular professions to predominant status, even when they are opposed by values equally prominent in our common moral framework.

None of these nonphilosophical observations is intended as an ad hominem argument: my arguments were all stated earlier in the text. An important question they do raise is whether the moral arguments can affect actual professional practice. To the extent that professional behavior, even ideal behavior as viewed from within the professions themselves, is to be casually explained in nonmoral terms, we might expect that moral arguments will be ineffective in influencing it. Traditionally new members were indoctrinated into the practices articulated in the codes in subtle and nonexplicit ways. Practice was inculcated simultaneously with factual knowledge, and the deeper moral questions were evaded in the professional schools. This has been changing. Furthermore, policing and criticism of professional practice is no longer an exclusively internal affair. Legislators and judges are increasingly invading the domains of businesses and medicine on the side of consumers; business managers are feeling pressure from stockholders, and in some cases membership on corporate boards has shifted; the courts have recently struck down some of the blatantly protectionist clauses of the A.B.A.'s code.

The increasingly open debate on professional ethics within and without the professional schools is itself another sign of change. Practices must change more slowly. The assumption by individuals of particular social roles, with their characteristic styles of conduct, patterns of internal justification, and accepted authorities, obligations and responsibilities, cannot be lightly altered or relinquished. Certain schools of psychology and sociology view personalities as conglomerations of the various social roles that individuals come to assume and identify with, and there must be some truth to this view. For a professional to alter his mode of practice and its central norms is for him to change his personality. One long in practice, who is already an admired member of his profession, cannot be expected to do this readily. The hope for flexibility and openness to rational moral persuasion is the hope that for the healthy and well-integrated personality, the Aristotelian ideal, the role of the good person, will at least limit all other roles the person may play.

NOTES

Chapter 1

1. American Bar Association, *Code of Professional Responsibility*, 1976. See especially section 7.

2. American Medical Association, *Principles of Medical Ethics*, Section 6. Reprinted, for example, in Tom Beauchamp and James Childress, *Principles of Biomedical Ethics* (New York: Oxford University Press, 1979).

3. Robert Veatch, "Medical Ethics: Professional or Universal?", *Harvard Theological Review*, 65 (1972): 531–59.

4. Compare Linda Bell, "Does Ethical Relativism Destroy Morality?", *Man & World*, 8 (1975): 415–23; also Geoffrey Harrison, "Relativism and Tolerance," *Ethics*, 86 (1976): 122–35.

5. See Veatch, op. cit.

6. For sustained application of this point to moral terms, see J. M. Brennan, *The Open-Texture of Moral Concepts* (New York: Barnes & Noble, 1977).

7. The most impressive defense and use of this contractarian framework is of course by John Rawls, *A Theory of Justice* (Cambridge, Mass: Harvard University Press, 1971).

Chapter 2

1. For examples, see M.B.E. Smith, "Is There a Prima Facie Obligation to Obey the Law?" in R. Wasserstrom, ed., *Today's Moral Problems* (New York: Macmillan, 1975); Rolf Sartorius, *Individual Conduct and Social Norms* (Encino, Cal.: Dickenson, 1975), Ch. VI; Robert Wolff, *In Defense of Anarchism* (New York: Harper & Row, 1970).

2. Referring only to this special obligation as the obligation to obey law as such is standard. See Wolff, op. cit.

3. This part of the law is called the secondary rules by H. L. A. Hart in *The Concept of Law* (New York: Oxford University Press, 1961). The position on the obligation to obey the law to be defended here bears certain similarities to the position of Hart. He holds that officials must accept obligations to the secondary rules for the legal system to be viable, while it is merely morally preferable that citizens accept such obligations in relation to the primary rules, i.e. that part of the law that applies directly to their behavior. I accept Hart's distinction, and accept his first claim while rejecting his second.

4. Compare J. C. Smith, *Legal Obligation* (London: Athlone Press, 1976), p. 65.

5. This point is made by Richard Wasserstrom, *The Judicial Decision* (Stanford: Stanford University Press, 1961), pp. 153–4.

6. Compare Sartorius, op. cit., p. 178.

7. This argument is given in Michael Bayles, "Obedience to Lawful Authority," *San Diego Law Review*, 15 (1978): 669–75.

8. M. B. E. Smith, op. cit., p. 392.

9. For elaboration on this point, see A. J. Simmons, "The Principle of Fair Play," *Philosophy & Public Affairs*, 8 (1979): 307–37.

10. This distinction is suggested in Sartorius, op. cit., p. 113.

11. M. Kadish and S. Kadish, *Discretion to Disobey* (Stanford: Stanford University Press, 1973).

12. Compare Kadish and Kadish, op. cit., pp. 90, 180.

13. Essays by Thomas Nagel, Bernard Williams and Stuart Hampshire in Stuart Hampshire, ed., *Public and Private Morality* (Cambridge: Cambridge University Press, 1978).

14. This thesis and some of the examples are found also in Michael Walzer, "Political Action: The Problem of Dirty Hands," *Philosophy & Public Affairs*, 2 (1973): 160–80.

15. Bernard Williams, "Politics and Moral Character," in *Public and Private Morality*, p. 53.

16. The example is from Walzer, op. cit.

17. This difference is suggested by Nagel, op. cit., pp. 83, 87. See also Virginia Held, "Justification: Legal and Political," *Ethics*, 86 (1975): 1–16; and Ronald Dworkin, *Taking Rights Seriously* (Cambridge, Mass.: Harvard University Press, 1976).

18. This question was put to me by Bernard Gert.

19. For a major statement of this view, see Richard Posner, *Economic Analysis of Law* (Boston: Little, Brown & Co., 1972).

20. C. Edwin Baker, "The Ideology of the Economic Analysis of Law," *Philosophy & Public Affairs*, 5 (1975): 3–48.

21. Posner, op. cit., pp. 98–9.

22. Ibid., p. 68

23. Ibid, p. 89.

24. Ibid, p. 311.

25. The phrase is from Dworkin, op. cit.

26. The argument appears to originate with G. E. Moore, *Principia Ethica* (Cambridge: Cambridge University Press, 1968), pp. 162–3. See also Barry Hoffmaster, "The Reliable Criterion Argument and Public Policy," *Social Theory and Practice*, 5 (1978): 75–93; Rolf Sartorius, op. cit.

27. This point is emphasized in Philip Devine, "The Conscious Acceptance of Guilt in the Necessary Murder," *Ethics*, 89 (1979): 221–39.

28. See Hoffmaster, op. cit., p. 88.

29. A reply to Walzer that develops this point is W. Kenneth Howard, "Must Public Hands Be Dirty?", *The Journal of Value Inquiry*, 11 (1977): 29–40.

Chapter 3

1. American Bar Association, *Code of Professional Responsibility*.

2. Ibid, EC 7–8, EC 7–7, EC 7–1.

3. Ibid, EC 7–8.

4. Ibid, EC 7–17.

5. Johns v. Smyth, 176 F. Supp. 949, 952 (E.D. Va. 1959).

6. ABA Code, DR 7–102, DR 7–105, EC 7–10.

7. See G. Hazard.

8. ABA Code, EC 5–1.

9. Ibid. EC 7–1.

10. Ibid, DR 7–103B.

11. ABA Committee on Ethics and Professional Responsibility, Informal Opinion 1057.

12. ABA Code, EC 7–19.

13. Ibid, EC 7–3, EC 7–4.

14. Ibid, 7, n. 3.

15. Ibid, EC 4–5.

16. Ibid, EC 4–1

17. Ibid, 4, n. 2, citing Baird v. Koerner, 279 F.2d 623, 629–30 (9th Cir. 1960).

18. Ibid, DR 4–101A.

19. Ibid, EC 7–5, EC 7–26.

20. Normally in such materials, sample hypothetical cases are simply presented and left for students and professors to analyze. I question the propriety of this standard law school pedagogic method here, presupposing, it seems, prior acceptance of moral principles from which to evaluate the cases. Perhaps the Code itself is most often presupposed as this standard of evaluation. If so, the inadequacy of such courses should be obvious from the ensuing discussion of its principles.

21. The example derives from Thomas Morgan and Ronald Rotunda, *Professional Responsibility: Problems and Materials* (Mineola, NY: The Foundation Press, 1976), Problem 2.

22. Ibid, Problem 46.

23. This case is from Jethro Lieberman, *Crisis at the Bar* (New York: Norton, 1978), p. 171.

24. The case is from Gary Bellow and Jeanne Kettleseon, *The Mirror of Public Interest Ethics*, manuscript unpublished as far as I know, Problem 3.

25. Compare Monroe Freedman, *Lawyer's Ethics in an Adversary System* (Indianapolis: Bobbs-Merrill, 1975), p. 204.

26. Ibid, p. 50.

27. Serving a client's interests and following his demands may require different courses of conduct. I do not emphasize this difference, as I do not accept the principle of full advocacy as interpreted either way.

28. See Freedman, op. cit., p. 33.

29. Compare Richard Wasserstrom, "Lawyers as Professionals: Some Moral Issues," Human Rights, 5 (1975): 1–24, pp. 10–11.

30. Compare Freedman, op. cit., p. 195.

31. These cases are described in Mark Green, *The Other Government* (New York: Grossman, 1975), pp. 98, 139.

32. See A. Goldman, "The Paradox of Punishment," *Philosophy & Public Affairs*, 9 (1979): 42–58.

33. See especially Geoffrey Hazard, *Ethics in the Practice of Law* (cited before); also Lieberman, op. cit.; Green, op. cit.

34. See Bellow, op. cit., p. 62.

35. Compare William Simon, "The Ideology of Advocacy: Procedural Justice and Professional Ethics," *Wisconsin Law Review* (1978): 30–144, p. 11.

36. This is the main argument of Charles Fried, "The Lawyer as Friend: The Moral Foundations of the Lawyer-Client Relation," *Yale Law Journal*, 85 (1976): 1060–89.

37. This point is made by Hazard, op. cit., pp. 27–9.

38. The notion is defined in John Rawls, *A Theory of Justice*, p. 86.

39. The analogy of Fried, op. cit.

40. Compare Wasserstrom, op. cit., p. 8.

41. Thus Fried's analogy is unhelpful, although he really views the preference not as contributing to the intrinsic value of the relation between lawyer and client, but as helping to realize the client's autonomy within the legal system. (see notes 36 and 39)

Chapter 4

1. American Medical Association, *Principles of Medical Ethics.*

2. I restrict discussion for the time being to competent adults. I assume for now that if they have rights to information or to make their own decisions in medical contexts, then parents or guardians not doctors, have these same rights in relation to children or the mentally incapacitated.

3. Compare Sissela Bok, *Lying* (New York: Pantheon, 1978), pp. 18–19.

4. See Gerald Dworkin, "Paternalism," in R. Wasserstrom, ed., *Morality and the Law* (Belmont, Cal.: Wadsworth, 1971).

5. Compare Norman Cantor, "A Patient's Decision to Decline Life-Saving Medical Treatment: Bodily Integrity Versus the Preservation of Life," in T. Beauchamp and S. Perlin, eds., *Ethical Issues in Death and Dying* (Englewoos Cliffs, NJ: Prentice-Hall, 1978), pp. 208–9.

6. Medical opinion seems to be changing on this matter, but we may accept the case as defined for the sake of argument.

7. I am grateful to Robert Goodin for this point.

8. Bernard Meyer, "Truth and the Physician," in Beauchamp and Perlin ed., op. cit., p. 160.

9. Compare A.R. Jonsen, "Do No Harm: Axiom of Medical Ethics," *Philosophy and Medicine*, 3 (1977): 27–41, p. 30.

10. Sissela Bok, op. cit., pp. 227–37, 240.

11. Allen Buchanan, "Medical Paternalism," *Philosophy & Public Affairs* 7 (1978): 370–90.

12. Compare H.T. Engelhardt, "Medicine and the Concept of a Person," in Beauchamp and Perlin, eds., *Ethical Issues in Death and Dying.*

13. One discussion of the Bayesian model is found in Isaac Levi, *Gambling with Truth* (New York: Knopf, 1967), ch. III.

14. In the introduction I spoke of two fundamental rights, that to autonomy, of which I speak here, and that to equality, to have one's interests considered on the same scale as those of others.

15. Compare Alan Donagan, "Informed Consent in Therapy and Experimentation," *The Journal of Medicine and Philosophy*, 2 (1977): 307–29, p. 315.

16. See Robert Veatch, "Medical Ethics: Professional or Universal?", *Harvard Theological Review*, 65 (1972): 531–59, p. 558.

17. Canterbury v. Spence (464 F 2d 772, 1972).

18. A good decision of recent court decisions and policies is found in Charles Montange, "Informed Consent and the Dying Patient," *The Yale Law Journal*, 83 (1974): 1632–64.

19. Ronald Munson, *Intervention and Reflection* (Belmont, Cal.: Wadsworth, 1979), p. 173.

20. Compare R.B. Brandt, "The Morality and Rationality of Suicide," in Seymour Perlin, ed., *A Handbook for the Study of Suicide* (New York: Oxford University Press, 1975).

21. The question of personal identity, of relevance here, is too large a topic to be treated in this chapter. I would maintain only that a person with an altered preference system in the future is still the same person in the most basic sense. This is the sense in which it is rational to be concerned about one's future even though one may predict altered values and preferences.

22. The example is from Kenney Hegland, "Unauthorized Rendition of Lifesaving Medical Treatment," in Beauchamp and Perlin, eds., *Ethical Issues in Death and Dying*, p. 196.

23. The analogy was pointed out to me by Robert Goodin.

24. For an argument against this equation of the desire for suicide with illness, see Thomas Szasz, "The Ethics of Suicide," in Beauchamp and Perlin, eds., *Ethical Issues in Death and Dying*.

25. A Goldman, "Abortion and the Right to Life," *The Personalist*, 60 (1979): 402–6.

26. Robert Veatch, *Case Studies in Medical Ethics* (Cambridge, Mass.: Harvard University Press, 1977), pp. 151–3.

27. Ibid, pp. 154–6.

28. Compare Joseph Fletcher, *Morals and Medicine* (Princeton: Princeton University Press, 1979), p. 62.

29. The Declaration of Helsinki, in Sam Gorovitz et. al., eds., *Moral Problems in Medicine* (Englewood Cliffs, NJ: Prentice-Hall, 1976), pp. 555–6.

30. Alan Donagan, "Informed Consent in Therapy and Experimentation," *The Journal of Medicine and Philosophy*, 2 (1977): 307–29, p. 315.

31. Cited by Tom Beauchamp and James Childress, *Principles of Biomedical Ethics* (New York: Oxford University Press, 1979), p. 106.

32. See, for example, W.D. Kelly and S.R. Friesen, "Do Cancer Patients Want to be Told?", *Surgery*, 27 (1950): 822–6.

33. Robert Veatch, *Case Studies in Medical Ethics*, pp. 24–5.

34. Compare Willard Gaylin, "The Patient's Bill of Rights," in Tom Beauchamp and LeRoy Walters, eds., *Contemporary Issues in Bioethics* (Encino, Cal.: Dickenson, 1978), pp. 141–2.

35. This is pointed out also by Alasdair MacIntyre, "What Has Ethics to Learn from Medical Ethics?", *Philosophic Exchange*, 2 (1978): 37–47.

Chapter 5

1. Compare David Novick, "Cost-Benefit Analysis and Social Responsibility," in F. Luthans and R.M. Hodgetts, eds., *Social Issues in Business* (New York: Macmillan, 1976), pp. 561–2.

2. See Milton Friedman, "The Social Responsibility of Business is to Increase its Profits," in T. Donaldson and P.H. Werhane, eds., *Ethical Issues in Business* (Englewood Cliffs, NJ: Prentice-Hall, 1979); also his *Capitalism and Freedom* (Chicago: The University of Chicago Press, 1962), pp. 133–6.

3. Friedman, *Capitalism and Freedom*, p. 94.

4. Compare Joseph Pichler, "Capitalism in America," in R.T. De George and Joseph Pichler, eds., *Ethics, Free Enterprise, and Public Policy* (New York: Oxford University Press), p. 27.

5. See, for example, Paul Heyne, *The Economic Way of Thinking* (Chicago: Science Research Associates, 1976), p. 42.

6. A point made by Charles Phillips, "What Is Wrong with Profit Maximization?" in W.T. Greenwood, ed., *Issues in Business and Society* (Boston: Houghton Mifflin, 1977), p. 81.

7. John Kenneth Galbraith, The Affluent Society (Boston: Houghton Mifflin, 1958), Ch. XI.

8. Compare Carl Madden, "Forces Which Influence Ethical Behavior," in C. Walton, ed., *The Ethics of Corporate Conduct* (Englewood Cliffs, NJ: Prentice-Hall, 1977), p. 7.

9. This reply to Galbraith is made by F.A. von Hayek, "The Non Sequitur of the 'Dependence Effect'," in Tom Beauchamp and Norman Bowie, eds., *Ethical Theory and Business* (Englewood Cliffs, NJ: Prentice-Hall, 1979).

10. Phillip Nelson, "Advertising and Ethics," in De George and Pichler, op. cit., p. 193.

11. Compare John Coppett, "Consumerism from a Behavioral Perspective," in Luthans and Hodgetts, eds., op. cit.

12. See also Thomas Garrett, *Business Ethics* (Englewood Cliffs, NJ: Prentice-Hall, 1966), pp. 25, 144.

13. Compare Robert Hay and Ed Gray, "Social Responsibilities of Business Managers," in Luthans and Hodgetts, eds., op. cit., p. 104.

14. See Peter Singer, "Rights and the Market," in John Arthur and W. H. Shaw, eds., *Justice and Economic Distribution* (Englewood Cliffs, NJ: Prentice-Hall, 1978); also A. Goldman, "The Entitlement Theory of Distributive Justice," *The Journal of Philosophy*, 73 (1976): 823–35.

15. See, for example, *The Miami Herald* (October 13, 1979).

16. Compare Robert L. Holmes, "The Concept of Corporate Responsibility," in Beauchamp and Bowie, eds., op cit., p. 158.

17. A similar point is made by Robert Heilbroner, "Controlling the Corporation," in Heilbroner, ed., *In the Name of Profit* (Garden City, NY: Doubleday, 1972), p. 240.

18. See the two works cited in note 2.

19. Fuller treatment than space allows here would distinguish between what is obligatory, commendable, and permissible for business managers, in relation to negative rights, positive rights, and utilities.

Chapter 6

1. There are exceptions. Mortimer Kadish, for example, drew the distinction in a lecture before the Institute of Law and Ethics, Williams College, 1977.

Index

abortion, 20–21, 156–7, 213, 228

access to professional services, 252; legal, 123–5, 130, 133; medical, 2, 156

adversaries (legal): interests of, 2, 7, 21, 95, 125, 127, 132, 146; lawyers' obligation to, 95, 146–7, 151

adversary legal system: justification for, 92, 97–8, 106, 109, 117–8, 120, 123; lawyers' role within, 92–101, 104–8, 116, 123; protection of autonomy within, 117, 123; truth-finding function of, 98, 106, 113–6

adversary tactics of lawyers. *See* lawyers, adversary tactics of

advertising, 248–9, 253; by lawyers, 124; influence of, 253–6, truth in, 255

American Bar Association Code of Professional Responsibility, 292, 293n, 294n, 295n; duty of confidentiality according to, 99–101, 104, 111, 114, 134; lawyer's role according to, 6, 90–101, 104–8, 114–5, 121; limits to advocacy within, 94–5, 104–5, 114–6, 121; organization of, 92

American Bar Association Committee on Ethics and Professional Responsibility, 92, 105–6, 115, 295n

American Hospital Association Patient's Bill of Rights, 224

American Medical Association: attitude toward medical ethics, 222–3

American Medical Association Principles of Medical Ethics, 6, 158, 293n, 296n

Aristotle, 292

authority: of corporate managers, 238–42, 246, 277–8; of doctors, 6, 11–12, 16, 24, 158–61, 172–3, 177–8, 187–8, 191, 196, 204, 209–14, 220, 223–7, 285; of judges, 24, 37, 45–6, 56–7, 84, 116; of lawyers, 111–2, 128–9; of parents, 5, 21, 210–12; political, 35, 38, 51, 57; strong role differentiation and, 4–7, 23, 38, 109, 173, 177–8; to act on direct moral perception, 81–9, 109–12, 116, 128–9, 154–5, 158, 173, 191, 198, 231, 238–40, 246, 288–90; to exercise rights, 28

autonomy: of citizenry, 52–6, 69, 112; of clients, 6, 19, 24, 31, 97, 107–13, 117, 123, 126–8, 138, 141; of lawyers, 129, 132–3, 141, 151; of patients, 24, 157–60, 166, 172, 176, 187–96, 200; of politicians, 87–9; of stockholders, 128; personal knowledge and, 160–1; responsibility and, 126, 217–8; rights and, 27–31, 54, 67, 69, 75, 89, 107–10, 117, 126–7, 141, 147–8, 154, 159, 164, 181–2, 187, 200, 203, 216–7, 284; value of, 11–12, 16, 86, 109, 126–7, 154, 159, 163–4, 180–3, 187–8, 191, 196, 227

Baker, C. E., 294n

Bayles, Michael, 294n

Beauchamp, Tom, 297n

Bell, Linda, 293n

Bellow, Gary, 295n, 296n

Bill of Rights, 69

blood transfusions, 171, 198–204, 210–11

Bok, Sissela, 174, 177, 222, 296n

Brandt, R. B., 297n

Brennan, J. M., 293n

Buchanan, Allen, 175, 177, 296n

businessmen. *See* corporate managers